Cousins

Cousins

A UNIQUE AND POWERFUL BOND

JOHANNA GARFIELD

AN AUTHORS GUILD BACKINPRINT.COM EDITION

Cousins
A Unique and Powerful Bond

AN AUTHORS GUILD BACKINPRINT.COM EDITION

Published by iUniverse.com, Inc.

For information address:
iUniverse.com, Inc.
5220 S 16th, Ste. 200
Lincoln, NE 68512
www.iuniverse.com

Originally published by Donald I. Fine, Inc.

ISBN: 0-595-13802-0

Printed in the United States of America

To My Cousins

CONTENTS

Effects of marriage and other life changes. Different roles at different times. Importance to gays. Importance as we grow older-as witnesses to parents and grandparents and to one's own childhood; as sharers of family secrets and conveyors of new information. Cousins in business-problems and solutions. Established and new businesses. Well-known and less well-known ones. How to make them work.

Special features of the cousin relationship in today's world.
Rebutting the skeptics. Class differences. Effects of mobility and smaller families. How and why people are increasingly seeking out their cousins-and should. Importance to mental health. (Why you need your cousins.) Tales of discovery and rediscovery. The cousinless child. The many roles cousins can play in today's fragmented society.

Some very candid opinions on their cousins from a seventh grade class in New York City.

HOW YOU'RE RELATED

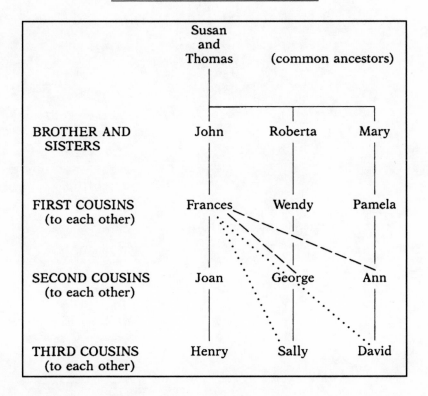

	Susan and Thomas	(common ancestors)	
BROTHER AND SISTERS	John	Roberta	Mary
FIRST COUSINS (to each other)	Frances	Wendy	Pamela
SECOND COUSINS (to each other)	Joan	George	Ann
THIRD COUSINS (to each other)	Henry	Sally	David

FIRST COUSINS ARE children of brothers and sisters, so Frances, Wendy, and Pamela are first cousins to each other. *Second cousins* are children of first cousins, so Joan, George, and Ann are second cousins, and so on.

A *first cousin once removed* (see dashes - - -) is the child of your first cousin, so George and Ann are Frances' *first cousins once removed*. (Sometimes, confusingly, also called "second cousins," though technically, they're not.)

First cousins twice removed (see dotted lines . . .) are children of first cousins once removed, so Sally and David are Frances' *first cousins twice removed*.

Cousins by marriage are simply those wed to your cousins of whatever kind. So that whomever George married would automatically become Frances' *first cousin once removed* with the additional tag "by marriage" at the end.

ACKNOWLEDGMENTS

MANY PEOPLE HELPED me along the way with *Cousins,* but I'd like to begin by thanking my husband Leslie for his consistent support as I was writing the book-and that includes keeping me company during otherwise isolated weekends in the country when I emerged only to eat the lunches or dinners he frequently, and uncomplainingly, prepared.

I thank my agent, Angela Miller, for her faith in the idea and her determination; my editor Susan Schwartz for the same, and for offering valuable pointers on structure; Hayes B. Jacobs for reading and critiquing many drafts, and the members of his New School workshop for many keen and helpful suggestions; Carole Klein for giving me numerous leads for interviews, for her ongoing enthusiasm about the concept and her generosity of spirit in sharing the resources other writers so often hug to themselves. Likewise Candy Schulman, who resisted the temptation to hang up when I'd call and say, "I know you're busy, but could I just run this by you for a minute?" And proceeded to "run it by" her for ten. Katheryn Clark saved me hours by cheerfully (at least, stoically) tearing apart hundreds of computer pages and twice as many perforated edges.

A chance meeting with my brother's associate, Professor Mike Brown of the City University in New York, is indirectly responsible for much of the anthropological and sociological expertise in the book, in that he steered me to Dr. Jerry Handel (also of CUNY), who knew just who to call and where to look for information. My deepest appreciation to both.

Not even counting my own cousins-whom I'll get to next-all the people I interviewed, or who wrote in response to my newspaper inquiries, gave generously of their time, but I'm especially grateful to Dr. Donald Bloch, Dr. Clifford Sager, Dr. Veva Zimmerman, Dr. Mio Fredland, Dr. Richard Schuman, Dr. Michael Fellner, Dr. James Framo, Anna Quindlen, Phyllis Diller, Jasper Johns, Celeste Holm, David Soyer, Lewis Burke Frumkes, Gloria Hochman, Neilson

Abeel, Barbara Lindeman, Fran Burton, Lew and Sue Brackley. And to the "real life" counterparts of Jean Allen, Tom Harwood, Eduardo Riccio, and David Forman, all of whom requested pseudonyms. But *they* know who they are.

Suzanne Davis and her seventh grade class at the Clinton School in New York contributed candid and refreshing opinions on the topic, and for these I thank them. Also, my friends from the Dwight-Englewood School in New Jersey, who were my first interviewees many years ago-especially Doris Gelman, for reasons only she and I know.

Finally, I thank all of my cousins-the ones who are mentioned or quoted in the book, and the ones who aren't. Many of them were enormously supportive and interested in the project, and Elliot D. in particular (most of my cousins' last names weren't used) was unusually generous with his time and open about his feelings and opinions.

The fact that some other cousins weren't brought into the book doesn't mean that I don't have specific and very meaningful memories connected with almost every one of them, or that I consider them unimportant, or that their individual stories weren't interesting. It just means that those stories or memories didn't help make or illustrate a point. Otherwise, the book would have been a chronicle of our family alone.

But *that's* another story.

Johanna Garfield

INTRODUCTION

WHY I CARE ABOUT COUSINS

In the field of family therapy, cousin relationships are not an issue we talk about, though of course they're very significant. In fact this is the first time anyone has asked me about it.
There is no literature on the subject. You're on your own and I wish you luck...

-SALVADOR MINUCHIN, A PIONEER IN FAMILY THERAPY AND RESEARCH PROFESSOR OF PSYCHOLOGY AT NEW YORK UNIVERSITY.

THEY'VE ALL BEEN explored, analyzed, chronicled: mothers and sons, mothers and daughters, fathers and sons, fathers and daughters, brothers and sisters. But the cousin relationship has, up to now, received surprisingly little attention. Why? Described by one friend as "magical siblings," the relationship can vary from genuine friendship to utter indifference, from love to hate, can have sexual overtones, and can reverberate throughout the memories of childhood and family with much of the same emotional intensity as that reserved for genuine siblings.

Certainly, when I was growing up, my two best friends, along with my primary role models and protectors, my first crushes, my most influential teachers (of everything from the facts of life to the piano)-even my severest critics and bitterest rivals-were all, also, my cousins. And though many years have passed since Helen and Clare, the two first cousins on either side I was closest to as a child, swore eternal fealty and pledged to name our first daughters (if we had them) after each other (we did both), we are still very close. These two, along with Fran, another same-age cousin with whom I've become equally friendly since we grew up, were the female tail end of a large clan of aunts, uncles, and older boy cousins who got together often for holidays, family parties, and musicales.

Not only did I see all these cousins regularly during the year, but during the summers we often trooped off together to whichever camp had been newly selected or deemed worthy of a second year by an unofficial committee of aunts and uncles. (Most of these choices, whose names read like a roster of Indian tribes-Waquaset, Watitoh, Taconic-were "progressive," weak on sports, and determinedly "creative," in line with the family veneration for the arts.) One summer, in fact, three of the four campers in my bunk, to say nothing of our counselor Phyllis, were cousins. Grace, the unfortunate outsider, left in the middle of the season, unable finally to cope with the "in" references and the sardonic family humor. Our joyous discovery of a leech curled up in her navel after she had dutifully gone for the required swim period in the muddy waters of that year's camp discovery was the final straw. (We had flatly refused to go in, and Phyllis-less an authority figure for being a relation-couldn't make us.)

All this, of course, I took for granted. Safely encapsulated within the family group, I never thought to question how other cousinless kids got along, to compare mine to other cousinly relationships, or to think about the nature of this special connection. Louisa May Alcott's *Eight Cousins* was my Bible, and I identified closely with every word, blissfully indifferent to the fact that the number of boys in our family (plus me) was closer to eighteen than eight, that there were four girls, not one, to share their affections, and that I-a hellion and a tomboy-in no way resembled the compliant, decidedly unliberated, and precociously maternal heroine, Rose.

But it all came back to me in a rush a few years back when I was reading about Maria Shriver's wedding plans. She told a reporter, "My cousins are my best friends. Basically, there's a group of four of us who are about the same age: Courtney Kennedy, Sydney Lawford, Caroline Kennedy, and me. The four of us grew up next door to each other. We hung out together and they will be my bridesmaids."

Her comment made me begin to think about the unique role these friend-relations played-and play-in my own life, and in the lives of others I know, to say nothing of in other cultures and countries. What is the nature of this mysterious blood tie, closer than an unrelated friend, yet not so inextricably involving as a sibling, a relationship described by my own cousin Helen as making her feel as though she was "entering a warm, welcoming room" whenever we got together?

I began to casually bring up the topic to friends and relatives, and was amazed at the response. "Boy, have I got a cousin story for you!" would be a fair example of the often near explosive reaction to my questions. People wanted to talk-about how they'd once been in love with a cousin, had been helped by a cousin, detested a cousin who'd competed for their grandmother's attention and otherwise made their lives miserable, discovered or rediscovered a long-lost cousin and felt a mysterious but undeniable sense of familiarity.

As for my own family, I was in for some rude shocks. On a personal level, I was chagrined to find out that some of the older cousins I'd adored had hardly been aware I was alive, though they'd certainly become more so as we all grew older. But even more startling was my discovery that the childhood togetherness I had naively considered near idyllic had been far from it for some of my cousins. I found out that a few had felt coerced into those frequent childhood visits; that invidious comparisons between them had sometimes been made by my aunts and uncles; that there was, to others, a "money hierarchy" in the family of which I was completely unaware. (My lack of awareness here may be explained by the fact that my parents were at the top of that pyramid.)

The hierarchy I'd noticed, and a clear-cut one it was, was based on musical talent. I saw early on that the rare, unfortunate child who lacked the usual Rosengarten gene for music was a second-class citizen in our family. (Rosengarten was my maiden name, and common traits-even among the married daughters who've taken their husband's names-are still referred to as "Rosengarten" traits.) His or her awful deficiency was never spoken of, as though the victim had some dread disease. The embarrassed parents of such a child-both parents, for whoever "married in" soon adopted musicality as an unquestioned value, willingly or otherwise-tormented these wretches with piano lessons year after unproductive year until at last, defeated, they gave up. Their offspring, relieved but still aware of their inadequacies, always seemed to me somewhat on the outskirts at family gatherings. To rescue them from complete ignominy, they were then deemed "good listeners," but their lowly status was very clear to me as a child.

Contrariwise, those with the most talent-like my cousins Ira and Phyllis (my camp counselor), a brother and sister who excelled at not just the piano but the flute, clarinet, and recorder-were high on the family pyramid.

Still, despite my discoveries of a few worms in the can, I found out that every one of my cousins, in his or her own way, had a tremendous sense of loyalty, love, and often great admiration for the others. In short, none of these revelations, interesting as they were, altered the basic sense I had that these were people who cared deeply for each other in a very special way, as did most of the people I interviewed.

And it was certainly other people I wanted to talk to, and did. Through ads in national newspapers and a lot of personal networking I reached people from all over the country, from rural and urban areas, from foreign countries. I talked to recent immigrants, to refugees who'd come over during World War II, and to people whose families went back five and six generations in the United States. And as I did so, I began to notice that certain patterns appeared and reappeared, especially in the stories told by some of my more verbal interviewees, aspects of whose cousin stories occur and recur throughout the book, as do my own.

To give the conclusions I was coming to some weight and to expand into areas that might not have occurred to me, I talked to psychologists, experts in family systems, anthropologists, and sociologists and researched historical cousin relationships here and around the world. And I found out many things I'd never been aware of. For instance, like most people, I knew that cousin marriage was and is frequent in royal families, but not that it was institutionalized in certain primitive tribes, and is still readily accepted in other modern countries.

It seemed a logical consequence then to check out the genetic risks involved in such marriages. And from there, just a short step to genetic connections between cousins in general. Are talents jointly inherited, for instance? This line of questioning led to some fascinating talks with people as diverse as artists Jasper Johns and Will Barnet, comedienne Phyllis Diller, musician David Soyer of the Guarneri Quartet, actress Celeste Holm, and others. While their answers to the initial question of mutual talents varied, other cousin stories emerged as we talked.

Not that finding experts with something to say was easy. I soon found out, as I'd suspected, that little work had been done on the subject of cousins in the field of psychology. The quote by family therapy guru Salvador Minuchin at the start of this chapter indicated that the pickings would be slim.

Dr. Ava Siegler, Dean of Training and Vice-president in charge of Academic Affairs at the Postgraduate Center for Mental Health in New York City, and an expert in family relationships, put it another way but essentially confirmed Dr. Minuchin's assertion. "I'm rarely at a loss for words," she said, "but this is a subject I've never really thought about much. I think it [cousin relationships] very much depends upon the family structure as to how important they become," she added. "Unfortunately, fewer and fewer families are large enough or connected enough to take advantage of the intense relationships one might have had with one's father's and mother's children in the past." (While no one will question the fact that few families are as large as they were, my research led me to some different conclusions about the loss of intensity.)

Fortunately, despite the lack of literature on the topic, I did find a number of psychiatrists and specialists in family therapy who had interesting and provocative things to say on the subject. But most of the observations I got from the authorities in this field were verbal ones, based more on personal observation and opinion than organized research.

As for general references, my original data search at the library in the late 80's had produced little I could use, and the *Library of' Congress Subject Headings* at that time went straight from "Couscous Industry" to "Coushatta Indians" to "Coutch Family" without even a backward glance for cousins. Similarly, the *Encyclopedia Americana* leaped from "Courtship of Miles Standish" to some famous people named "Cousins" to "Cousteau, Jacques." My children's *World Book* did indeed provide the chart that was the basis for "How You're Related" (see page x) but had no other information. In fact, the *Encyclopedia Britannica* was the only general source I could find with anything to say on the subject.

A search of the internet for this edition, while it had numerous sites for "cousins," in fact added little to what I'd discovered years ago. Most turned out to be specific family genealogies or web pages or newsletters. Only one, which mentioned a book on cousin marriage in America to which I refer in the chapter on that subject, provided fresh information.

At first, the fields of anthropology and sociology seemed equally barren of material, except for studies of cousins in exotic cultures involving elaborate diagrams of kinship systems which, interesting as they may be, were not what I was primarily after. But just when I'd pretty much given up on the experts in those fields also, and was well into writing the book, a chance tip led me to Dr. Jerry Handel, a professor of sociology at the City University of New York. He directed me to at least a few colleagues who had studied the subject, or had opinions on it. Some had even written about it.

As it turned out, the belatedness of these discoveries had its benefits because, while I might have accepted as gospel some of the gloomy forecasts for cousinly togetherness made by a few sociologists when I started out, by the time I unearthed the new material, I had enough evidence of my own to do some refuting. And I had also figured out why the relationship had been so neglected.

In short, though I qualify as an expert in none of the "-ologies," I was eventually able to move out of the anecdotal where necessary and to draw some conclusions-and question others-that were based on more than my own experience or interviews, however wide-ranging.

I began to tune in to cousins in the media-to notice how they were presented: sometimes as the butt of jokes (on one episode of Mary Tyler Moore, she teases a friend about how she doesn't want to spend another quiet evening at home "watching the movies of your cousin Harry's son's bar mitzvah"); sometimes as the basis of TV series. The basic premise of two very popular television shows, *The Patty Duke Show* of the 60's, and later, *Perfect Strangers,* is that of cousins raised in completely different cultures-and with completely different temperaments to boot-who are thrown together and become firm friends. In *thirtysomething,* Michael (Ken Olin) and Melissa (Melanie Mayron) were first cousins with a close relationship, and in fact it was she who, in a widely watched episode, convinced him to attend services at his former temple, when he was conflicted about doing so because of what he perceived as a possible disloyalty to his non-Jewish wife.

And speaking of the thirties, I was able to talk with Anna Quindlen, formerly author of the much admired *New York Times* column, "Life in the Thirties," and later a regular on the Op-Ed page, about many aspects of her cousin relationships. Like me and like the Kennedys, she'd grown up surrounded by an enormous group of cousins, with many of whom she remains extremely close to this day. Referring to the issue of cousins' importance in her life, she said, "I think it's a real interesting issue, because about half the people I know I don't even have to discuss this with, because it's so much a part of their lives, too. The other half are people who are totally perplexed by it. Like, each of their parents had maybe one sibling, and they lived in Arizona or somewhere else far away. And they just don't understand." She also told me that she based a number of the characters in her novel *Object Lessons* on her cousins, and that it includes a number of cousin relationships.

I began to remember other books I'd read-books besides *Eight Cousins*-in which cousin relationships were important. The close friendship between the two male cousins in Laurie Colwin's novel, *Happy All the Time,* for instance, or the tragic love between the cousins Simon and Mariella in Rosamond Lehmann's *Dusty Answer,* a novel I found deeply moving as an adolescent.

In two more recent novels, Mary Gordon's *The Other Side* and Ursula Perrin's *The Looking-Glass Lover,* cousin relationships are central to the stories. Jane Austen's books are full of cousinly romances and cousinly friendships, and she herself received a marriage proposal from a cousin. I recalled Truman Capote's relationship with his beloved cousin Sook, about whom he wrote *A Christmas Memory.* ("We're cousins-very distant ones-and we have lived together, well, as long as I can remember. We are each other's best friend. She calls me Buddy in memory of a boy who was formerly her best friend. The other Buddy died in the 1880s, when she was only a child. She is still a child.") In Gerald Clarke's biography of Capote, he tells more about Sook and about the young Capote's relationship with the other three cousins who raised him in Monroeville, Alabama.

I learned that the young Truman also had a cousin contemporary he'd been close to, his boyhood pal Jennings Faulk Carter, and that Carter's stories of their escapades and growing up in Monroeville were the major source of Marion Moates' *A Bridge of Childhood-Truman Capote's Early Years.* (An interesting footnote: Capote and Harper Lee are said to be the real life counterparts of Dill and Scout in Lee's *To Kill a Mockingbird,* and Carter may well have been the model for Jem.)

I also began to listen for cousin relationships in the movies. The very popular French film, *Cousin, Cousine*-remade in 1989 as *Cousins,* in America-of course springs immediately to mind, though in fact the two principals who become romantically involved were related by marriage rather than blood. In the 1988 movie, *Everybody's All-American,* the bond between the sports hero Gavin Gray and his bookish cousin Cave forms the cornerstone of the story. Daphne DuMaurier's mystery *My Cousin Rachel* became a starring vehicle for Richard Burton and Olivia DeHavilland in 1952. And *Shy People,* of a few years back, features Jill Clayburgh and Barbara Hershey as cousins and friends.

Still, what most interested me were the personal cousin stories I began to hear. Could they answer the questions I'd begun to think about? I must admit that gradually I discovered another motive besides fond recollection and simple curiosity for exploring this rarely discussed relationship. I realized with regret that my own children did not have the same bond with most of their first cousins that I had-and still have-with mine, though, interestingly, they were close to several second cousins or first cousins once removed. (The aforementioned chart, p. xi, provides a graphic explanation of these often confused terms.)

As my cousin Fran said, "We often talk about getting the younger generation together, but somehow we don't. If it felt comfortable, we would. But it doesn't. They didn't have the shared experiences, the summers at camp together, the aunts who'd pop in to see the whites of our eyes if our parents were out of town. So now we can talk about things we felt the same about then. We all bemoan the fact that our children don't have that, but you can't force something."

Why had this come about? I began to wonder. Was it something very personal in our own family circle, or perhaps something more insidious and general in the ways families operate today?

From there it was just a small step to larger questions. How do good cousin relationships get formed? Why are some cousins close and others cool or even hostile to each other? How important are differences in age? differences in gender? What is the cause of the magical connection some cousins feel? Most importantly, were my family and others losing out on relationships that could be of great benefit to them? And if so, what can and/or should be done about it?

Other questions followed. If indeed the failure to connect with cousins is a real, recent and general phenomenon, how much has shrinking family size been a factor? What do cousins mean to the children born into today's smaller families, and especially to the only child; could cousins perhaps take up the slack left by fewer or no siblings? And reflecting back on my own experience and looking at the other end of the age span, what is the special significance of cousins to us as we grow older? How do they help us understand who we are, where we're coming from, and in some cases, where we're going? How do cousins provide role models, both good and bad? (Michael Dukakis, for one, is remembered by all his cousins as a powerful and positive role model.) Furthermore, with so much uprooting of upwardly mobile parents in search of better jobs nowadays, can the enduring cousin relationship, less likely to be permanently severed by geographical separations, compensate-at least in part-for the friendships left behind when families move on? In short, how has the cousin relationship helped us in the past, and even more importantly, how can it help us now and in the future?

1

WHY COUSINS ARE SPECIAL

THE SENSE OF CLAN

We feel a shock of recognition. It's this feeling of 'Oh yes, of course. This person knows. This person understands where I'm coming from.'

-Anna Quindlen

I have family all over the world, and cousins are the thread that ties us all together. Actually, it is just their difference from siblings that we treasure.

-Phyllis Lerner, real estate broker.

These relationships are intense by choice, not need.

-Berta Walker,
Acting Director, Fine Arts
Workshop, Provincetown, Mass.

WHAT'S SO SPECIAL, then, about the cousin relationship? Why is it unique, and how is it different from either a close friendship between siblings, or from that between unrelated friends?

Though I spoke to a number of psychiatrists and psychologists about this, some of my clearest answers to these questions came from Anna Quindlen, who was the eldest of twenty-nine first cousins on her father's side and the youngest of "a bunch" of older cousins on her mother's, though she had a lot more to do with her father's side because they lived closer.

"In recent years, I've had very probing conversations with my cousins," she said. "Actually, they've often taken the form of letters, not oral conversations, about how they saw me and about how I saw them, and about how it impacted on our lives. And these conversations were incisive and emotionally candid in a way that they could never be with siblings. There's just too much at stake with your sister or your brother, whereas with cousins you're close enough to share blood and history, but far enough away that you can get right into it in a way you can't with siblings.

"And another thing is that though you share this blood and history, at a certain point you diverge, so that during one of the exchanges I had with one cousin, she told me that she thought she knew me better after reading *Living out Loud* [Ms. Quindlen's 1989 collection of essays from the *Times*] than she had from knowing me all these years.

"And it seems to me the difference from good friends also came clear to me during one of these conversations," she continued. "My cousin was writing to me about how wonderful it was to have my mother, who was so gentle and so kind, as an aunt, and my father, who was so funny and outgoing, as an uncle. And I wrote back to her and said, 'Oh, it seemed so great to me, too, to have your parents who were so this and so that. There isn't an arm's-length kind of thing like there is with your friends, where it's 'Mr. and Mrs. Quindlen.' It's that 'Aunt Pru and Uncle Bob' thing that gives them enough closeness to really know your parents in a way outsiders don't, and yet, again, there's enough distance that they don't feel the same kind of self-identity wrapped up with your parents as you do."

As for what's so special? "Though I don't stay in constant contact with them, there's always this sense of 'Gee, Wow' kind of discovery whenever we see each other. We feel a shock of recognition. It's this feeling of 'Oh yes, of course. This person knows. This person understands where I'm coming from' "-a comment so incisive I felt it should head the chapter.

As for the professionals I spoke with, Dr. Donald Bloch, head of the Ackerman Institute for Family Therapy in New York City, saw it this way: "The cousin relationship is distinctive in that, of all blood relationships, it tends to be the least toxic-it's not a 'hot' one-and the most generally supportive. There's enough distance so that cousins are not deeply competitive and antagonistic, yet they're clearly family with a common heritage. This makes for a nice mixture of closeness and distance. In a way, you have the best of both worlds. If you want to encourage the kinship, it's O.K., and if you want to ignore it, that's all right, too."

Dr. Clifford Sager, emeritus Director of Family Psychiatry at the Jewish Board of Family and Children's Services and now Clinical Professor of Psychiatry at New York Hospital-Cornell Medical Center, agreed. "There's an ongoing relatedness, yet there's not the daily bickering you have with siblings," he said. Dr. Ann Gorelitz, a Chicago family therapist, added that in her long experience as a family therapist, she could think of only one case with direct cousin involvement as a serious problem, a case of sexual abuse that will be discussed later on.

Herein, I think, lies at least part of the answer to why the subject of cousins has been so ignored for so long. It's not because these relationships aren't intense, meaningful and, as Dr. Minuchin said, "very significant," but because-unlike almost every other intense family relationship-they are generally easy, natural, taken for granted, and *rarely a problem*. And because they are relatively (no pun intended) painless, they've been overlooked. No pain-ergo, no gain, at least in terms of attention being paid.

Dr. Veva Zimmerman, a psychiatrist who is associate dean of the medical school at New York University, drew an excellent analogy. "Cousins are one step removed from being brothers and sisters in much the same way that grandparents are one step removed from being parents. A lot of the direct conflictual interaction is minimized, which makes it very nice."

Speaking of her own experiences, she said, "I quickly became involved with my husband David's cousins when we married, because he has a large number of very involved cousins in both areas of the country where we hang out [Chicago and New York], to say nothing of elsewhere. Since neither my brother nor sister married, this has meant an enormous fine family experience for my children. We have huge reunions at least twice a year-I'm the Thanksgiving cousin and a cousin in Boston is the Seder cousin.

"But what's especially interesting to me is that there's never any fighting. Yet these are people who all have aggressive and successful lives outside. There are tensions between us, but no fighting. I mean, it's not as though people are on their best behavior. It's just that everyone feels warm and related and they just don't feel like arguing."

Dr. Richard Schuman, a psychologist, had this to say: "The closeness comes out of a strong tribal feeling-what you might call a sense of clan. Unless there's been a rupture in the parents' generation or you live so far apart that you just can't get together"-though I found many cases where even these problems were overcome-"you're likely to meet and re-meet over and over again, even if you don't like each other. With friends, you can easily drift apart. But because of the family tie, you're almost forced to stay in touch with cousins-especially while you're kids, but often, even afterwards."

"The Clan" is in fact the title of the second chapter of *Eight Cousins,* and when Rose first sees her seven boy cousins, "a sight that nearly took her breath away-all ages, all sizes, all yellow-haired and blue-eyed, all in full Scotch costume," Archie says, "Don't be frightened. This is the clan come to welcome you." Though at that point Archie is referring to their partly Scottish heritage, the term "clan" also reflects their sense of family unity.

Probably the most dramatic theory about cousin special-ness was put forward by Dr. Mio Fredland, a psychiatrist at the Payne Whitney Hospital in New York. "Even people who grow up and don't like their cousins feel a primordial, atavistic togetherness, an inexplicable pull towards each other," she said. "In the case of cousins of the opposite sex, the pull resides in the substituting from early life of the passionate but forbidden feelings for the mother, father, sister, or brother, and is often romantic and sexual.

"But even when cousins are of the same sex, they're often unaccountably drawn to each other. It has to do with some primitive feeling about blood ties," she said. "The initial barriers are broken down, even when cousins haven't met before. People feel immediately that a distance has been bridged. Cousins are drawn together by something more than common interests. The feeling of blood-bonding makes them willing to put up with shortcomings that they'd never put up with in a stranger."

I noticed that the word "blood" kept appearing and reappearing in the comments people made. Said Dr. Zimmerman, "Obviously, it's a blood relationship versus a non-blood relationship that's important, and cousinships are only one step removed in everybody's mind, no matter how many genealogical steps they are removed from siblings."

The "blood" aspect of the special connection was interestingly described in anthropologist David Schneider's book, *American Kinship: A Cultural Account*:

> The relationship which is 'real' or 'true' or 'blood' or 'by birth' can never be severed, whatever its legal position. Legal rights may be lost, but the blood relationship cannot be lost…Two blood relatives are 'related' by the fact that they share in some degree the stuff of a particular heredity. Each has a portion of the natural, genetic substance. Their kinship consists in this common possession…
>
> The unalterable nature of the blood relationship has one more aspect of significance. [It] is a relationship of identity. People who are blood relatives share a common identity, they believe. This is expressed as 'being of the same flesh and blood.' It is a belief in

common biological constitution, and aspects like temperament, build, physiognomy, and habits are noted as signs of this shared biological makeup, this special identity of relatives with each other."

He concludes that "The fact that the relationship cannot be ended or altered and that it is a state of almost *mystical* [my italics] commonalty and identity is also quite explicit in American culture.

As "mystical" as this may indeed sound, many people confirmed Schneider's and the others' theories about blood-bonding, shared history, unaccountable ease and attraction, the "shock of recognition."

Certainly this was true in the custody case of little Elian Gonzalez, who became a political football between the United States and Cuba in late '99 and into 2000. In all the excitement over parental rights, it was easy to forget that one of the most powerful magnets drawing the child close to his Florida family was the quick and passionate attachment he formed with his cousin Marisleysis, 21 to his 6 years. The connection he felt with her, substituting her in his mind for the mother he'd lost despite her constant reminders that "I'm not your mother, I'm your cousin," tells us something about the instinctive drawing together of blood to blood, the subconscious recognition of someone immediately and peculiarly familiar, though in fact Elian hardly knew Marisleysis before his rescue.

Said Academy Award-winning actress Celeste Holm, who catapulted to fame as the original "Ado Annie" in *Oklahoma,* and is still seen on TV or in movies (*Three Men and a Baby* among them*)* "I have one hundred twenty-five cousins-admittedly, some by marriage-and I like all of them and feel close to them. There's a lot of delving into instinctual knowledge in the teaching of semiotics I do with actors, and sometimes I wonder about it. Because I think a lot of acting is instinct. And clearly, as far as cousins go, it's a matter of instinct, too-what I'd call 'trained genes,' designated genes that come down to us over thousands of years that draw us together. My cousins on my father's side all grew up in Norway, and I didn't even know them as I grew up, but when I met them, as I said, there was an instinctive recognition. In fact, one I hardly knew from there just came over, and I had a great sense of relationship with her right away."

Neilson Abeel, a real estate broker in his 40's, had never met his second cousin Griselda, an editor twelve years older than he, and a number of other cousins until a relative from England suggested a family get-together a few years ago. "I definitely felt more comfortable than I would have with a new group who were just friends of friends," he said. "Griselda and I in particular have picked up a friendship with each other. We're very direct. I don't know-somehow it's different. It's the assumption of family. You don't have to be quite on your guard or think you're going to lose the friendship just because of one stupid thing you might say. You don't feel 'at risk.' "

Frances Kaufman Doft, who has lived all her life in Canada, said, "Though I grew up knowing my cousins on my mother's side through frequent visits to the United States, there were thirteen cousins on my father's side who lived in Israel whom I didn't meet until 1975. This was because my father had come to Canada as the oldest of five or six children-he followed my mother so he could marry her.

"Anyway, the others got caught in the war [World War II] and the four who survived went to Israel. The first time I went, it was a very moving event. I felt an instant bonding with those cousins, a very special feeling. I met one who was named after the same grandmother as me. That was so exciting! They had a huge cousins party in Tel Aviv. Actually, they don't get together that often, but if visitors come from the United States, they do. To me, it's such a luxury to have these cousins, as well as the ones in America. It's a very special and comforting feeling, an anchor, a lateral support."

"Comforting" was also the word used by Harrison Rainie and John Quinn, in their 1983 book *Growing Up Kennedy,* to describe the early relationships of the twenty-nine Kennedy cousins (coincidentally, the same number Anna Quindlen grew up with). They said, "They constitute an entire spiritual ecosystem-self-sustaining, self-regulating, self-regenerating, self-informing, self-enhancing. They need one another as they need air to breathe. It is an amazingly buoyant and comforting circumstance."

They go on to quote young Teddy Kennedy as saying, "I've probably spent more time with my immediate family and my cousins than with any other person or group of persons. I enjoy them. It's partially out of knowing that we've shared so many of the same things. And it's partially that this is the way we were raised."

Obviously, the tragedy of David Kennedy's drug addiction and death, and the problems Chris Lawford, Bobby Jr., Joe (to a lesser extent) and others had as they got older show that a cousinly support system is not enough to overcome every personal-and in the case of the Kennedys, public-problem. Still, in the growing-up years of the Kennedys, it seems the "comforting" aspects and the strengths of the relationships far outweighed the weaknesses-and in most cases still do.

The sense of comfort was also mentioned by Gloria Hochman, a writer from Philadelphia and winner of numerous awards, including the 1989 first prize from the National Mental Health Association for her article "A Brilliant Madness." "There were four of us-all girls, who grew up near each other. I'm three years older than my sister, and there was one her age, and one a year older. There were also four cousins on my father's side with whom I've maintained close friendships. The point is, I feel an enormous sense of comfort and safety with these people. Cousins give me a very secure family feeling. I know they're there when others won't be. I feel a strong sense of continuity and a shared past. And even though we have very different lifestyles, we're not judgmental. At the same time I feel perfectly all right-in fact, I feel a responsibility-about giving advice if I feel it's needed, as they do with me, recognizing that they have every right to reject it. As I said, it's all very safe."

And Barbara Lindeman, a career counselor from New Jersey who spent every Sunday of her childhood visiting with her twelve first cousins at their grandmother's house, said, "At family gatherings, we still have a very special feeling for each other, though with only one does the relationship transcend the cousin-ness."

Lewis Burke Frumkes, a writer of humor with a radio interview show, and many books to his credit (the most recent being *Manhattan Cocktail),* stressed the sense of continuity and comfort based on what Dr. Schuman had called the "sense of clan" and Dr. Fredland the "blood-bonding." "As you get older, your friends change, and as your life develops there's not a sense of stability and permanence. With cousins, whether you like them or you don't, you know that they're there, and that they're blood-related from the past and all the way into the future so that suddenly, at a mid-life point, they've become very important to me. And this is something I feel good about-knowing that these people are there, and will go out of their way for me."

And Susan Fisher, an art dealer now living in New York who grew up in Milwaukee, Wisconsin, said, "Just two years ago, I met a first cousin I never knew who'd come down from Syracuse to visit. She was just ten years older than my kids, and ten years younger than me-right in between. I found her amazingly easy to talk to, and found I had a really strong family feeling towards her. I told her all about some of the other relatives-she hadn't been to almost any family occasions-and I wouldn't have felt it an intrusion if she had asked me for help."

I heard it over and over again: "These people will be there when no one else is"; "I know I can rely on them"; "They were an incredible support system for me."

Gloria Hochman tells of coming in from Philadelphia on business, and falling and breaking her arm in New York City during the twenty-three-inch snowstorm of a few years back. "After I got back to the apartment where I was staying from the emergency room with this paralyzed hand and immobile arm, I called my sister in Baltimore who got in touch with my cousins in New York. They came through the snow that night to rescue me. They helped me dress and pack and took me on the train all the way to Baltimore, so that my sister could take care of me."

Gloria remembers playing the role of supporter to one of her own young cousins even as a child. "I guess I was about seven and Milly was five when this happened," she said. "Milly had done something really mischievous-taken all the linens out of the closet to hide, or something like that. My aunt-Milly's mother-called up my grandmother's house, where I was staying at the time, and told my grandmother, 'I just can't deal with her. If she stays here, I don't know what I might do. She'll have to go to your house tonight.'

"Well, usually we loved to go to my grandmother's. She was wonderful, and besides that my grandparents owned a bakery shop that they lived above, so we grew up on jelly doughnuts. But this time, when Milly came over, she was really upset. I remember spending hours comforting her, and telling her that her mother would feel differently in the morning and let her come home. Which of course is exactly what happened. But she later told me that my being there had made an enormous difference to her."

And Pamela Freemont, who runs a leather goods business, said, "I've always been close to my cousins. We are always in touch. But I most appreciated them when my husband of thirty years walked out on me for another woman last year. They all rallied around me and were enormously supportive."

Dr. Schuman told of a case where barely-known cousins had formed a support group that almost literally saved the life of one of his patients. A young woman had come to the city from the Midwest after a divorce and fallen into a deep depression which led, unfortunately, to a suicide attempt. "Her parents wanted her to go back home after that," he said, "which would have been fatal-both because she didn't get along well with them, and because her ex-husband lived nearby. Her brother only accused her of worrying her parents, and her sister lived too far away to be of any help."

On a hunch, Schuman suggested she call some cousins who lived in New York, but whom she knew only slightly. "It was amazing," he said. "They immediately befriended her-and even more importantly, through a contact, one found her a job as a hostess in a restaurant-a job for which she was overqualified, but which lent structure to her life and gave her a chance to pull herself together and feel competent. All in all, they joined forces and played an enormous role in her recovery."

But perhaps the ultimate story of cousinly support and rescue was sent to me by Berneice Lunday, who runs a writing service in Bismarck, North Dakota. "My ninety-one-year-old mother-in-law, Martha Duschka Lunday, had the misfortune of being put in an orphanage when she was young because her father had died, and soon after, her mother became ill and could no longer care for her. One day Martha had some visitors-her cousin Leona and her parents. When they got done visiting, Leona said, 'Let's take Martha home with us,' and they did. They adopted her and Leona's father even gave Martha a farm when he died."

Finally, Rainie and Quinn also describe the Kennedy cousins as offering each other ongoing "strong support." They quote Father James English, the family priest, as saying, "They see their main job as telling each other that each is doing all right and that the others in the family should do the same. It is an immensely strengthening activity that comes from their grandparents."

As mentioned earlier, these rosy descriptions may overlook some of the darker complexities that surfaced later. Still, there is strong evidence that, as Theresa Fitzpatrick, governess to Ted and Joan Kennedy's children, said, "They're their own best friends and their own best fans." Which brings us to unrelated best friends or good friends as distinct from best friends or good friends who are cousins. Besides the blood bond and the mystical sense of kinship, are there other differences? (And there are those who insist there are none.)

Schneider makes some nice distinctions:

"Friendship and kinship in American culture are both relationships of enduring…solidarity. What distinguishes friends from relatives [for our purposes, cousins] is that, as informants tell us so clearly, you are born with your relatives, but you can pick your friends. If you can pick them, by the same token they can be dropped at will and without obligation…In this regard, friends and enemies are alike in being chosen.

"But a friend is dropped if the friend fails to maintain desirable standards of loyalty, or solidarity, or fidelity. Performance in a friend is everything, for there is nothing else.

"Friends are relatives who can be ditched if necessary, and relatives are friends who are with you through thick and thin whether you like it or not and whether they do their job properly or not. You can really count on relatives…"

He concludes by discussing the old saw, "A man's best friend is his dog:" "Here, of course, the contrast with one's [relatives] is the clearest. One expects solidarity and loyalty from one's relatives. But if they turn mean, they cannot be taken to the local humane society to be 'put away'. They are yours and you stay with them as they stay with you."

Another way in which cousins experience a special feeling harks back to the concept of "magical siblings" expressed by my friend Stephanie Low a few years back. This is especially true of only children. My own cousin Clare says, "In my experience as a child, they represented pure magic-maybe because I wasn't with them all the time." (Like Gloria, she grew up in Philadelphia but had many relatives in New York.)

"Somehow they became the siblings I didn't have. I certainly experienced the 'big brother-ness' of your brother Frank when I visited [my brother was three and a half years older than we were] and also of Frank D." In our family, and in others I've heard of, though more often in Protestant or Irish Catholic families than in Jewish ones like ours, the sense of clan was promoted by a tendency on the part of aunts and uncles to use the same or similar names for their children, especially the boys. There were two Franks, a Frances, and a Clare Frances, two Elliots, two Phillips, and a Phyllis. We cleared the confusion by referring to them as, for instance, Elliot D. and Elliot R., but the similar names were another constant reminder of the family tie and history. And rightly so, since they were all versions of parents' and grandparents' names.

"Frank D. lived with us for a while when he was going to college in Philadelphia," Clare continued, "and he acted as a buffer between me and my parents. I remember being sent from the table one night, and Frank intervening on my behalf. I don't know what he said, but I know I was asked to come back a few minutes later."

Gisela Marks, a jewelry designer and only child who was forced to flee from Europe with her parents during World War II, told me that she lost all her aunts and uncles and most of her cousins during the Holocaust. "But a few of my cousins survived and came to America," she said, "and they are actually now my family. I feel the same way towards them that I'm sure brothers and sisters feel towards each other."

And Margot Levin, a teacher and librarian who comes from Joliet, Illinois, said, "I was an only child till I was sixteen, but I grew up surrounded by aunts, uncles and four cousins, all of whom lived within a block of each other. Being an only child is a stark existence. You feel different from other children, so you reach out, and somehow cousins are accessible and permissible. I thought of them as my brothers and sisters.

"I especially thought of the one cousin on my father's side who lived far away in New York as a sister, since she was three years younger than me and also was an only child. But what makes it even better is that you don't have the burden of a real brother or sister, where you're obligated to them, so you do these things from choice. There's nothing like a cousin," she concluded. "It's special-like a cult, a secret bond. In fact," she joked, "you'd better stay close, because these oldest friends could be your oldest enemies. They know everything about you, so even if you wanted to change your past, you couldn't."

Dr. Bloch confirmed Margot's point about doing these things from choice. "The relationship can be comfortably ignored in a way that the real sibling relationship cannot," he said.

Besides Margot's, I heard of many other cases of cousins as substitute siblings. Said Dr. Michael Fellner, a prominent dermatologist in Manhattan who writes frequently on skin care, "A cousin can be such an enriching experience, especially for an only child like me," he said. "I have a darling cousin, Doris, who's my age, and when we were kids I treasured my time with her. We did all kinds of things together-I particularly remember roller-skating. I also had other cousins I was very fond of. I've always felt that I'm really able to share with them even more than I could have with a brother or sister, who would be too close."

Barbara Oskamp, of El Cajon, California, wrote me, "My cousin is about two years older, and we're both only children. Our families lived next door for a few years while we were kids, so we spent a lot of time together. I feel she is the sister I never had.

"After college and marriage, we went our separate ways with little contact. But in the early 1970s we were both divorced and both living in the Los Angeles area and became very supportive of each other. I wrote on her birthday card: 'To my cousin who is also a friend. To my friend who is also a cousin.'"

Susan Newman, author of *Parenting an Only Child*, mentions the importance of cousinly ties as a means of giving the only child a sense of family and of overcoming his or her feelings of isolation. "Say to your only [child], 'Do you think cousin Michael got into college yet? Let's call tonight.' Simple statements reveal your strong attachments and make the only child truly a part of a family that is not present...If your daughter uses a phrase that's familiar, tell her, 'That's just the way cousin Lisa would word that.' "

She particularly emphasizes how single parents, who tend to worry even more than couples about what will happen to their children if anything happens to them, can and do use cousins as substitute siblings. "Admits Lynn Murphy, 'I worry about my health, and I've always been healthy. I make an effort to build a relationship with my son's older cousins so that they will view him as a brother. I talk to them openly about my concern.'"

Perhaps the most poetic description of cousins as substitute siblings to only children can be found in Mary Gordon's novel *The Other Side*. Speaking of Cam and Dan, a girl and boy raised by their grandmother Ellen, she says,

> Ellen allowed the child [Dan] to bring her to life...She said to

him, 'You can live here.' And made a place for another child, a girl, his cousin Cam, his sister. She could see they both were orphaned, saw them huddling together, warming each other with their breath.

...And later [Cam] saw that he suffered, and she would always act to keep back suffering from this boy, more than brother, orphaned even more than she and bereft.

Not that cousins can be substitute siblings to only children alone. Frances Kaufman Doft, the woman from Canada who had discovered her Israeli cousins only recently, said of those she'd known as she grew up, "I was the eldest of three, but my brother was six years younger, and my sister twelve years younger, than me. My girl cousins represented sisters-the older ones were role models, and the one two years younger was 'my bratty younger sister,' though now we're very close and try really hard to get together. In fact, she came in from Arizona just last week to see me and another second cousin."

Similarly, Frank D.-who died, tragically, towards the end of World War II, and whom I personally remember only slightly-became a surrogate brother not only for my cousin Clare but for my cousin Phyllis as well, who like Frances Kaufman Doft had a sibling far apart in age. "Frank became my big brother because Ira [her real brother] was more than seven years older than I was," she said, "and we didn't have that much to do with each other then. Frank really seemed to like me. He might have said 'Get lost, kid,' but he never did, and we spent a lot of time together because our mothers were always visiting."

Dr. Gorelitz summed up the many different ways in which cousins can be substitute siblings: "Even if you have a sibling of a different sex, you may wish you had a sibling of the same sex, or want an older brother or sister, or contrariwise, want a sibling very close in age. Cousins can supply all that. And sometimes, you both want a sister or a brother and you don't want one. This way you know there's a blood relationship but there's neither the intense rivalry nor the forced intimacy nor the responsibility."

And Dr. Walter Toman also mentions, in his book *Family Constellations,* that

"The inclusion of cousins in the family life can result in good...This is particularly true when one or both of the merging families have unbalanced child configurations, if one perhaps has only boys, the other only girls, or one family has two children with a large age difference and the other family has three children whose ages fit between them."

Further validation comes from anthropologists Elaine Cumming and the previously quoted Dr. David Schneider who, in a paper entitled "Sibling Solidarity" also note that, lacking siblings, a person will tend to be close to his cousins. And Bert N. Adams, professor of sociology at the University of Wisconsin, comes to the same conclusions in his book *Kinship in an Urban Setting,* noting that "substitution might occur either when the individual has no siblings...or when the individual has no same-sex siblings."

Certainly, my own experience confirmed several of these additional uses of cousins as substitute siblings, my cousins Clare and Helen becoming the same-age sisters I didn't have.

Dr. Schuman's comment about the strong tribal feeling that was part of the sense of clan points up another reason for the almost mystical sense of kinship between cousins. Because of their common background, their mutual grandparents, and the value systems families tend to share, it's perfectly natural for them to think alike-often to the extent of finding the same things funny-or even, at times, to look alike.

Rainie and Quinn also refer to the Kennedy cousins' sense of clan, adding that "In a sense, the publicity that came with the tragedies has served to increase the cousins' instinctive tribalism."

To share a history; even more, to hear a certain turn of phrase, have a mutual talent, see a certain facial configuration in the voice or features of another who is not a brother or sister, is an intriguing, even a fascinating phenomenon. To this day, people who have met Clare and me-or Helen and me-separately, often comment spontaneously, "My God, you sound just like each other!"

And why not? Together we tried to affect the casual insouciance of Ginger Rogers in *Top Hat* or other old movies seen on TV, wrote each other letters patterned on the elaborate wit of S.J. Perelman, and absorbed through our collective pores the speech patterns and thought processes of our mutual aunts, uncles, and grandparents.

And speaking of letters between cousins, the recent discovery of the long-term correspondence between Mary Shelley-author of *Frankenstein* and wife of Percy Bysshe Shelley-and her Australian cousin Elizabeth Wollstonecraft Berry and Elizabeth's husband Alexander, changed entirely the general perception of Mary as a helpless widow overcome by grief to one of an active, highly intellectual, and opinionated woman with strong views on the British monarchy and feminism, among other things. And many of T.S. Eliot's frequent letters to his cousin Eleanor reveal the whimsy that would some day result in the book *Practical Cats,* the original inspiration for the Broadway show *Cats.* At 26, he entertained her with installments of "my great ten-reel cinema drama EFFIE THE WAIF."

The common genes, along with the experiences, are also there. In our family, for instance, there were enough good amateur musicians to form a family orchestra-far more than would be likely in a random group of even the closest friends. And Clare and I harmonized constantly. To this day, we are known for our mid-July renditions of "It Came Upon a Midnight Clear."

Iseult Froelicher, who works in publishing and has only a few cousins widely disparate in age, said the same about her family. "Maybe because there are so few of us, we make a real point of getting together, especially for birthday celebrations, and I must say I think there's a definite artistic and musical gift in our family. We all play instruments, and at these birthday parties, every single person either writes a poem or composes a song, or does something else creative. And they're really good!"

Well-known examples of cousin pairs who have clearly emerged from the same talent pool are actors Sissy Spacek and Rip Torn, singers Dionne Warwick

and Whitney Houston, journalists Gay Talese and Nicholas Pileggi, Hearst Trade
Book Group president/writer Howard Kaminsky and comedian/writer Mel
Brooks. Conductor André Previn's family came from Europe to Los Angeles
when he was a boy because an older cousin was a conductor at Universal Studios.
In the 1890's, cousin collaborators Edith Somerville and Violet Martin (who
used the pseudonym "Martin Ross") wrote the novels *The Irish R.M.* and *The
Real Charlotte,* on which the Masterpiece Theatre productions were based. The
protagonists of the latter? Two female cousins.

Celeste Hoim, who has so many cousins, said that while none of her cousins
were in the theatre, many were musically talented or otherwise artistically gifted,
including a very successful weaver of tapestries in Norway. Painter Will Barnet
and his cousin, flutist Phil Kaplan of the Boston Symphony Orchestra, whom
young Will often sketched as he was growing up, also seem to demonstrate that
genetically shared creativity sometimes takes different artistic forms. And
Guarneri Quartet cellist David Soyer is the first cousin of artists Moses, Raphael,
and Isaac Soyer.

Said David Soyer: "The fact that we followed those different art forms all has
to do with our early exposure. My sister and I were exposed to music early and
received a lot of support when we wanted to pursue it. [His sister was a pianist.]
Raphael and Moses, whom I didn't actually meet till I was in my teens, knew very
little about music, and had very little interest in it, I think. They were much
older, too, so while I admired them we weren't that close. But in their family, art
was more important. We did have a mutual forebear who was very talented-my
father's father, who was my grandfather and Raphael and Moses' uncle. They told
me stories about his carving figures out of soap, and how fascinated they were
with this as they were growing up, and that may have drawn them towards art."
As for other similarities, he was hesitant, except about one thing. "Both our
families were Leftists," a very important bond in those days.

Other cases of prominent cousinly pairs using their mutual talents in different
ways aren't hard to find. Though Olympia and Michael Dukakis are in unrelated

fields, their drives for success and strong personalities may well arise from nature as well as nurture. Another good example is the Tisch family (their positions have ranged from running CBS to running the U.S. Postal Service) in which business acumen seems to have been equally spread among seven cousins and their fathers. And comedian Henny Youngman is the first cousin of Sybil Simon, who headed the New York Arts and Business Council for many years.

The genes for some surprising physical resemblances are present, too. My own daughter looks more like my brother's son than she does her own brother. Even more unexpectedly, she bears a strong resemblance to a second cousin whose father-my first cousin-in no way resembles me. Margot Levin and her New York born cousin Dana Pollock both have a white streak in their black hair, and have had it since birth. Mel Brooks and Howard Kaminsky look very much alike and apparently share ebullient personalities and a capacity to talk for hours on the phone. (Genetics are discussed in more detail in Chapter V, "When Cousins Marry.")

While my cousin Helen and I had only a vague family resemblance and somewhat similar coloring (I was pudgy, she slender; my features were large, hers delicate and fine), we often tried to emphasize the similarity by wearing our long, brown hair alike and dressing in similar clothes-at camp, or at home. As I mentioned, when people asked us if we were sisters-or better yet, twins-we were thrilled.

On the long summer evenings, when we talked in bed, Helen and I became "Twinks" and "Twinkie," famous twin movie stars. And when Clare joined us we were the triplets "Pris," "Pat" and "Penny"-successful career girls in the big city, a fantasy I enjoyed less than the one of cinema stardom, though in retrospect it strikes me as gratifyingly liberated for the time. Helen had a huge pile of *Photoplays* and *Modern Screens,* and our heads were filled with tales of sudden and unexpected discoveries by talent scouts-in drug stores (Lana Turner), at ski resorts (Jeanne Crain), or in small Southern towns (Ava Gardner). It was clearly not just a matter of being in the right place at the right time, of looking enough alike to do a twin act, or talented enough to sing in harmony, we decided, but of being prepared when the moment came.

Therefore, based on our real or contrived resemblance, and our somewhat inflated idea of our mutual cousinly talents, Helen and I readied ourselves for our discovery by rehearsing an elaborate song and dance routine one summer at camp. The choreography was nothing if not unique, consisting as it did of running around with long scarves trailing behind us (shades of Isadora Duncan, of whom we knew nothing), rushing together with scarves flying aloft, and then dashing off in different directions, only to reunite once again.

At the end of the summer, as we waited at the station in Hinsdale, Mass., for the train home, we decided to perform our "number." (We had shrewdly deduced that our chances of being discovered there were somewhat better than in the apple orchard behind our bunk.) Too astonished even to laugh, our campmates watched us, joined by a few startled strangers on the platform. To our intense disappointment, none of these strangers whipped out a card and proclaimed himself a representative for MGM. Down, but definitely not out, we continued to rehearse our twin act back in Cedarhurst, Long Island, where I grew up, during Helen's frequent weekend visits from the city.

A strong case for genetic similarities of personality was made by both Riva Castleman, Director of the Department of Prints and Illustrated Books as well as Deputy Director for Curatorial Affairs at the Museum of Modern Art, and her cousin Fran Burton, who when she left Michigan to move to New York City was the senior Cadillac saleswoman in America. "One reason I moved to New York was to be near family," said Fran, "to be near my sister and daughter, and to reestablish contact with my cousins."

Fran and Riva had met only a few times as children (Riva, who grew up in Chicago, recalls only one meeting; Fran, who grew up in Omaha, recalls three or four, but that may be due to her being six years older). As adults, they'd met twice, but only when surrounded by many others, so they'd never had a chance to really talk.

"When I contacted Riva and told her I was here, we went out to dinner and caught up on our lives," said Fran. "It was amazing. I felt an instant sense of comfort. It wasn't like meeting a stranger at all. I found we had a delightful meeting of the minds. But most amazing, as we've gotten to know each other"- they now talk to each other at least twice a week and see each other often-"is that we've found uncanny similarities that nothing in our backgrounds would necessarily produce.

"First of all, we're both very adventurous and experimental; we like kooky, off-the-wall things. She knows I'll be a viable companion to do something that most people would say 'Nyeh, I don't want to do that,' to. We'll try different kinds of food or offbeat kinds of theatre that other people find hard to take. We both love clothes and jewelry, which isn't so unusual, except that we found out we're a lot alike in our handling of them. One day we had lunch and went to Saks, and Riva was all worried about what she was going to wear to a museum opening that night. She said, 'I always know just what I'm going to wear till the last minute. Then I panic and change my mind.' Well, so do I!

"But it extends to a lot more than just taste in clothes or idiosyncrasies. Last week we went to see *The Heidi Chronicles* [the Pulitzer Prize-winning play by Wendy Wasserstein] and found we reacted exactly the same to it. We both liked the first act and didn't like the second. But that's not all. We said to each other: 'Oh, we're such smart women, what would we have done at the end?' Well, we came up with six possible alternative endings, and in the process discovered that we could build together creatively. It definitely has to do with thinking alike in some special way, and it was great fun.

"I've been trying to understand the women in my family," she continued, "and I've decided that our resemblances must come from not only environmental factors but genetic ones-particularly our grandmother, who was an extraordinarily strong and capable woman. From what I hear, she really ran the roost, and the family business, too!

"She came over to America from Russia just after the Civil War, and somehow, though most Jews who came here then stopped in the east or Chicago, she and her family moved on to Omaha. There was a pioneering spirit in her, and I think in all of us"-Frances felt the same was true of her own and Riva's sister-"that made us strong women, survivors. We're all risk-takers. And I do feel that these traits were passed on and developed due to both environment and genes."

Riva echoed this concept, saying, "There are definite Castleman traits that I can see in both of us: a way of talking, of thinking, of speaking out."

"All in all," Fran concluded, "it's been a fascinating rapprochement for me, and very rewarding."

Similarly, Lillian Schuman, who now lives in Los Angeles, re-met her cousin Vivian Rothenberg, an actress twenty-five years her junior, at the bedside of their dying uncle just ten years ago. "I can't explain it," said Lillian, who is now in her late eighties. "I hardly knew her before, and within hours, we developed the most fabulous relationship. We are so alike that it's almost spooky. In fact, we call each other 'clones.'

"To begin with, we're both interested in literature and the theatre, and react emotionally and intellectually the same way to almost everything we see or read. We even have the same tastes in food. I'll say, 'I can't stand squash!' and Viv will say, 'I can't believe it. Neither can I!' Even her kids can't get over it. I'll say, 'I love something' or 'I hate something', and her kids will say, 'That's amazing! Mom feels exactly the same.'"

Lil's health prevents her from making the trip east, but she said, "Viv and I are in touch all the time now, and she comes out to visit me on the coast regularly. Having so much in common has got to come out of something beyond mere chance and family in common, though of course we discuss all the relatives we both knew a lot." (The importance of such talks and memories are explored in depth in Chapter 7, "The Test of Time.")

Margot Levin and her cousin Dana Pollock, who also grew up halfway across the country from each other, share more in the way of similarities than the unusual white streak in their hair. "We see things the same way," said Margot, "including the idiosyncrasies of our very peculiar family. That is always there-and it all seems funnier because we're related. We're also alike in our personalities-we're both very direct and accurate. Too direct, maybe. This is hard for some people to take, but it amuses and satisfies us.

"We have a natural affinity, too, that's got to come from something alike inside us, because although I did see Margot four or five times as we were growing up, we were basically raised in completely different environments-she in the rural Midwest, which I guess I romanticized, and I in the East in the city. At twenty-two, Margot came to New York for a year and lived with me, and it was then that we discovered most of these similarities. We like a lot of the same things-books, movies, etc. We also both like to do everything in bed-read, write, eat, study-you name it. Our closeness was obviously as much intuitive as based on time spent together," she said. "I mean, I would feel this way about Margot even if we weren't related, but it makes it nicer and more special that we are."

Lewis Frumkes, the writer, who had never gotten to know his cousin Mel, a successful Florida lawyer now in his sixties, till a reunion a few years back said, "I couldn't believe how much Mel was like my father. [Their fathers were brothers.] First of all, my father had a mannerism-an odd way of touching his nose with his thumb. I noticed right away that Mel was doing this, and I thought, My God, maybe this man is my half-brother, and not a cousin! But even more importantly, there was a remarkable meeting of the minds. We definitely talk on a level that's more sympatico than it would be with a new friend, or even with the other cousins. The gene pool is really fascinating."

Anna Quindlen also notes cousinly similarities. "A lot of us have a real anecdotal relationship to the world. We are a big storytelling group, though I'm the only writer. It tends to be the kind of family where you can't get a word in edgewise. There are some quiet ones, and I do have a quiet brother, but overall it tends to be a very volatile group. We also tend to find the same things funny, and to do the same things at the same time. In fact, we're even having kids at the same time!"

The sense of clan and of a special shared history is enhanced by what Dr. Michael Kahn, associate professor of psychology at the University of Hartford, and coauthor, with Steven P. Bank, of *The Sibling Bond*, calls the "family mythology"-stories about mutual grandparents and great-grandparents, eccentric aunts, uncles, great-aunts and great-uncles that get passed along, that can be both more interesting but perhaps less accurate than family history per se. Who else would know that great-grandfather Philip was a tyrant who had once cowed the now-formidable Aunt Madeline? (But was it true he had a photographic memory?) Or that my maternal grandfather was a saint, my grandmother an unmitigated shrew when her daughters were young? Though these stories no doubt had elements of truth, they always seemed a bit too black and white for me, especially when I recalled the sad and quiet old lady my grandmother became.

As Elizabeth Stone says in her fascinating book *Black Sheep and Kissing Cousins,* subtitled "How Our Family Stories Shape Us":

> Like all cultures, one of the family's first jobs is to persuade its members they're special, more wonderful than the neighboring barbarians. The persuasion consists of stories showing family members demonstrating admirable traits, which it claims are family traits. *Attention to the stories' actual truth is never the family's most compelling consideration. Encouraging belief is* [my italics]. The family's survival depends on the shared sensibility of its members.

But it takes more than blood or common traits or shared mythology to create close cousin relationships. Because sometimes all of these elements are present, and cousins remain indifferent or hostile to each other. Why some cousins are central to each other's lives and others aren't, why some cousins love each other and others don't is what I wanted to find out next.

2

COUSINS WHO LOVE

Message on a greeting card under Relatives"~
"So much more than just being cousins...I'm glad
that we're friends."

"Our shared history transcends any differences"

-CAROLE KLEIN, BIOGRAPHER

WHY THEN DO some cousins get along so well? (Which is not to say that even among the friendliest of cousins, differences never exist.) Said Dr. Kahn: "The relationship between the parent siblings is a very strong factor in how cousins will interact. Cousins are often proxy delegates for their parents."

Dr. James Framo, Distinguished Professor of Family Therapy at the U.S. International University in San Diego and a past president of the American Family Therapy Association, describes this phenomenon as part of the "family systems theory"-an awesome term that, reduced to its simplest level, means that relationships of family members are interconnected and tend to persist from one generation to another. "For instance, if brothers and sisters get along, their children are likely to," he said, to which Dr. Kahn added, "If the parents had a good relationship, they will often actively work to encourage contact and a positive relationship between their children."

It is this last factor-the active encouragement of parents and often of grand-parents-especially when combined with proximity (though, as has already been shown, this is by no means always a condition) that I found was true not only of my family as I grew up, but of many others.

Said Anna Quindlen, whose childhood and adulthood, along with my own and that of the Kennedys began to emerge as a prototype of cousinly togetherness, "My father and his five brothers and his two sisters all lived close to each other and saw each other with great frequency either at their parents' house, or at one another's houses socially. So whether I liked it or not-and I generally liked it-I was thrown together with my cousins all the time. We were all over each other, and even if we didn't see each other directly, our paths intersected at our grandparents'. You'd see a toy truck or a doll you hadn't seen there before, and say, 'Where did that come from?' And they'd say, 'Oh, Casey and Robert were over last week.' So they were a presence, even if not actually present."

Supporting Dr. Kahn's opinion, she concluded, "I do think that a lot of how you interrelate with your cousins has to do with how close your parents were."

And often, with the influence of your grandparents. Says Dr. Bert N. Adams, "Grandparents, when living, are a focal point of much ritual kin inter-action." And Rainie and Quinn stress that, "Towering over each of the six sep-arate families of this generation of Kennedys are a dead grandfather's still vital memory, and one grandmother's living exceptional presence...The [cousins'] commitment to each other came from deeply programmed responses that were taught to their parents."

They quote Chris Lawford as saying, "The fact that we all feel so strongly about one another and the fact that we all really have the same core of values and beliefs means that it had to come from somewhere-and that place is our parents and our grandparents."

Again, the shared history was an important element and one especially stressed by Rose Kennedy, who would invite a few cousins over at a time, grouped by age, to talk about "things suitable to their age and experiences," and especially to tell them about the family. As she herself wrote: "Naturally, as I see them sitting there, often in the same chairs where long ago their parents sat, I want them to get a little sense of family history, our family life-where they are, where they come from, what it was like, what good times there were."

There is another powerful positive force in uniting cousins: the real family stories they pick up, separately or together, as opposed to the often embroidered family mythology. Elizabeth Stone, whose book *Black Sheep and Kissing Cousins* was already mentioned, is eloquent on this subject. "In the beginning, as far back in my family as anyone could go, was my great-grandmother, and her name was Annunziata." She goes on to tell how the name was handed down from genera-tion to generation, eventually becoming anglicized as "Nancy" and then says:

> I never met that first Annunziata, but my mother often told me a family story about her which, as a child, I knew as well as I knew the story of Cinderella and loved better [a story of that first Annunziata's elopement in defiance of her father's wishes].
>
> For me it was always the stories that held the spirit and meaning of our family…Some were old and ancestral, but some were new, about my mother's generation or mine…Some relied only on a well-developed scene-like the one in which [in their native town in Italy] my great-grandfather and his half-dozen sons were playing music after dinner in the courtyard as people came 'from miles around' to listen. And still others were simply characterizations of people-'You had one ancestor who was a court musician' or 'You had another ancestor who was an aide to Garibaldi.' These qualified as stories in the way haikus qualify as poems.
>
> These stories last not because they're entertaining, though they may be; they last because in ways large and small they matter…The family is our first culture, and, like all cultures, it wants to make

known its norms and mores. It does so through daily life, but it also does so through the family stories which underscore, in a way invariably clear to its members, the essentials, like the unspoken and unadmitted family policy on marriage or illness. Or suicide. Or who the family saints and sinners are, or how much anger can be expressed and by whom."

So whether she intended to or not-and it appeared she was at least partially conscious of the effects-Rose Kennedy used the family stories to unite the cousins on family values, family policies, family expectations and aspirations.

Furthermore, Maria Shriver says that their childhood was "like a camp organized around ourselves. There was always the sense, the very strong sense, that the family was the most important thing in the world."

The cousins also traveled together often (many still do), and during their summers together at Hyannis Port-a powerful force in uniting them as, I see now, were the summers together at camp for my own family-they did a lot of things besides competitive sports and sailing. They participated in political discussions and wrote and produced plays such as *The Wizard of Oz* and *Cinderella* for each other and for their parents and grandparents. (Maria Shriver is recalled as the most prolific playwright.)

Even after his stroke in 1961, their grandfather is remembered by most of the cousins as "the predominant pervasive force in their childhoods," according to Steve Smith, Jr. Say Rainie and Quinn, "On his birthday, they would stage an especially extravagant production, line up to give him a kiss, and then stand back in choir with their parents to sing 'Happy Birthday."

They also honored Rose Kennedy, one of the last plays being "The Story of Rose," starring young Rory Kennedy, that described in dramatic terms her participation in the JFK presidential campaign. On her ninetieth birthday, in 1981, they staged a parade in Hyannis Port. And earlier, for her eighty-fifth birthday, Bobby Shriver, then an editor at the *Yale Daily News,* had all the cousins put together a book of tributes that said, in Chris Lawford's words, what all the cousins believed: "My grandmother is very, very special."

If "all happy families are alike," then it may explain the remarkable similarity between at least one of the cousinly activities of a family of second generation Jewish immigrants in Joliet, and that of the Irish Catholic Kennedys. Said Margot Levin (the teacher and librarian who was previously described as having grown up an only child until age 16, but surrounded by cousins, aunts, uncles, and grandparents all living within a block of each other), "We were always putting on plays for the parents and grandparents. As a girl, I was the Statue of Liberty. Some of the others would be the new arrivals in America, dressed in babushkas and carrying baggage. Grandpa always cried."

And moving to still another ethnic group, amazing parallels exist between the childhood of Eduardo Riccio, an Italian raised in the Bronx in New York during the Fifties, and the seemingly remote and rarefied Kennedys in terms of family values. Eduardo, now a teacher of comparative religion at the Horace Mann School in Riverdale, described it this way: "We grew up in the Bronx in this very tightly knit community. We all lived in houses on Zerega Avenue, and all our life was with our cousins. Our best friends were our cousins; we did everything with aunts and uncles. Our regular family outings would be going to Pelham Bay Park"-which I began to see as the Hyannis Port of the Riccios-"with grandfather, grandmother, all the mothers and fathers, and then all the cousins. We would then walk to Orchard Beach and have a swim, and if it was a good day, the police would come by on their horses.

"It was a tightly knit cousin community. I had no friends besides cousins. Other people were regarded as outsiders-as strangers [another parallel with the Kennedys]. Our Sundays were completely communal. The men would line up on Sunday morning, talking. The women and children went to church, and then the women came home to prepare the midday meal. About two o'clock everyone was eating, and then you would visit-and play with the cousins, who were across the street, or upstairs, or around the corner."

Like the Kennedys, also, the family often traveled together as a group. Many of them still do. "Constance, Maria-" he said, "they all go to the Jersey shore together. In fact, they're always together, especially the girls, even though they don't live on the same block anymore. And they're having their children grow up together. Even though my sister lives ten or fifteen minutes away now, she will drive her kids over to play on the block with their cousins."

The importance of proximity in promoting close cousin relationships can't be overemphasized. Says Dr. Bert Adams, in the chapter of *Kinship in an Urban Setting* entitled "Best-known Cousin and Secondary Kin":

> One reason why a particular cousin is known better than other cousins may be because at a crucial stage of life close contact was afforded by residential proximity
>
> Almost seven out of ten of the 261 respondents [in his study] who knew a cousin quite or extremely well now were characterized by residential proximity in childhood, frequently continuing into adulthood…At the other extreme, about six out of ten who do not know their…cousin too well at present never lived close…at all or for more than a few years.
>
> …Hunting buddies, shopping partners, sharers of activity both at home and in the community: all but six of these eighty-two pairs of [close]cousins spent their childhood in close proximity and developed through the years a companionship based upon common interests which exceeds the superficial obligation for secondary [non-nuclear] kin contact. They…refer to their cousin as 'not just a relative, but a good friend.'

And speaking of obligations, as with the Kennedys, family obligations among the Riccios were not taken lightly or left to chance. "My father inculcated an enormous sense of duty and responsibility towards aunts, uncles and cousins. He was always reminding us of it. When one of my father's sisters emigrated here, it was my responsibility to get my cousins to school and show them around the city. And believe me, there was no discussion about that. Even when I was in college, if I came up to visit on a Sunday, I didn't just visit my parents. I was expected to make the rounds to visit all the aunts and uncles-I particularly liked to see Aunt Sophia and Uncle Felice, who were like second parents to me-and of course the cousins."

Theorists are of two minds about the obligations of the cousin relationship. Some support Dr. Donald Bloch's and others' earlier comments about the tenuousness of the cousinly connection as an indirect advantage. (Adams: "The very weakness of the obligatory link…makes possible a close association between feelings towards him or her and frequency of contact.")

Others see it as no advantage at all. Adams later quotes Barrington Moore, in *Political Power and Social Theory,* as describing the "barbaric 'obligation to give affection as a duty to a particular set of persons on account of the accident of birth.'"

Still others assert with vigor the strength of the sense of obligation. Robin Fox, the anthropologist, says in his book, *Kinship and Marriage,* "We may be a relatively 'kinshipless' society (although sociologists have probably exaggerated this tendency) but the sentiments of kinship still linger. Would we not, if a long-forgotten first cousin turned up having fallen on hard times, feel *some* obligation towards him *simply* because he was a cousin." Returning to the "blood" theme, he concludes, "Blood, as the old adage has it, is thicker than water."

Fox was referring to the sense of obligation aroused by a crisis situation, such as the one described earlier, in which cousins rallied to help a previously unknown-and suicidal-cousin get her life together. The less extreme demands of regular family visits (such as those in the Riccios, the Quindlens, or my own) were mentioned by many others as the tie that binds.

Whether out of obligation or love, or a bit of both, career counselor Barbara Lindeman says she's sure it was a combination of the warm personality of her grandmother and the willingness of her mother and her mother's six brothers and sisters to gather every Sunday at her grandmother's house that created the "special" feeling the thirteen first cousins still have for each other. "The wonderful thing about her was that she made us all feel that she loved us best. In fact, I recently got together with one of my cousins who made some passing remark about having been 'grandma's favorite.' I was completely shocked, and I said, 'I always thought *I* was her favorite.' Then we looked at each other and realized that that was her genius. All of us thought *we* were her favorites. She made friends out of all of us; she made us all feel good, and there wasn't the slightest rivalry. Actually," she mused, "those Sundays are my happiest childhood memories."

Barbara did say that after her grandmother died, and as they got older and moved out of range of each other, there had been some fragmentation. "She was what kept us in touch, and though we still will always see each other on happy and sad occasions and feel very close, when she died, so did the ongoing connectedness."

Which brings up an interesting point: In certain families, one person, rather than a group of parents or the group of cousins as a whole, will become the catalyst who makes the real effort to keep the cousins united. In Barbara's case, and in many others, like the Kennedys, it is the grandmother. But sometimes it can be a member of the younger generation who consciously or unconsciously, takes on this responsibility.

I became aware of this when a cousin of my own recently mentioned that I was the one who kept the family flame burning. Till then I'd never thought about it, but when he said it, I realized it was at least partly so. Certainly, I wanted to stay in touch myself, which led inevitably to my thinking in terms of seeing my cousins on occasions that went beyond the obligatory weddings and funerals. Similarly, Frances Kaufman Doft told me that she was considered by others in her family to be playing this role, "although till someone said so, I'd never thought of it. Maybe it was because I needed it and missed it so much as a child."

Frances' is a good case to illustrate how determined parents can to some extent overcome the lack of proximity. (She'd grown up in Toronto, and all her cousins were in Chicago or New York.) "I certainly missed seeing my cousins during the year," she said. "Through them, I felt connected to the world at large. They were my extended family. But at least we would spend summers with some of them"-and these were the ones she had turned into her "substitute siblings."

Likewise, when Edith Beer and her relatives came to the United States from Switzerland during World War II, she said, "We actually didn't live very near each other. Some moved to the city, some to Westchester, and my family was out on Long Island. But every Sunday the aunts, uncles, and the first, second and even third cousins-among them my 'Aunt' Yetti, and 'Uncle' Max (he was actually my first cousin once removed)-came over to talk and reminisce," she fondly recalled. "They kept me in touch with the family and that's how I learned all the family lore. Today we're still very close."

But it's undoubtedly easier when parental encouragement and proximity coexist. Gloria Hochman, the writer from Philadelphia whose grandparents owned the bakery, said, "We lived nearby-within a ten-minute walk-and saw each other all the time. I was very close to my aunt, as well as to my grandparents and my cousins."

And Neilson Abeel, who hadn't known any of his relatives on his father's side till his English cousin suggested a reunion, said of his mother's side: "We spent all our early summers together at my grandfather's house in Matapoiset, and were very close. We all sailed together and had a wonderful time. I was terribly upset when the girl cousin five years younger than me died at twenty-five of cancer. It was devastating. But the boy and I are friendly to this day."

An extreme example of proximity as a factor is that of Nancy Smoller, who grew up in the same house in Boston with four of her cousins. "My parents had to move together with my aunt and uncle for economic reasons during the Depression," she said, "and though they certainly liked each other, they always felt guilty about the fact that we had so little space. In fact, we had only one bathroom for the nine of us, and that wasn't so great. But apart from that, we all thought it was wonderful. I slept on the porch with my cousin Joey, and it was like one big, extended family." (She and her husband still talk daily with Joey and his wife Lillian and see them every week, though Joey lives in Boston, and Nancy in Westchester.)

A final example of the happy combination of parents, grandparents, and proximity contributing to positive cousin relationships seemed to me to be found in the story told to me by A. Lewis Brackley, Jr., a realtor now living in Natick, Massachusetts. Until he was 8, Lew and his sister Sally, two years younger, grew up in Malden, Mass.; his cousins Ellen and Bill Quinn lived in Marlboro, just ten miles away. "Ellen was just three months younger than I was, and Bill was Sally's age. We saw them all the time, because we all had fun together and because Ellen's mother and my father, who were brother and sister, were very close," he said. "Also, our grandparents lived with Ellen and Bill, so we saw them all the time, too.

"We moved to Maine in 1941, when the war was just starting, and lived there for ten years, and this had a big impact on our relationships with our cousins. As soon as school was over, they and my grandparents would come up and spend the whole summer with us. And Christmases we were together, too- either with them in Malden or in Maine with us. We've always felt that Ellen in particular was one step removed from a sister." (She is close to Lew's wife Sue as well as to Sally and her husband.) "But it was all really an extended family."

Over the years they've all remained unusually close, and Lew and Sue see Ellen and her husband Ron often, to play bridge or just to get together. Ellen has no children of her own, but has taken a great interest in both Sally's and Lew's children, and in fact was planning a wedding in Massachusetts for Sally's daughter with Lew and Sue when I talked to Lew, since Sally and her family now live in Georgia. "And whenever there's a problem situation in Sally's family or mine, we get on the phone and discuss it with Ellen," said Lew. "In fact, there's a kind of female triumvirate now, of Ellen, Sally, and Sue."

Sue suggested that perhaps they'd all have been friends anyway, and that maybe the same thing could have happened even if they weren't related, an opinion Lew did not share. "If the chemistry isn't there, and you don't like a cousin, maybe you'd ignore them. But if it is there, you have more reason to pursue it. There's definitely more of a connection." Echoing the feelings voiced by other close cousins, he said, "There's a special attachment-a communication you don't have if they're just friends."

Adams supports this point, noting that next to proximity, the second condition for closeness to one's cousin in adulthood is "a similarity of ideas and interests and minimal obligation, the same attributes considered to be crucial to friendly relations." However, he stresses that "Childhood proximity, while the best predictor of adult closeness, is far short of being a sufficient condition for it."

Lew pointed out the contrast in his relationships with another set of cousins, where neither parental closeness nor proximity was an early factor. "My mother's sister's children lived in San Diego, so we didn't know them very well, and my mother and her sister didn't make much of an effort to get together. But two of them went to college in Maine and came to live with us, so I got to know them better. But I don't have the same relationship with them as with Ellen and Bill, and now we don't contact each other much."

As in Lew's case, when closeness in age is added to parental encouragement and proximity, the mixture is even more powerful in forming close cousinly relationships among children-though it should be emphasized, and will be demonstrated later, that these differences become increasingly unimportant as cousins grow up. Certainly, the awe with which I regarded some of my older cousins as a child mellowed into friendship when we began to relate as grownups years later. Still, as children, the fact that Clare, Helen, Fran and I were all born within a year of each other was an important element in forging our lifelong friendships, as it was to Maria Shriver and her bridesmaids. To this day, theirs are the only birthdays, besides those of my immediate family, that I never forget.

Another case in point is that of John Baker, now Assistant Director of Preservation at the New York Public Library. "I was always happy to see all my cousins," he said, "but I was definitely closest to those nearest my age. In fact, I think I was closer to those my age than I was to my own brother and sister, who were five and seven years older than I was."

He, too, described a childhood "of old-fashioned togetherness, as I look back on it. On my mother's side, there were nine siblings, all of whom had children, and I have clear memories of all of us roasting weenies together during our summers together in Cape Ann. We had a big old stone house there, and I also remember singing old American songs, and of skating and skiing parties during the winter. For several years we got together for the Christmas holidays, too, and when my grandmother and grandfather were alive, we would have annual family dinners."

Arnold Kauffman, 67, was born three weeks after his cousin Milt, and they have been best friends throughout their lives, a fact Arnold attributes at least in part to their close ages. "We all grew up in Brooklyn and were all very poor," he said, "but we had a lot of fun. Everybody would gather in our backyard to play. In fact they used to call it 'Frank's Place.' (My father's name was Frank.)

"All our lives Milt and I have stuck together," he said. "When I was in the Marine Corps and he was in the Seabees, we found out we were both located in the South Seas only twenty miles apart. Somehow he found me, and he managed to wangle a visit with me. We Marines were living like kings-we had ice cream, tents, movies, fresh meat-and he had nothing like that where he was stationed, so we had a great time. Then we were both stationed in San Diego for a while. I claimed he was my brother and got him out on liberty. In fact, I consider him my brother more than my cousin.

"After the war, we always lived near each other-first in Massapequa Park on Long Island, then Laurelton. When he moved to Florida a few years ago, I followed him, and now we live just a few blocks apart. When my wife died, and I started to go out with other women, I always brought them to him to be checked."

Eduardo Riccio, the Horace Mann teacher who grew up in the Bronx, said that though he was close to all his cousins, his closest friend as a child was his cousin Tony, who was also closest to him in age. "We went all over New York together on the subway, exploring the city," he said. "In fact we did everything together-played street games, got part-time jobs together, dated together, everything. We also got into plenty of trouble together. When we were teens, we got all the boy cousins to build a big clubhouse with wood we found from a house that was being built. We used the supports behind a big billboard as the frame. We had floors and everything. But when it was built, we made so much noise that the adults got together and rounded us up, and made us shut up. Anyway," he concluded, "I've always assumed our being so close in age was part of the reason we were so close."

Being contemporaries, then, can create a powerful bond between cousins. But the admiration younger cousins feel for older ones, who often become role models and teachers, is another.

Dr. Clifford Sager, with whom I discussed the subject both for his professional and personal views, confirmed the importance of cousins as role models and said that in fact an older cousin who was not only a physician but also a great outdoorsman and ecologist had given him the idea to study medicine.

"I also had another cousin for whom I felt nothing short of hero worship as I was growing up," he said. "He was an outstanding football player, and always gave me great advice. One thing I remember in particular is his saying, 'If you're going to get in a fight and can't avoid it, make sure you hit the other person first.' I learned a great deal from him."

Alice Pareles, a former executive secretary at IBM, said, "I had a cousin, Mary, who was three years older than I was and very smart, very pretty, and very talented on the piano, which I played, too. I remember how my uncle bragged about it when she skipped a grade. I really worshipped her, though I see now that I also felt very inferior to her. But somehow, it didn't get in the way of my admiring her, and in fact I still do, and I still love her because she was so helpful to me.

"Anyway, I seemed to follow in her footsteps in a lot of ways. In high school,

I kept up with the piano because Mary liked me to play duets with her, and she taught me lots of pieces. And she always included me in things that really widened my horizons. For instance, in high school, she was part of a social club I'd never have joined without her. And she was in the glee club, so a few years later, I got the idea of joining, and even became the accompanist after her. Because she went to college, I got the idea of going, too, and I did, though my father wouldn't let me go away to school like her."

Another case of a cousin acting as an inspiration for higher education was related by Eduardo Riccio. "Even though my cousin Tony wasn't a role model in the usual sense, since we were so close in age, in many ways he was the reason I ended up going to Columbia. He was really the first one in the neighborhood to go to college. He was going to CCNY, so I went with him a couple of times. And when I decided to go, and got through my own college applications, I had a scholarship at St. Johns and Manhattan. (You know, they wanted us to go to a Catholic college.) Then by accident I saw a Columbia bulletin, and called them, and when they asked me to come for an interview, of course I went to my cousin. And he said, 'Well, it's just a few blocks down from CCNY.' So we went together for the interview. We walked around the campus, and we were in awe of how beautiful it was. We had no idea there was anything like this in New York City. I was finally accepted, and it was at least partly because of Tony. Later, he was impressed with me because I went there."

David Forman, an art dealer in New York, told a fascinating tale of a cousin as a longtime role model. "You have to start with the picture of this very repressed family I grew up in," he said. "My parents, and in fact all my aunts and uncles and most of my cousins, never expressed anger or talked about their real feelings. Also, we were a family of intellectuals. Sports weren't considered important. Well, I had this cousin Peter, ten or twelve years older than I was, who was big and strong and who wrestled. I thought he was terrific!

"After college, he was offered a job on Wall Street, and he took it, although I'd already heard he wanted to be an artist-another unheard of thing in our family. Anyway, one day I guess he got fed up with the job and the long hours, and went in to tell his boss he wanted to quit. They must have gotten into a fight, because the next thing you know he decked the boss. My parents were shocked, and talked about it in hushed tones with my aunt and uncle, but I was thrilled. To me, a weak kid of twelve who always felt everyone was stepping on him, it seemed very brave and heroic, though I have no idea if the attack was justified or not.

"The next thing I knew I heard that Peter had sought out this really important Italian artist, Carlo Alfieri [not his real name], whose work he admired, while Alfieri was visiting in New York. Somehow, he persuaded Alfieri to come to his studio. Alfieri stayed for an hour and ended up saying to Peter, 'You must come to study in Florence with me.' And Peter did, and stayed there for fifteen years.

"Now comes the most important part, his influence on me as an adult," continued David. "I hadn't seen Peter after he went to Florence for about ten years. Then I went to Italy on a trip-just a vacation. I had no idea what I was going to do with my life, but it looked as if I was headed for the family business. Anyway, I'd almost forgotten about Peter, but then I remembered he was living in Florence, and I decided to call him when I got there. He seemed delighted to hear from me, and invited me to come to his house. God, I remember getting completely lost looking for it, but finally, after about an hour of wandering, I found it. When Peter opened the door, he shouted *'Cugino!'*-that's Italian for 'cousin'-and threw his arms around me. That really scared me. I thought, Is this guy gay or something? It hadn't occurred to me that he might just be really glad to see me, and be willing to show it.

"Anyway, he showed me some of his paintings, and I was really impressed. Then he insisted we go out to dinner. On the way to the restaurant, Peter peed in a street urinal, and that startled me, too. I thought: This is unbelievable. Who opens his pants in the middle of the street and pees? But then I began to think about it and to realize it really made sense. I mean, if people have to pee, they have to pee, and why make it difficult?

"Finally we got to the restaurant. We spent two hours drinking a wine called 'Fiasco'-I remember thinking what a funny name it was for a wine (I later found out it was the name for the bottle, not the wine)-and telling stories about the family. I found I could be honest with him about how things were handled in our family in a way I'd never been before. Somehow, we cracked through a layer of family bullshit I'd never thought could be broken, and I began to see that people could be honest-I mean, not just people, but me. If I had a cousin who could be like this, maybe I could, too.

"But the most significant thing that happened was that after dinner, in our drunken state-we'd had coffee but it had absolutely no effect-we went wandering through the streets and came to these statues. I saw Michelangelo's 'David' for the first time (it was a copy, but I thought it was an original) and just twenty-five feet away, Cellini's 'Perseus.' I don't know if it was the wine or what, but I couldn't get over how beautiful they were. That was a turning point in my life in a lot of ways. I really think it was that night that I decided to pursue art in some form as a career.

"Also, the sculptures of the Sabine women were there. They were very sexual sculptures, and that has to do with another way in which Peter opened new areas for me. I saw him a lot during the next ten days, and he had this beautiful girlfriend, Isabella, who was living with him. Their relationship was very openly sexual, and I was fascinated. I was still a virgin then, but soon I got a girlfriend, too, a wonderful girl who was studying Italian history in Siena, but who lived in Florence. She spoke no English, but we got along in French. Well, I lost my virginity just a few days later, and somehow, I knew that Peter had validated the whole thing for me. He even said, 'You've got the equipment; you might as well use it.'

"As I think about it," he concluded, "I realize he actually influenced almost every area of my life-my personality, my work, my sexuality-everything."

Artistically at least, writer Walker Percy was also enormously influenced by a second cousin who became the guardian for him and his two brothers after their parents' early deaths. In a *New York Times* review of editor Carolyn Anthony's book, *Family Portraits,* Jill Ker Conway says that this cousin "showed the three Percy brothers what it meant to live for literature, why great art mattered, how to breathe in ideas like the Southern air of Jackson, Mississippi."

Many women, like Ann Pareles, who saw their older cousins as career or school models, also regarded them as models of beauty or sophisticated femininity.

"I idolized two of my older female cousins," said Barbara Lindeman. "One was two years older, one four years older than I was, and they knew things I didn't. They seemed wonderfully worldly and exotic to me. They had movie stars' pictures on their wall, and that seemed to me to be the height of sophistication."

Anna Quindlen also had two older cousins she looks back on as having been role models-each in a slightly different way. "One I thought was just the smartest, most together person in the world, mainly because I was eight and she was thirteen," she said. "The other just happened to be very pretty and sort of delightful, and I remember thinking *"That's* what I want to be like!"

Said Frances Kaufman Doft: "I had a cousin five years older than I was, and I wanted to be just like her. She dated before me; she went to nursing school and I wanted to be a nurse, and so forth. As children, I know she was more important to me than I was to her, but as we grew up it evened out, and now we definitely connect as equals. In fact, she was maid of honor at my wedding."

Perhaps the part that cousins play as role models for women was expressed most poignantly by Elizabeth Fishel in her book *Sisters.* Speaking of her five-years-younger sister Annie, she says,

> I wonder if Annie watches me for clues as I puzzle, blunder, navigate the next step, the way I watch our two older cousins, raised almost like sisters to us, for signs and hints as they work, marry, have children, separate, carry on. 'Only be afraid of the big things in life,' said one of my cousins in all seriousness when she was fourteen, I was nine, 'like going to the dentist.' Later I asked them whether it hurt the first time and how they decided whom to marry and what it felt

like to give birth to and raise a son. I planned and measured my script against theirs. Now I wonder if they felt as ambivalently worldly and wise as I do on the sidelines of Annie's passing parade. I wonder whom they watch for clues.

Anne Leventhal, a writer from Hartford, Connecticut, remembers her cousin Harriet, twenty years older, as a teacher more than a role model, "Probably because she was really old enough to be another mother-and in fact she used to babysit for us when she went to Florida with us. But whenever I do certain things I always think of her, because she's the one who taught me things like how to cut an onion, and how to make a pizza with cheese on an English muffin."

Today, she added, the twenty-year difference made no difference, and she said the same phenomenon had occurred with other cousins who as a child had seemed too old to be her friends. "All the other cousins were much younger or my sister's age-four years older. I felt then that 'She has cousins; I don't.' But once I grew up and we all started to have children, the age differences didn't matter at all."

This brings up another important factor that helps maintain lasting bonds between cousins-a factor that will come up again in other contexts, but should at least be touched on here. As Dr. Schuman had said, "Because of the ongoing tie, you're almost forced to stay in touch with cousins-even with cousins you may not like." Negative as this may sound, it often results in the discovery that a cousin you once disliked was not so bad after all, and that a cousin who seemed remote and much too far apart in age to be a friend can become one.

Said one woman I spoke to: "I remet Karen, a cousin I had often treated as a child with an unkindness that makes me blush in retrospect, at a family gathering about five years ago, and now she's a close friend. We discovered we had both changed in ways that drew us closer. To my great relief, she recalled my occasional cruelty as a child with a lot more understanding than I'd have believed possible. Knowing the family *gestalt,* she knew a lot more about why I was acting so mean (and hating myself for it) in those days. Yet without the family connection, it's unlikely we'd ever have seen each other again when we were adults. Certainly we wouldn't have sought each other out."

A story from my own experience illustrates how periodic meetings over the years can afford a forum for resolving long-term misunderstandings. Furthermore, it demonstrates how friendships that are formed between cousins of far different ages later in life can be no less powerful than those between contemporaries.

When I was about seven, I began to realize that there were three age levels of cousins in the family in relation to me. First of all, of course, the three cousins my age; then a group five to eight years older-one girl, Phyllis, the two Elliots, and Charles, brother to my cousins Fran and Elliot R. And finally, there were five much older boy cousins-Frank D., brother of Elliot D.; the brothers Bernard, Saul, and Henry Jaffe; and Ira (Phyllis' brother). This last group especially seemed very old to me then, but actually ranged in age from about eighteen to thirty-one, and I thought them very glamorous and worldly.

I especially admired Ira and Henry, who seemed to be around our house more than the others. Henry, already a successful lawyer at age thirty-one, knew famous people in the movies and theatre (many, in fact, were his clients), adored my mother, and was often her tennis partner.

Ira, an aspiring pianist who had taken on a few piano students in our area to earn some money, was very muscular, handsome and, I thought, extremely witty in the dry style of the Rosengarten clan. To Ira was handed what I realize now was the more than challenging task of taking over my piano lessons just after three or four teachers before him had given up on me in rapid succession. This was, I should add, no reflection on either my musicality or their talents as teachers, which were no doubt adequate to most situations.

But I was at a difficult, rebellious stage, angry at the world because an administrative mix-up at my school had put me in the humiliating position of being a year behind my same-age cousins, and anguished because a nurse I loved had left at the same time.

Into this cauldron of inchoate emotions came my unfortunate cousin, the hopes of my parents for my musical future, and of other relatives as well, pinned on him to teach me and bring me into line.

We both remember what ensued with pain and sadness. (This I only found out years later.) I developed a tremendous crush on Ira, and fearing that I couldn't possibly win his attention by practicing and playing well-an impossibility in any case, since every time I saw him my hands began to shake-I chose other ways to make him notice me, chiefly, being bratty, disrespectful, and unprepared. After a few months, when it became obvious that this teacher-student combination, too, was doomed to failure, a merciful halt was called to my lessons with Ira.

Still, instead of never seeing him again, which would have been the usual consequence of such an unhappy match-and was, with the other, unrelated teachers-we continued to meet as I grew up and we both grew older; in fact, his wedding eight years later took place at my parents' house in Cedarhurst. But we remained somewhat distant, circling each other warily for years, and it was a rare occasion, if we were together and did talk, that one of us didn't make some glancing reference to that experience. Mine tended to be kiddingly apologetic; his sarcastic.

Finally, only a few years ago, when by chance we were seated next to each other at a family wedding, the whole thing came out in the open. I have no idea how it came up, but I think it had to do with the fact that an old recording on which Ira had accompanied my mother, a singer, was played. We were both very moved at hearing it, and since it was cut at about the same time as the failed lessons, it evoked that era poignantly, as music so often does. Perhaps that's why, later, one of our usual half-joking comments was picked up by one or the other of us and not allowed to pass as casually as it always had before. And I discovered, to my surprise and delight, that he had been as pained, saddened, and embarrassed by the whole episode as I was, and had had no idea that I, too, had been feeling genuinely regretful about it for years. And so, fifty years later, we straightened it out and have been much closer ever since. The fifteen-year age gap seems quite unimportant now.

According to Dr. Sager, this is the right way to handle such problems, though it was quite unplanned in our case. "It should be talked about if there's a problem-even if it's many years later," he said-though ideally, before fifty years has elapsed. Once again, this was a case where the built-in continuation of the relationship due to family gatherings, gave us a chance to work things out, and where the difference in ages dropped away as time went by.

As for Henry, who went on to become the producer of such early TV hits as *The Dinah Shore Show* and *The Bell Telephone Hour,* though I never quite got over my childhood awe of him-which his natural reserve and sardonic manner did nothing to dispel-he and I, too, eventually became good friends thanks to the ongoing family connection.

He'd come in from California, where he'd moved, to visit my by-then very aging parents about ten years ago. I'd made a point of being at their apartment, too, since I knew that, sadly, my mother and dad could no longer sustain much of a conversation. Though they couldn't-and Henry was terribly shaken by the changes in them-he and I could, and did. He told me, among other things, that in fact in those early days, as the oldest, he'd felt more like an uncle than a cousin to many of us.

Since that meeting, we've been in touch regularly by phone and letter, and whenever he comes to New York or I go to California, we see each other. And there is no denying the very special feeling towards each other that we have both acknowledged. As almost every person with close feelings for their cousins said: Whatever the age differences, the shared history and sense of clan exert a powerful pull, and the visits and gatherings reinforce it.

There are the obligatory family gatherings-and then, of course, there is another kind, the kind that falls into the general category of "cousins clubs," though some people shudder at the term. But whatever you call them, these voluntary meetings can also do a lot to create and keep good cousin relationships going.

I was well aware that the phrase had taken on a certain tacky cast nowadays, and even I, a champion and spokesman for cousinly togetherness, knew that to many it evoked images of huge crowds of near strangers brushing ants off hot dogs, and of shrieking babies carried by fat people in polyester pant suits. So it was with some trepidation that I called Larry Levine, a successful New York lawyer who handles the affairs of some of New York's top art dealers, to check out a friend's report that he was part of just such a group.

Sure enough, his first response was one of pained distaste. "It's definitely *not* a cousins' club," he maintained. "In fact, it's not a formal group at all-it's an affinity group of people who really like each other and who also happen to be cousins." He went on to explain that every one of his cousins, who now range in age from thirty to fifty-five, is either an academic, a lawyer, or a doctor.

Having cleared up that prickly point, he relaxed and told me that in fact on several occasions in recent years, he and his many cousins had taken a place in Maine where they could gather with their wives and children to be together. And this was on top of the holidays and other family occasions at which the group often saw each other.

He mentioned that in addition to the social aspects of such reunions, a great deal of professional and personal networking took place. "It's a terrific support group, a great resource," he said. "My cousin who's a professor of medicine at Cornell found a special physician when one of the kids was having a puzzling medical problem. And so forth."

Furthermore, he told me that five of the male cousins who live in Manhattan get together every third, fourth or fifth week, just to talk. "The wives-dedicated feminists all-objected at first," he said with a laugh. "But now they think it's a good idea. It gives us a chance to discuss male issues of mid-life, and these are the people I feel most comfortable doing that with."

I asked him what factors had led to the strong sense of togetherness he described, and everything he said fit into the group of positive factors I'd found in other close families. "First of all, four of the five parent siblings were very close to each other, so we start with that. Since they saw each other a lot, and made a point of bringing us along, we had early and frequent exposure to each other. My mom and dad liked all of their nieces and nephews and actively inculcated the idea of family as a value, too. The big family seders were the high point of the year. Of course, I was closest to the cousins closest in age, but as time has gone by, that's much less important.

"I also have to say-without sounding boastful, I hope-that we were a very high-achieving group with common interests, both athletic and intellectual." He concluded with some fresh observations on the "specialness" of the cousin relationship. "These are people who care for you without an objective critique. Their love is gratuitous, not something you have to constantly earn and reinforce. Of course, it could wither if it wasn't nurtured, but it's reinforced by all the weddings, seders, bar mitzvahs, and funerals. And I do think our all being in the metropolitan area as we grew up helped a lot."

But a "cousins' club"? Not at all, he said. "And we don't need a newsletter to keep in touch either." Newsletters, however, can be a very effective way for cousins who live all over the country to keep up with each other. Lew Brackley told me that after his daughter Martha married Rich, a boy who'd hardly met his cousins until they came in from around the country for his wedding, the newly-weds were added to the list receiving the cousins' newsletter. "The kids," who he said had formed the kind of quick attachment described so often between cousins, "were thrilled, and really look forward to getting it. They also contribute their own news."

Whether they're called cousins' clubs or affinity groups-I concluded it was largely a semantic difference-such voluntary get-togethers can do a lot to keep cousins in touch and on good terms. Pamela Freemont said that she and her twenty-two first cousins and "innumerable second and third cousins" took turns having the whole cousins' group to their houses twice a year. At Thanksgiving, they and all the other relatives, who number over one hundred, have to go to a country club to find a place big enough to hold them all. "But we love it," she said. We all look forward to it-the kids, the grownups, everyone."

Some of these clubs are strictly social and some are devoted to tracing origins and family history. Berneice Lunday, of North Dakota, whose mother-in-law had been adopted by her aunt and uncle at her cousin Leona's urging, told of putting together a cousins directory, listing the names and dates of birth of all the first, second and third cousins for the North Dakota centennial. But she didn't leave it at that. "At the end," she said, "I had everybody write down their most inter-esting memories-the funny things, the crazy things they remember. And when it's done, everyone will get a copy."

An interesting combination of the social and the historical/genealogical was the Lehman family reunion, which was written up in the *New York Times* in June of 1989. The event drew 170 family members from around the world to view the family tree and discover or renew connections. Among the visitors: two English knights and an English shepherdess of five hundred lambs.

Through yet another piece in the *Times,* I heard about a group with similar social/historical goals and an even wider spread. This is the Cousins, an organiza-tion of more than three thousand black people in twenty-three states, and con-tacts in Nigeria, Tanzania, Liberia, Jamaica and Barbados. A mere six hundred, who ranged in age from five weeks to eighty, were at the all-weekend New York meeting covered in the article.

Organized by Roland J. Hill, a seventy-five-year-old Brooklyn restaurant owner, the group began in 1970, when "a dozen family members gathered around a table in Pittsburgh and agreed to arrange an annual reunion of all their known relatives. They read the research of a deceased relative, a schoolteacher named Aida Arabella Stradford, and studied census figures, family Bible records and other documents...

"All the members can in one way or another trace their roots back to that day in 1805 when a young member of the Yoruba tribe was auctioned to a Camden, South Carolina, planter. The slave took the name of Scipio Vaughan," and established a reputation as a gifted artisan who fashioned iron gates and fences. Several descendants were legislators during the Reconstruction period, and the group includes many teachers, doctors, and lawyers.

Besides the Vaughns-who lost their second "a" somewhere along the line-the Cousins has traced seven main family lines: Barnes, Brevard, Bufford, Cauthen, McGriff, Peavy, and Truesdale. The publicity generated from Alex Haley's *Roots* "helped the organization grow at an exponential rate."

"When we contact people and tell them they're related to us, they are usually amazed,' said Oscar Vaughn," who is national chairman. "Often they bring us more information about our history." With the help of name tags, the various branches identify those in their own and other lines and altogether have a marvelous time exchanging "tidbits of family lore." The sense of pride and belonging the Cousins has created among its members was implicit throughout the piece.

Another such gathering, which didn't make the *Times* but sounds like it should have, was described by Lewis Frumkes, the humorist. "A distant cousin on my father's side-a really dynamic woman named Lynn Gilbert, who runs an executive employment agency in the city-started to put together a family tree a few years ago. Out of that came the idea of getting all the cousins together for a reunion. Well, that first one was so successful that now a huge group of us get together annually in some remote spot.

"Such wonderful things have come out of this," he said. "First of all, we've all gotten to know each other a lot better than we did years ago. And what I especially like is meeting each other's children, and learning about their accomplishments. I've really loved getting to know the second generation of kids, and having our kids meet each other." Besides reconnecting with Mel-the matrimonial lawyer from Florida who had the same mannerism of touching his nose as Louis' father-he reestablished contact with other cousins five to fifteen years older as well. Echoing others, he added, "When we were kids, Mel seemed so much older. The others, too. Now it doesn't matter at all.

"Also," he said, "we got such a kick out of the big reunion that one of us in the city started a local sub-group. He threw a dinner at the Regency"-unlike Larry Levine's subgroup, this one includes wives-"and now that's become a regular event, though not always at the Regency."

The reasons Lewis hadn't seen his cousins for years had to do with a bitter family quarrel over business years before. "Basically," he said, "three of the four fathers were in business together, and they went to war over a company. After that, though we'd previously always celebrated Thanksgivings together and so forth, our parents never talked to each other."

Yet Lewis and his cousin Don, who lived nearby, remained friendly, and the recent reunion of the clan illustrates a seemingly completely contradictory reason for close ties between cousins: this is the amazing determination of some groups of cousins to stick together not because of, but in spite of their parents. Such comings together would appear to defy all the previously stated conditions for creating good feelings, yet it would be less than honest to deny this phenomenon.

Examples abound, among them a few from my own family. When my father and his brother, who also had been partners, had an angry breakup of their business partnership, my uncle's daughter Fran and I, as well as his sons Charles and Elliot R. and my brother Frank, were relatively unaffected. I continued to see Fran regularly over the years, Charles occasionally, and was close to both Elliot R. and his wife when he married. (I should add that this is usually possible-especially when kids are young-only if parents tacitly go along with it by not interfering.) My parents also continued to have a cordial relationship with Fran and an even closer one with Elliot R. and his wife that seemed quite apart from the fraternal one. I, too, remained on good terms with my uncle and aunt. In other words, the damage was contained, the quarrel confined to one generation.

Similarly, Sandy Shapiro, an editor, said that her mother's older brother had married her father's sister-an interesting pairing that one would think would lead to having a great deal in common. Instead, said Sally, the two sisters-in-law hated each other. Between them, they had six children within five years, and these are the cousins of whom Sandy said, "Even though we don't live near each other and our parents made no efforts to get us together, we've developed a very close connection, and stay in touch by phone all the time. I think having to fight to keep the relationship going has strengthened it."

A case of individual cousins deciding to stick together despite a dispute among the "grownups" was told by Carla Schwartz, a photographer. "When I was a child, there were two cousins who became my instant temporary friends whenever I saw them at family parties. The boy, Harry, was unusual. He had a pet monkey and raised snakes in his room. But I liked him anyway and always looked forward to seeing him and his sister Jane.

"After there was a rift in the family, I lost track of them for about ten years. But one day, I found out that Harry was living near me in the city. Somehow once I knew that he was in the area, I felt compelled to call him up. He seemed really glad to hear from me. We discussed the family argument-as you can guess, it had to do with business-and decided that if we got together it was one topic we just wouldn't talk about.

"We were both lonely and single at that point in our lives, and we began to hang out together. We'd have dinner together on Saturday nights, or we'd go to the movies if we didn't have dates. Sometimes we even went to the singles bars together, and it was kind of fun having a male escort that you didn't have to impress. I was amazed at how completely comfortable I felt with him. All those shared memories of the same relatives and our childhood peculiarities (I had mine, too) put us totally at ease. When my mother found out about it, she didn't seem to mind at all. Now I'm sorry for all the years we missed."

In a related phenomenon, sometimes it is the alliance of the kids against the grownups that can create a bond. Said Doris Gelman, a teacher friend, "I had twenty-one first cousins, and five of them were girls around my age. We were all very close-at least partly because we had to form a kind of alliance system against the neurotic aunts and uncles." She added that, as they were for me and many others, "the older cousins served both as protectors and as role models."

And Margot Levin, who lived on the same block as four of her cousins said, "Though the aunts were always wonderful to us as nieces and nephews, each of us had trouble with our own mothers, and the three of them, who were sisters, really didn't get along at all either. In fact, we used to kiddingly refer to them as 'The Three Horrors.' The way we helped each other was by making jokes like that. It was like a cult; a secret bond. And now we can verify things for each other. Like when I thought I remembered a day my mother buried a piece of the dog's tail in the ground because she heard he'd never wander away if you did that (of course he was never seen again), and one of my cousins said, 'You're not crazy. That really did happen.'

"Actually, it's still a bond, and our parents-especially the mothers-are jealous of our friendships and of the secrets. My mother always says, 'What do you talk about all the time?' and I say 'You!' (I don't think she believes me.)"

These final cases of cousin friendships despite parental quarrels or as an alliance against the older generation, however, are already moving away from the pretty picture of cousinly togetherness described up to that point. They begin to hint at a darker side to cousin relationships, and it is this darker side, the side that includes deep rifts, long-term rivalries, and bitter resentments that will be explored in the following chapter.

3

WHEN THE MAGIC TURNS BLACK

COUSINS WHO HATE

I don't like interviews and I don't like my cousin.

-VLADIMIR HOROWITZ-, WHEN ASKED TO TALK ABOUT
HIS ONLY LIVING RELATIVE.

MAESTRO HOROWITZ' PITHY comment notwithstanding, I have to say that I had to hunt to find really bitter cousin stories. I found that most people I talked to were either genuinely fond of their cousins or, at worst, indifferent. Some of the more negative comments had to do with rivalry; others with the notion of cousins as bores and drags-obligatory relatives one has to visit; still others with external factors such as differences in age or gender. (As has already been shown, the last two tend to dissipate with time, thanks to the re-meetings and the chance to get a new perspective discussed earlier.)

Alienations due to divorce, where parents actively prevent or discourage their children from seeing "your father's/mother's side of the family" can be a factor, and relatedly, lack of proximity can lead to lack of contact, and subsequently, lack of interest. Primarily, of course, there is the obverse side of positive parent and grandparent relationships resulting in positive cousin relationships. As Dr. James Framo said, "If the adult sibling relationship was negative or competitive, it may result in the same rivalry between cousins and their parents that the siblings themselves felt. ('My kid is in medical school; yours isn't')."

"In such competitive relationships, the shared history and mythology often get distorted," said Dr. Michael Kahn. "Who did what to whom twenty-five or thirty years ago is heard and passed on with so many changes that by the time the second or third cousins hear it, it's hopelessly confused."

Even if the sibling relationship has been close, when children are born to both (nephews and nieces to the siblings; first cousins to each other), intense rivalry over their children's status with the grandparents can sour the good feelings between the parents.

Said Evelyn Gates, a literary agent, "About a year ago, my daughter Carrie made a date to stay overnight at my mother's house, and she was really looking forward to it as her special time with Grandma, without having to share the attention with her brother and sister. Or maybe that's how I saw it. Anyway, when we got there, my brother's daughter Alice, who's an only child and spends lots of time with my mother, was there, too. I was furious, though I tried to hide it. I felt like screaming, 'What's *she* doing here? This is Carrie's turn to spend time with you alone.' But when I asked-a lot more tactfully than that-my mother just said, 'Oh, Alice heard Carrie was coming, and she wanted to come, too.'

"I was so angry that Alice was there, and I began to get angry at my brother and sister-in-law for sending her. I began to imagine that they'd heard Carrie was coming, and were afraid Mom would prefer her to Alice, so they'd sent her over. But I couldn't say a word about it. I don't even know how Carrie felt. For all I know she might have been glad to see her cousin. But I certainly wasn't. I really resented Alice's presence, though I hope I didn't show it to her or Carrie."

If this kind of unspoken parental rivalry continues, it will undoubtedly seep down a generation at some point, and in time affect the cousins directly.

The cure, as Dr. Sager recommended about other long-standing resentments, is an honest discussion of the issue between the adult siblings, but this is a touchy and difficult subject to bring up.

I can speak from personal experience on the matter since I experienced feelings similar to Evelyn's when my brother and his wife sent along his son to visit on a day my daughter had a long-planned play date with a cousin she adored but rarely got to see (Phyllis' daughter, in fact). Since the date was at Phyllis' house, I felt I couldn't say anything, but I secretly felt that my attempts to foster a special friendship between the girls were being sabotaged, however unwittingly. The result: I was very upset, and at the same time so ashamed of feeling that way that I wouldn't have dreamed of admitting it to my brother, his wife, or even to Phyllis.

Since the problem didn't recur, it may have been just as well that it didn't become an issue. But this kind of parental guarding of one's own child's interests is clearly not unique nowadays, and may well be a result of the more recent generations' close involvement with their children's feelings and perceived needs.

Looking at it from the child's point of view, Lucy Davis, a social worker in New York City, recalls that while she was fascinated to see her parents relate to other young people in the family on those rare occasions when they got together, she was upset that her parents seemed "far more accepting and casual, far more indulgent and less critical with my cousins than they were with me. I knew they were doing it to please their sisters and brothers, and because they wanted their nephews and nieces to like them, but I still thought it was hypocritical."

And Carla, the photographer who had been reunited with her cousin Harry after ten years and often went out with him, said similarly of his sister Jane, "She was younger, and even though I liked her, I was always sort of envious of her because I saw that my parents let her get away with a lot of things they wouldn't let me get away with-like putting my elbows on the table. And I guess there was some subtle competition to be my grandmother's favorite, too."

Before getting into the more usual kind of rivalry, the kind consciously or unconsciously fostered by parents or grandparents, one thing should be pointed out: the closer and more frequent the encounters between cousins, as with Helen and me, the more the relationship is likely to resemble that to a sibling-including the intense rivalry. Those are the times when the "magical" connection is black magic, and the spell seems more evil than benign.

I was startled to find out recently that my sporadic but bitter envy of Helen-for her sultry beauty, her slimness, her handsome and affectionate father-was matched by her envy of my rosy cheeks, my ability at sports, and my seeming confidence. I was enraged by my brother's favoring of her in almost all our arguments, even as she, an only child, envied me my sibling, our large house in the suburbs, and our apparently stable family life.

At times, I even envied the tragedies in Helen's life-a painful ear operation and her parents' divorce at a time when divorce was still relatively rare-which made her an object of sympathy and pity to others. The result of that divorce was that my Aunt Polly had to struggle hard to make a living as a milliner (she once worked for Lilly Daché), and was so short of money that, despite my father's frequent loans, she was forced to live with Helen in one-room "kitchenettes" in the Henry Hudson Hotel or other west side apartment hotels, and often had to cook dinner on a hot plate.

No matter. I envied their straitened circumstances, too. Their life together seemed so cozy and reassuring compared to my own spread-out existence in our Long Island house, and I especially envied her "only child" specialness to her mother.

And while I, a jacks champion and far better athlete, was often her declared protector at camp, refusing to join either baseball team till she was chosen by one of them and defending her right to non-participation in all other sports, she reminded me recently that from time to time we also had vicious fingernail fights in which I invariably had the advantage, since she was an incurable nail biter. After one of these gouging sessions, she retaliated brilliantly by signing "To Sloppy Jo and fat stuff" in my treasured autograph album for all to see. Those words rankled painfully for years.

Similarly, when Clare and I were teenagers, our lifelong loyalty was sorely tested when we were both interested in the same boy, a friend of my brother's who visited often. I was far more threatened by what I perceived as her attempts to flirt with him on a prolonged visit from Philadelphia than I'd ever have been if she were just a friend-especially since she knew I'd both met and cared about him for a long time. (He'd been the subject for several months of long-distance phone confidences.)

The situation was never really resolved. Between Clare's guilt at feeling disloyal, and my own barely concealed resentment, the atmosphere at our house became so charged that the boy, sensing something beyond his emotional grasp, faded out of the picture as a possible boyfriend for either of us, probably the best outcome for a situation that was a torment for both Clare and me. (We didn't discuss it till years later, and it was uncomfortable even then.)

Just as an innate understanding between cousins can blossom through close contact, long-lasting enmities are intensified when cousins not only see each other very often, but actually live together.

Edie Lauderdale, an administrator at a private school in New Jersey, recounted just such negative feelings. "During World War II, five red-haired cousins, who were refugees from the blitz, came over to stay with us till the war ended. I was told I should love them like brothers and sisters, but frankly, I didn't. They got all the attention, and everybody felt sorry for them."

And Greta Sawyer, an English teacher at the same school, describes a catastrophic cousin relationship. "I had a girl cousin three and a half years older than I was, and her parents and mine shared a house. I suppose when I was born, she was jealous. But all I can say is that she was awful to me from the day I was born. We vied for my grandmother's affection, and I particularly remember the time she came home from school and kept telling me that she had met a first person, a second person, and a third person. She kept saying how nice they were, but she wouldn't tell me their names. It was years before I realized she was just teasing me about a grammar lesson.

"Anyway, when I grew up and started to live with Ted, she wanted to come to see us. But I told Ted, 'I'll never see her again.' I told him how she'd been to me as a child, and how much I feared we'd repeat the relationship in some form as adults. And you know what? I never have seen her, and I've never regretted it, though I think she was pretty shocked, and her parents never forgave me."

An even worse story of the mental cruelty older cousins can inflict was told to me by comedienne Phyllis Diller, a story that shows how older cousins, far from being friends, supports, or positive role models, sometimes pick on their younger counterparts in much the way older siblings do. "When I was a kid, I was often taken care of by a cousin who was married and twenty-two years older than I am. As it happened, on the way to their house from my parents', we had to pass the local orphanage-that's what they still called them in those days. Well, every time we'd drive by, they'd tell me they were going to leave me there, and I'd cry and cry and they'd laugh and laugh. They really thought it was hysterical! I've never forgotten how terrified I was."

Unlike Greta, however, Ms. Diller has forgiven her cousin over the years, lending support to Dr. Bloch's contention that cousin relationships, even if far from ideal, tend to be "less toxic." She in fact regularly visits the woman, who is now ninety-four, in the nursing home where she lives. "After all, as far as I know she's the only first cousin I'm aware of, and what did they know about psychology then?" she said. "She's led a small, narrow life in Indiana, and is really not that educated or smart, though she's certainly a feisty old lady. In fact, would you believe it, she still thinks that story is funny! I know, because a few years back she reminded me of it when we were looking through some family pictures. I guess it was then that I decided to stop being mad about it, and use it in my act. So I actually developed a routine about it. The first line was: 'My cousins used to take me to the orphanage and tell me to mingle.' Of course, everyone thought I was joking. They'd have been shocked if they knew it was true."

More often, the problems between cousins who see each other often or for concentrated periods are between near contemporaries. Close as they were, as the Kennedy cousins grew older, intense rivalries surfaced between some of them from time to time. In their 1984 book, *The Kennedys,* Peter Collier and David Horowitz eloquently describe the jockeying for position that went on among some of the cousins during Ted Kennedy's abortive attempt to get the Democratic presidential nomination. They tell a particularly unpleasant story of how Bobby, Jr. tricked Chris Lawford into making a completely inappropriate toast at Courtney Kennedy's engagement party that embarrassed Chris in front of a large group of friends and relatives.

Nor can it be ignored that Chris Lawford, Bobby Jr., David, and for a while, Joe (the latter three, sons of Robert Kennedy) aided and abetted each other in their increasing drug use, clear evidence that cousins-to say nothing of brothers-can be powerful negative as well as positive role models.

Cousins as negative influences appear to be especially common in the drug cultures of inner cities. While reading a terrifying first person account of this world by Phillipe Bourgois *(The New York Times Magazine,* Nov. 12, 1989), I was particularly struck by the frequency with which cousins were mentioned as companions in drug use or drug selling-one on almost every page.

Near the start: "By the time I caught up with Jesus...he was telling the story to his cousin [who] was on her way to the crack house. Her emaciated face and long sleeves made it likely she was a coke mainliner...Finally, she said she needed the money she had lent him the day before to buy a new supply of marijuana-he had spent it on crack instead-and that she was disgusted with him."

On the very next page: "After a close encounter with the police, Julio...begged his cousin for a job in his crack house."

And a few paragraphs later, speaking of Julio's girlfriend Jackie, whose husband was "upstate" serving two to five years for selling cocaine and possessing firearms, the author says: "Her husband's cousin, who had taken over the crack franchise...while her husband was in jail...hired her to sell 'twenties of rock'-$20 foils of cocaine."

Two columns later: "The admonishments of his cousin.... could not have been clearer: Jesus was not going to be upwardly mobile in the underground economy."

And finally, a column after that: "Once Julio told me he was nervous about a cousin of his who had started hanging out at the crack house, feigning friendship. Julio suspected him of being in the process of casing the place for a future stickup."

The frequency of this kind of cousinly influence and involvement may represent a dark side of the tight kin networks that often exist in the inner city. But they are by no means confined to it, as several of the Kennedy cousins demonstrate. Their involvement with drugs and with each other was compounded by the strong competitive streak underlying their friendships. Collier and Horowitz say that David and Chris Kennedy particularly envied Bobby Jr.'s ability to ingest large amounts of drugs and still function publicly at a high level-at least for a while.

And these rivalries existed between cousins who basically cared deeply for each other and whose parents weren't directly involved in fostering bitter competition, though of course the presumably good-natured one-upmanship among the Kennedys is legendary. When parents and grandparents do stir the pot, there's bound to be trouble.

Hilberto Ramos, a twelve-year-old at the Clinton School in New York City, put it this way in a composition on the subject of cousins: "When my family gets together, the grownups start talking about the kids...They start talking about how we are doing in school. They start braging [sic] about how good their son is in sports. They are serious bragers...they would say anything to be more popular and better than the others."

There's no question that, as with siblings or even friends, comparisons between cousins can be disastrous, especially when they go on for years. Debbie Bates, a tall, striking brunette now working as a paralegal in Texas, told a story of lifelong comparisons-and ultimate revenge. "I was raised as an army brat," she began. "We traveled all over the place, but when I was growing up, no matter where we were during the rest of the year, every summer we went back to my dad's home in Cape Hatteras to spend the summers with his mother-my grand-mother-and the rest of the family. Well, I had this cousin just a year younger than I was-Kathy-and my grandmother openly preferred her. I was fat and had to wear braces, and all I'd ever hear from my grandmother was about how pretty Kathy was, and how some day she'd go to Hollywood and all that. And her mother encouraged it, pushing her into wearing panty hose and padded bras when she was still a kid.

"It was as though I didn't even exist! My grandmother had pictures of Kathy and the other cousins all over the house, but none of me. One day my mother said, 'Where's Debbie's picture?' and my grandmother kept saying she didn't have a frame. So my mother went out and bought one, and she still didn't put out my picture. When my mother asked her why, she said, 'Oh, the picture did-n't fit,' which I knew wasn't true, because my mother had measured it. And one of the worst things was that my father never defended me. He just chose to ignore the whole thing. I felt like saying, 'Hey, I'm your daughter. Defend me!' But he never did. It was really hard for me, and I got so I hated Kathy, even though it wasn't entirely her fault. But she wasn't too nice about it either, to tell you the truth. I think she just ate up being my grandmother's favorite.

"Then, when I was thirteen we went to the Orient for three years and did-n't come back in the summers. During that time, I lost a lot of weight, got rid of my braces, and if I say so myself, I really looked terrific. You know, the old ugly duckling story. Well, when we went to North Carolina the next summer, nobody could believe how I'd changed. Kathy was so jealous! To show you how much: when I decided to graduate a year early, the very next year she did the exactly same thing. She couldn't stand the idea that I was going to be out of school two years ahead of her.

"At that point the tables really turned. I went on to college, and Kathy-well, she became pregnant at eighteen and had to get married. Still, in that small town, that was considered better than what I was doing. Getting married and having kids was all they thought a woman should do, so in a way she was still ahead, even though I happen to know she isn't that happy with her life. She acts like she is, but I know she isn't. Well, wouldn't you know I met this great guy in the navy and last year, at twenty-six, I got married, too.

"Boy, when we went back to Cape Hatteras, it was a great moment for me. Here I was married to this naval officer who was in a much higher rank than Kathy's father had been. She was green. I couldn't help but say, 'Well, you never went to Hollywood, did you?' I guess it was nasty, but after all those years, I just couldn't resist. And my mother said to me, 'What goes around comes around.'

"Another expression my mother uses is, 'It's all water under the bridge,' but I still resent Kathy, and even more that my father never stuck up for me. He's still going along with it to some extent. He loves to tell me when Kathy gets a new car, or something like that."

Laraine Newsome, a middle-aged woman who lives in New York's Greenwich Village and is studying to be a guidance counselor, related a very similar story, but with one different twist: in her case, the rivalry was handed down from the two mothers to the two daughters. "My cousin Barbara and I were exactly the same age and grew up together. We even went to the same school. I was a pretty good singer, but Barbara was a great ballet dancer and an Olympic-quality runner. In fact, she was supposed to run in the Olympics, but she fell in a hole and had to miss them. Secretly, I was so glad.

"Later on she always seemed to be just a little bit ahead of me. Her husband got a great job in Paris and she stopped off to see us with these two beautiful daughters. (She'd moved to Chicago before that.) Then she got to go to the Cordon Bleu cooking school. I have to admit I was really jealous. But I do think our mothers caused a lot of the bad feeling because I knew that they were very rivalrous and were watching every move we made to see who came out on top." In other words, the two girls were a perfect example of Dr. Michael Kahn's "cousins as proxy delegates for their parents."

Even in a family as "together" as the Riccios, there was an element of parental involvement and competition. Said Eduardo Riccio, "In spite of all the positive things, there was certainly some rivalry as we all got older: who did better in school, who got a better job-these were all things that we and our parents were somewhat caught up in. And when there were fights between us, our parents would get involved, too. I once had a fight with my cousin Maria, and for years my mother Josephine and her brother Giuseppe, who was Maria's father, wouldn't talk."

Sometimes it is only one parent who promotes the rivalry. Said Amy Harter, a dark, attractive woman who runs a philanthropic fund in New York, "I never had any trouble with my aunt, and my mother got along quite well with her, too, but my mother was always comparing me to my cousin Donna, who was blonde, and vivacious, and very popular-in other words, all the things I wasn't. I was quiet and studious. And I do have to say that I get a lot of satisfaction out of the fact that she eventually got divorced, and that I happen to know she envies me my job and my apartment. I don't really hate her, but I think we'd have been much better friends if my mother wasn't always comparing me to her."

This leads directly into the closely related matter of forced role models, which, though similar to rivals, are actually somewhat different. These are not cases of direct comparison so much as implication-the implication being that the child being lectured to "be like so-and-so" is decidedly lacking not only in those areas in which the cousinly paragon excels, but in every other way. "I always resented Sarah," said a young cousin of mine, now in her 20's, of a second cousin. "My mother always held her up to me as a model of how I should be: talented, sweet, and so forth. As a result, I really hated her."

Another case from my own family is that of Elliot D., one of the middle range of boy cousins five to eight years older than me. "As a kid, there were two sets of cousins-well, one set and one individual-who were held up to me as models of perfection. The 'set' was the three Jaffe boys-my mother was always telling me about their wonderful scholastic achievements; the individual was Ira" (my erstwhile piano teacher). "Whatever he did, my mother thought was great. I heard a lot of 'Why can't you do what Ira does? *be* like Ira?' All of them were displayed to me as: This is the way children should be, and I really resented it." (How Elliot worked through all this and became close friends with Ira and a number of other cousins much later in life is a story by itself that is told in the final chapter, "Cousins Today.")

Anna Quindlen says that though she herself was not made to feel inferior by implication, she suspects that some of her cousins "got real sick of hearing, 'Oh, guess what Anna Marie did!' In fact that's what one of my cousins just wrote to me," she said. "I was the eldest on my father's side and kind of the golden girl. I don't think I was ever held up consciously as a forced role model, and I do think some of the uncles and aunts were really proud of me. What I mean is, they certainly weren't *trying* to make their kids feel bad by implication. But I guess it was pretty hard for some of my cousins to take."

Still another form of rivalry can occur over possessions, such as the quarrel Helen and I had over a doll given to both of us to share by my Aunt Rose. (Aunt Rose was one of my mother's three childless sisters who took a gratifying interest in her nephew and nieces, though clearly child psychology was not her *forte.*) I don't recall who ended up in possession of the doll, but I do remember to this day the rage and resentment I felt-and again, the guilt about feeling that way towards a favorite cousin. (Helen tells me she felt the same.)

Though Helen's father had very little money, he never came to visit her at camp without bringing her some wonderful gift. And while my mother might bring lollipops for everyone, she and my father rarely brought anything just for me. I especially remember a Brownie camera Helen's father Jules brought her, because I suppose he noticed that I was looking very unhappy when Helen got hers. To my delight, when he returned in the afternoon, he had bought one for

me, too, on which he had carefully incised my name with a pin. Though my
mother and Aunt Polly could never say enough bad things about Jules then or in
later years, that one gesture was enough to win my lifelong loyalty.

Said Conrad Fernandez, who teaches special education in New Jersey, and
whose description of his childhood in a Puerto Rican neighborhood in New York
sounds a great deal like that of Eduardo Riccio in terms of cousins as a cohesive
unit, "In my family, the cousins were always coming over, and there was a lot of
rivalry over toys. Actually, most of the time I got the fancier ones, and it caused a
lot of bad feelings. One time my cousin came over and my dad gave me this terrific battleship, and him a cheap airplane. To this day, he feels bitter about it!"

And to show how such rivalries can cross national boundaries and oceans,
my friend Françoise Rambach, a writer and program director of the Drawing
Society told me of how much, as a child in a small town in Belgium, she had
resented having to wear her cousin Bernadette's hand-me-downs. "Their family
was much wealthier than ours, and she always had such beautiful clothes. But I
got no pleasure out of the dresses when they came to me, even if they were in
good condition."

The rivalry took other forms as well. "I wasn't a good student and she was;
she had a big wedding and I wasn't married, and so forth." But like Debbie Bates,
she feels it all evened out in the end. "Her family had financial reverses; then she
got divorced, and now she doesn't know what to do with her life. Meanwhile, I
came to the States, went to school, became a guide at the U.N., met a wonderful man and married him. And would you believe it, now I send her my clothes,
and she's happy to have them. What a reversal!"

Unlike Debbie, however, Françoise feels she has made her peace with her
cousin now. "After all, it wasn't her fault her family was better off," she says. "And
I can't say that she or her parents ever consciously tried to make me feel bad. I
think I did that all on my own."

Then there's the kind of rivalry that can come from the sense of being displaced in the family-much as a child feels when a brother or sister is born. My cousin Phyllis, who reigned supreme as the only girl cousin for years-and was actually much closer to being a real life parallel to Rose in *Eight Cousins* than I was, having exactly eight older boy cousins and no competition-recalls distinctly the day she heard there was a new arrival.

"When Clare was born, I knew that was the end," she said drily. "I remember the day perfectly. I even remember what I was doing. I was combing my hair, getting ready for school. My mother came running in, and said, 'I have the most wonderful news: Aunt Jessie just had a little girl.' I felt absolutely terrible. I'd never thought about my position among my boy cousins before, but then I did. And I thought no one would ever talk to me again. Then when I saw her-that rotten kid" (at that point, Phyllis was kidding) "with those big blue eyes and that curly hair, I hated her."

But, in a typical cousinly reaction, Phyllis soon recovered. As Dr. Bloch suggested, and we have seen, cousinly rivalries are rarely as deep or as long-lasting as those between siblings. Said Phyllis: "After a while, I got over it. She was so cute. And when I got the 'wonderful' news that *you* were born a year later, I didn't even care. By then, seventy girl cousins could have been born. I thought, 'Well, that's nice. They can all play together.'"

A curious kind of rivalry can also occur when there's a close friendship between same-age cousins, and a younger or older sibling of either resents it. Such was the case with Jean Allen, an artist who grew up in Columbus, Ohio. She first met her cousin Paul, who lived in Ramsey, New Jersey, at two or three. "He was exactly my age and we hit it off right away-even as little kids," she said. "When I got a little older, for several years I'd spend three weeks of the summer with my aunt and uncle [Paul's parents] and his sister Betsy-she was four years younger-at a summer house they had on a lake.

"Then, when I was around thirteen and began to have some serious personal problems, I needed to get away from home for longer periods. At that point,

I began to spend the whole summer with them. Paul and I always had a great time-the same things struck us funny, we liked to paint and make things out of clay, and when we were older, we'd do things like going into the city to museums, things like that.

"The trouble between Betsy and me started during those long summers. Besides the fact of the age difference, I guess it seemed to her as though Paul and I had this closed, exclusive little club, into which she was definitely not invited. Actually, I think it was more that I just never paid much attention to her, but it turned out that she was convinced I was stealing Paul's affection and interest away from her. After all, when I wasn't around all year she had this great older brother all to herself. And later on, when she began to go out, she accused me of swiping her boyfriends, too. My lousy self-image made that last charge seem really ridiculous. But my main problem with Betsy had to do with Paul, and to this day I don't think she trusts me. The fact is, we still don't get along."

My own resentment of my brother's invariable support for Clare or Helen over me in any quarrels also fits into this category of "triangle" problems, though here the resentment was directed more towards my sibling than my cousins. And speaking of triangles, what happens when a beloved cousin marries someone you don't like is a sub-topic that's covered in the chapter entitled "The Test of Time."

Leaving the realm of cousin rivalries in their many forms, I found a number of other problems that led to hostility or dislike between cousins.

Surprisingly, one of these was the exact duplicate of what had seemed to be a very positive factor in the cases cited earlier. This was the regular weekly or bi-weekly visits to relatives so many cousins felt had contributed to their sense of bonding. In some cases, I discovered, quite the opposite had occurred. Said my cousin Elliot D., with some vehemence, "When you're young, your cousins are thrust upon you-unlike friends, whom you can pick. I can never remember being asked if I wanted to go to visit. It was just: 'Today is Sunday, and we're going to visit Aunt Eva, or Aunt Leah, or Aunt Clae." (Clae was my mother.)

"And even though I did like some of these people and some of these visits-especially to your house, which was a place I always felt you could really be yourself-everything seemed to me to stem from the fact that I felt these weren't *my* relationships; they were an extension of my mother's." (Ilse Schrag, wife of the noted artist Karl Schrag, told me a nice phrase from the German, *Wahl Verwandte*-which means "relatives of your choice"-as opposed to just *Verwandte*, presumably "obligatory relatives.")

Artist Jasper Johns was also acutely aware of a lack of choice when, at age 7, he went to live for a year with an aunt, uncle, and three cousins in Allendale, South Carolina-a case where not having an option, even more than obligation, did not have happy results. "I had always looked forward to holidays and summers with my cousins before that," he said. "In fact, two of the cousins were about my age. But at the end of that particular summer, I was asked if I'd like to stay on with them, and I soon realized it really wasn't up to me." This, he explained, was because his parents had divorced and his mother couldn't keep him with her at the time. As a result, while he didn't actively dislike his cousins, he developed a sense of distance from them despite the proximity in distance and age. "I never felt at home there," he said.

Johns also noted, in response to my question on shared familial talents, that neither those cousins nor any of his others were artistically gifted, and that in fact the only paintings he saw as a boy were some his grandmother had done before he was born, which he suspected were copies.

Truman Capote's reaction to being sent to live with his much older cousins in 1930 was remarkably similar, despite his devotion to the childlike Sook. Not that the cousins weren't very fond of him. Says Gerald Clarke, in his biography, *Capote*, "If they did not take to him immediately, as Sook had done, Jennie and Callie soon did so. 'I fear if there is such a thing, we all love him too much,' Callie confessed in one of her reports to Arch's mother [Truman's paternal grandmother]. 'He is a darling sweet boyÉhe is the sunshine of the house.'"

Nonetheless, Clarke continues, "Compared with Sook, both Callie and

Jennie were viewed as cold and unloving, as purse-mouthed and pinchpenny spinsters." But in the end, "Truman's complaint was not that Jennie was short-tempered, that Callie was a nag, or that there was not enough money. It was that none of the Faulk sisters, even the beloved Sook, could take the place of his real parents."

As for the more usual short-term obligatory visits, I asked my cousin Elliot D. if he'd felt the same sense of coercion about seeing his father's relatives (a group I knew only a little) as his mother's, and his answer led to another cause of cousinly distancing, if not dislike. "My mother never wanted to visit my father's side of the family," he said. "As a result, I really didn't get to know them very well. Somehow, my father went along with it to a large extent. I guess he got tired of arguing about it."

Similarly, Barbara Lindeman, the career counselor whose grandmother had been the magnet that drew her mother's side of the family every week, said: "I had cousins on my father's side, too, and I liked them, but there was always a quarrel between my parents when my father wanted to see his side of the family, and usu-ally my mother won. It was odd, because they were even in the same towns we were-Mount Vernon-yet we rarely saw them, so of course I didn't get to know them as well."

By contrast, I never remember feeling there was any differentiation made between between the aunts, uncles, or cousins on either side. It seemed to me they all mixed freely and frequently at many family gatherings, and in fact several of my mother's four sisters were close friends with my aunts on my father's side.

However, my cousin Helen (on my mother's side) recently told me she did feel excluded and uncomfortable from time to time. She especially remembers the time a photograph of all the younger cousins on the Rosengarten side was taken at a wedding-Ira's, in fact-and she wasn't included. She concedes there was no outright attempt to leave her out; in fact, a girl who was even less related but happened to be standing nearby when the picture was taken was included, which made Helen feel worse when she saw it a few weeks later.

Quite simply, no one had thought to go looking for her, since she wasn't related on the same side-a sin of omission rather than commission. Still, almost because she and her mother Polly had been so much a part of the family in other ways, she felt terrible about it. So much so that when we came upon the picture a few years ago, a shadow crossed her face, and she told me she still vividly recalls how hurt she was at the time.

Professor Bert Adams comments on the whole question of favoring sides in his summary to *Kinship in an Urban Setting,* posing the question, "What is the relation of marital power relations to involvement with one or both kin networks?" and answering his own question: "It is quite possible that the agreement of both spouses that they should be close to both sets of kin, or neither, or one and not the other, is enough to keep peace within the couple and with kin and in-laws. However, a struggle for power may be manifested in those cases where a choice must be made..." Though he was referring more to the choice of where to live than who to visit, the statement actually applies to both.

Even on the same side, certain relatives are often given preference, and as a result, their children have much more of a chance to build friendships. Said my cousin Phyllis:

"Even though Charles is exactly my age, I never got as close to him or [his brother] Elliot R. as I did to Frank D. or Elliot D. This was because my mother and father almost always visited Madeleine and Max"-who, ironically, were the parents of the much put-upon Elliot D., the cousin who felt so strongly about having been an extension of his mother.

Though cousins of different sexes are often good friends, especially when they're close in age, as were Jean Allen and her cousin Paul, most people mentioned that at least as children they had socialized mostly with cousins of the same sex. Anna Quindlen said that "Though I certainly like them, I'm not particularly close to any of my boy cousins. I have more in common with them now than I did then, but I think in terms of our cousin situation we broke down in real straightforward gender lines." (The special category of sexual attraction between cousins is the topic of the next chapter.) Says Adams, "[There is a] strong tendency to know best a cousin of one's own sex."

Also, as has been touched on before, large age differences can certainly put a barrier between cousins as children. As my oldest cousin Henry said, "I felt more like an uncle than a cousin." And Margot Levin, the librarian who grew up in Joliet, Illinois, said, "While I was having all that fun with my cousins, my sister wasn't even born. She came along when I was sixteen, and I have to tell you that that has made a tremendous difference in how she feels about those people. She's told me she felt-and still feels-very shut out and neglected; that nobody cared when she excelled, which she did, or went ga-ga over her kids when they were born. Unfortunately for her, the four of us were all contemporaries, and no one else came along in her generation."

As discussed in different contexts, unless parents make a real effort to get kids together, the lack of proximity can be another reason cousins end up alienated or indifferent. Said Suzanne Ponsat, a fundraiser for Carnegie Hall in New York, who grew up here, "A few of my cousins lived in Denver or California, but most of them were in Cleveland, where my parents come from. I do remember visiting them a few times as a child and loving it. When I'd come home, I'd feel really upset, because I could see how wonderful it could be to have all those kids who were related to play with. And also to have aunts and uncles who cared about you. But we went out there so seldom that I never really established close ties. And I guess I substituted my parents' friends for the aunts and uncles, and their kids for my cousins. But I'm sorry about it. And when one of those Cleveland cousins moved east recently, I became very friendly with her, even though she's seven years older than I am."

David Harris, a piano accompanist and singer who grew up in upper New York, said, "All my cousins lived in Richmond, Virginia, and I hardly feel related to them. First of all, they're all ten or more years younger; secondly, we don't seem to have much in common. None of them are into music at all. I feel there are too many gaps that can't be filled now to make up for all the years we didn't see each other. In fact, I really have to prepare before I call them. I have to refer to letters to remember who they are and what's happened. I don't know why my parents didn't visit them. They hardly talked about them, in fact. I guess that's why I don't have any real feeling for them."

Why do such separations occur so often nowadays? For herein lies the answer to much of the alienation and indifference between cousins today. I discussed this question with Jerry Handel, the professor of sociology at the City University of New York who was so helpful with leads and has long been fascinated by the topic of cousins. Though stressing that his observations were more speculative than proven, he said: "This is a very individualistic and career-oriented society, and people pursue economic opportunity where they find it, so families tend not to live so close together. Middle-class families even more than poorer ones are likely to go to different cities if they have a chance to advance that way. It's not that middle-class families don't care about separations, but being close to relatives is a less compelling reason for the middle classes to stay where they are." Sociologist Bert Adams, who has done a great deal of research on the subject, supports these opinions, stating flatly that "The middle classes are more mobile residentially."

Tied in with middle-class aspirations is the matter of social class. "I suspect that social status has to do with the possibility of cousins being close or not," says Dr. Handel. "As some succeed and others don't, their contacts with each other are likely to diminish and their children's contacts are likely to be less. There tends to be some discomfort about associating across social status levels. People tend to be socially mobile, and one of the requirements is that they sometimes have to be able to leave behind friends or relatives from the earlier status level because they have to learn to interact in new ways at a different status level."

Anthropologist David Schneider agrees, but approaches the question differently. "What, then, determines whether a relationship with one person on a given genealogy will exist or not? The reason Americans give is that one is 'close' and the other is 'too far away.' Distance, then, is said to be the deciding factor.

"But what is distance? Distance means one of three things. The first is simple physical distance…So one hears it said: 'We never see them. They're too far away.' 'Too far away?' 'Yes it takes almost an hour to get there.'"

Secondly, there's "a complex composite of what might be called socio-economic distance. This in turn can mean anything from a mystical feeling of identity or difference, a feeling of emotional warmth and understanding-or the lack of it-to the fact that certain important prestige symbols are either similar or different…One informant said, 'No one has much to do with them…It's a matter of the kind of life and education-hardly any of the people in Harry's family have been to college and that sort of thing."

His third distinction-genealogical distance-isn't relevant to the issue of how physical distance or social differences separate cousins here, but in fact is important enough to be the subject of a chapter of its own ("The Outer Inner Circle") later on.

A different cause for alienation between cousins in today's world, and an all too common one, was inadvertently brought up by Sue Brackley, who with her husband Lew is so friendly with Lew's cousins Ellen and Ron. Sue said, "I knew I had some cousins on my mother's side, but I never heard about them. And for some reason, I wasn't and still am not even curious about them. I don't know how to explain it except that in our house it was as if they didn't exist."

We talked about why this unusual degree of estrangement had come about, and Lew speculated that perhaps it was symptomatic of today's nuclear families. Somehow this didn't seem to satisfy Sue. "They did live far away, in Texas," she mused (Sue grew up in Massachusetts), "but that still doesn't quite explain it. I never even met my grandmother on my mother's side, though my father's mother lived with us."

The most important reason was revealed when Sue recalled that she hadn't even known that her mother had been married before, to a man who lived in Texas, until she was twelve. "My parents were very embarrassed about it," she said. Sue found out, through a late and dramatic disclosure ("I heard my father threaten to tell the truth to us when he and my mother were having a fight") that, as my cousin Helen had learned, divorce was still considered shameful by many people in the late 30's and early 40's. "I suppose that's why it was such a secret, and of course it explains why I never met or heard about those cousins. They were part of a life my mother was trying to hide or forget. But they are my first cousins, and there must be quite a few of them, because my mother was one of seven children."

Sue's alienation from her cousins due to divorce was the first but far from the last case of this kind I heard about. In fact, in today's world, divorce is frequently an important factor in creating schisms. Said Dr. Handel: "Again this is speculative, but it would seem logical that the children of two intact marriages would be more likely to have friendly contact than those where one parent in a divorce takes some of the cousins far away, and is on bad terms with his or her in-laws."

Unlike Sue, however, many cousins feel deep regret about the separation, especially where there has been regular contact that is suddenly cut off. Such a case is that of Andrea Wechsler, who is now in college, and her two younger brothers. The problems arose when her uncle (her father's brother) and his wife divorced. "I was about ten at the time," Andrea recalled. "After that, the two cousins we were close to, Matthew and Steven, went to live with their mother, the ex-wife. I guess she was pretty mad at my uncle, so she didn't encourage their getting together with our side of the family. Then my uncle had two kids with his new wife, and whenever he did come over, he'd bring the two little ones, who were cute, but much too young for us to play with. Besides, we wanted to see Matthew and Steven. But my uncle never wanted to go and pick them up, and they lived too far away to travel by themselves. The only time we did see them for a few years was on alternate Passovers. We'd complain a lot about it, asking,

'Is he bringing Matthew and Steven?' when my uncle came to visit, but the answer was always no. It was really frustrating. Heartbreaking. We're really family-oriented, but not seeing them year after year eventually began to make them fade from my consciousness.

"But recently, things have begun to get better," she said. Now that we're all older, and can drive, we've begun to try to get together on our own. Matthew called me recently and invited me to his high school graduation, and said he really wants to see more of me and my brothers. I don't know if we'll have anything in common after all this time, but I certainly hope we do."

If cousins can hold out long enough, then, they can take control of the situation themselves. But all too often, by then their cousins have "faded from consciousness," never to reappear. Katie Weiner, my first cousin once removed (she is the daughter of my close cousin Clare), told a story that combined both divorce and distance as fragmenting elements. "First of all, we lived in Australia for three years before I was thirteen," she said. "But even before that, I rarely saw my first cousins on my father's side, because we were always moving all over. (Katie's father was a professor of drama and taught in Ohio and Wisconsin as well as Australia.) "Then, when I was thirteen and my parents divorced, I was completely cut off from them. I really feel bad about it-more as I've gotten older. But the fact is, now I feel the opportunity has been lost.

"I always envied my mother's position vis-à-vis her cousins. I've come to appreciate having the connection with you and your family enormously." (Katie and I are close, as are she and my daughter.) "It's as near as I'll ever get to the kind of family togetherness you had. And I do think this is because we were always off in Timbuktu somewhere and also because of the divorce."

And speaking of my own family, and divorce, it's at this point that I must in all honesty deal with what I've come to recognize as at least part of the reason my children and their first cousins (my brother's children) have such different relationships from those I had to my cousins as a child. And this was despite the fact that their ages match quite well, and that there are two boys and a girl on each side.

Divorce did indeed deal the final blow. But the essential problem started even earlier, and seemed to be-as it so often is-among the two sets of adults; mostly between my sister-in-law Marty and me, and to a lesser extent between my brother and my husband, though not so much between Frank and me, the direct siblings. Only later did the differences between my brother and his wife surface.

Though I had always enjoyed Marty's volatile and bohemian style as an individual, when we began to get together as couples with our kids at my parents' house in the country (my parents no longer used it), I found that we had profound differences in our approaches to raising the kids and to keeping house.

Whereas we favored intervention in our own kids' fights at the point when they began to draw blood, Marty believed in letting hers "work out their hostilities," no matter what. Result: both sets of kids were getting mixed messages about the limits on physical violence. (Incidentally, these fights were never between the cousins; they were between the siblings.)

We also had completely different concepts about meals: theirs a catch-as-catch-can one; ours more planned. The same applied to doing dishes, which meant that my husband and I-more orderly, or perhaps more compulsive-ended up doing them almost all the time.

Not that I felt Marty and my brother didn't have every right to raise their children any way they wanted. But in the forced proximity of weekend sharing, the differences we might have overlooked with less intense and frequent contact became impossible to ignore.

As a result, by the time the kids ranged in age from about six to eleven, it was decided that sharing the place didn't work out-the first separation of the cousins, but not the last. In the years that followed, though we both made sporadic attempts to get the kids together, and occasionally did so at my parents' apartment in the city, the real continuity was cut. Sensing the charged atmosphere between the sets of parents, the cousins gradually stopped requesting the visits, and by the time my brother divorced and remarried years later, they were cordial, but not really close.

Still, I have to say that I realized recently that something had been gained, even through those brief years of early contact. When my mother died, and both my brothers' and my children came to our house after the funeral, my former sister-in-law Marty came over as well. One of my kids took out some photo albums of pictures taken during those long ago country weekends. Three hours later, they were still happily reminiscing about "the time Danny planned the wedding of Dairy Queen and Burger King," of going to a horror movie at the drive-in, and of the neighbor's dogs who scared them when they hiked the two miles down to the local store. Suddenly, I felt faintly optimistic.

Like my niece Katie, Fran Burton, who rediscovered her cousin Riva Castleman just recently, also attributes the years of unfamiliarity to both divorce and distance. "We lived in Omaha; they were in Chicago. In addition, Riva's parents were divorced, and to add to the fragmenting factors, my dad was a snob and never thought my mother's family was good enough for anyone, so of course he also looked down on Riva's dad, who was my mother's brother. Between that and the divorce, you can imagine that opportunities to get together were few and far between. Of course we've really made up for lost time, but I do regret all the years we could have been friends before."

To end on a hopeful note, I can relate a story of divorce, distance, and wonderful cousin reconciliation that was sent to me in response to an ad in *USA Today*, by Melanie Cease, of Arlington, Virginia.

"My mother is a native of Washington, D.C.," she wrote. "In the early 1940's my grandmother and grandfather were divorced. Out of spite, my grandmother refused to let him or his side of the family see his children. My mother eventually married and moved to Florida, where we grew up.

"My grandfather died in the late 50's. Then, two years ago my grandmother died. We flew to Washington for the funeral. My grandfather's sister (my great-aunt) just happened to notice the obituary in the paper and came to the funeral. My mother and I were quite shocked, but overjoyed at the prospect of finally getting to meet some of our lost relatives. Six months later we had a family reunion with all of my grandfather's relatives. As it turns out, several of my cousins had migrated to Florida many years ago. So we had all been living less than an hour from each other all those years and never knew about each other.

"Now it seems like we have known each other all our lives. (Yet another example of the inexplicable connection cousins so often feel, even when they haven't met before.) We really regret all the years we spent living so close and never knowing about each other. It is somewhat ironic that my grandmother tried so hard all her life to keep us apart, yet it was her death that brought us all together. I now live in D.C. and spend every spare moment with my cousins, sharing family secrets and memories."

And on that happy note, the discussion of the more conventional cousin relationships comes to a temporary halt. The next two chapters will deal, instead, with the rarely discussed (though privately acknowledged) matter of sexual attraction and experimentation between cousins, and the phenomenon of marriage between cousins in our own and in other cultures-not as unusual nowadays as you might think, and even more common in the past.

4

SEXUAL ATTRACTION AND EXPERIMENTATION BETWEEN COUSINS

What made these contests thrilling was the presexual tension that I always associated with the competition-that I always associated with [my cousin] Hester in particular.

-JOHNNY, IN JOHN IRVING'S *A PRAYER FOR OWEN MEANY*.

My cousin, Kay, thirteen and flirting, lets us look into her shirtfront while we hoe our rows of corn. Kay leans, pretending she is innocent, and bobs across from me…

-OPENING OF "COUSINS," A STORY IN *ESQUIRE* BY WILLIAM TESTER.

SEXUAL ATTRACTION TO a cousin (sometimes, but by no means always, reciprocated) is not uncommon. And when the depth and sense of mystical connection that draws cousins together is mixed with the powerful dynamics of animal magnetism, there can be surprising results. The experience of those who have acted upon their intense but generally forbidden longing (in our culture, at least), has been described by those who experience it as everything from "comfortable" to "explosive."

Certainly the two brothers in the *Esquire* story were consumed with desire for their cousin, and in fact fantasizing about Kay is the central topic. "Her dampened T-shirts sieved her skin...We watched her seashell-colored nipples on her body where she hoed...I'm nearly crazy watching Kay! She bends and lifts inside her shirt...I make a hard-on watching Kay. Inside of her, inside her body, I imagine all the hollowness of her."

But the desire is fulfilled only by his brother Jeab, to the painful frustration of the younger narrator, who hears them having intercourse in the next room. ("Our girl on our farm in the whole wide world is the sound of my brother on her.")

Jared Diamond, a professor of physiology at UCLA, delved into the causes of these attractions, seeking to find how we develop our ideal "search image" for a mate or lover. (A "search image" is "a mental picture against which we compare objects and people around us in order to be able to recognize something quickly, like a Perrier bottle among all the other bottled waters on the supermarket shelf.")

The first thing he found was that, "On the average, spouses resemble each other slightly but significantly in almost every physical feature...Experimenters have made this finding for people as diverse as Poles in Poland, Americans in Michigan, and Africans in Chad...We develop our search image of a future sex partner as children, and that image is heavily influenced by those of the opposite sex whom we see most often"-i.e., Mommy or Daddy, Sister or Brother. He stresses that factors like religion and personality affect our choices more strongly, but that physical resemblances do have an influence. However, the incest taboo, learned or trained, stops us from acting directly on these impulses with our actual parents or siblings, even extending to adoptive brothers and sisters, or children raised together in the same peer group, as on a kibbutz.

Not so with cousins, Diamond found. In one experiment using quails as subjects (sounds a bit ridiculous, but apparently they are good substitutes for humans) and measuring the degree of sexual attraction between familiar siblings, unfamiliar siblings, unfamiliar first cousins, unfamiliar third cousins, and total strangers, the quails found unfamiliar first cousins most desirable, and familiar siblings least. This experiment, at least, seemingly demonstrated that the exotic charm of the unknown, when combined with the familiarity of subtly recognized family resemblances, was a powerful factor in their choices.

And similarly, though the peer groups on the kibbutzim who were raised together until adulthood showed no adolescent or adult heterosexual activity, among those raised together only until age six, there were thirteen marriages. Again, as with cousins, the combination of familiarity from early childhood, combined with enough later separation to break down the incest taboo, would seem to have made the relationships both more viable and more alluring than that with total strangers. (Quite possibly Kay, in the story, had come to help out on the farm for a season, and hadn't lived there all along.)

Closer to home, I heard a story of cousin attraction that was about as close to the "quail tale" as one could come. Said Sue Brackley, whose sister-in-law Sally had moved to Georgia with her family years before, "When my son David met his cousin Dory after a separation of fifteen years there was a definite romantic feeling between them, though I'm not sure they were aware of it. But Sally and I were. You couldn't help but notice how they were always hugging or putting their arms around each other or horsing around in some very physical way.

"They'd seen each other a lot until they were about five; then, when they re-met they definitely clicked-not just in that way, but altogether. They really liked each other as people." Added Lew, "I've thought about it and think it comes out of the fact that since Sally and I were raised alike, and basically have the same attitudes and sense of humor, so do our kids. So they had this common basis and the early connection. When they were separated and then reunited at twenty-one, it was almost like lovers who'd re-met after a long separation."

Dr. Mio Fredland, the psychiatrist at New York's Payne Whitney, whose theory of "blood bonding" was quoted earlier in the discussion of what was special about the cousin relationship, approached it in a more Freudian way than did Dr. Diamond. "Sexual attraction between cousins is not at all unusual," she began. "The big thing is that the cousin relationship provides an opportunity for a lot of incestuous sensual venting of sexual feelings. "(This aspect will be explored in depth in the chapter on cousin marriage-especially in Victorian England.)

"There is a lot of displacement of feelings, and often, a lot of passionate and romantic sexual exploration. Even cousins who grow up and don't like each other feel a primordial, atavistic togetherness. When they see their cousins, they often hug and kiss and feel a sexual pull. That pull resides in the substituting from early life of these passionate feelings for the mother, father, sister, or brother. It goes so far that even cousins who've never met till they're middle-aged are mysteriously drawn to each other. It is a romantic and sexual attraction."

Dr. Fredland cited some examples from her own experience. "I met a male cousin I hadn't met before just a few years ago," she said, "and I felt inexplicably related. It was that sense of blood bonding with a faint sexual overtone. I became particularly aware of this when I realized I also felt an antipathy to his wife."

Going way back, she recalled having a boy cousin one and a half years younger whom she "used" for sexual experimentation. "He was my toy," she said. She also remembered being in love with an older cousin who was twenty when she was just four or five. "I made him come to the playground with me. Then I'd hang upside down so he'd see my panties."

Similarly, Anne Leventhal and many others recalled finding out about how boys and girls were different by playing doctor with their cousins. "I had a boy cousin about three years older than I was, who was very interested in the fact that

I had a crack that went all around. This was prepuberty, mind you, but I do recall that I was always the one who did the undressing, and I remember being absolutely humiliated when my mother came into the room one day and found us. After that, I was never allowed to be alone with him."

Other cousins devised less direct ways of looking at each other. Dr. Clifford Sager recalls a patient's story about how he and a male cousin enticed their girl cousin three-and-a-half years older into playing strip poker, so they could see her undressed.

One benign benefit of the subtle attraction and interaction between opposite sex cousins, said Dr. Sager, is that they often learn boy-girl social skills from each other, like dancing.

He also noted that older cousins "frequently enlighten the younger ones about sex-correctly or incorrectly." I can personally recall hearing from one of my authoritative older cousins that babies were created "when the man makes wee-wee inside the woman"-a horrifying prospect that I was glad to learn was untrue a few years later.

I also heard about rape for the first time when my boy cousins came over one evening and gathered in my brother's room to talk. A girl in Inwood, the poorest of the towns near Cedarhurst, had been raped, they said, and she wouldn't name the rapist. Something about the way they lowered their voices to be sure no grownups would hear them talking made me aware that this was a forbidden topic.

Ashamed of my ignorance, but curious, I asked for an explanation of the word. I couldn't believe the definition. "You mean, he does it to her even if she doesn't want him to?" I kept asking, finding this concept impossible to accept. The basic procedures of intercourse, even with both parties, incredibly, willing, had seemed terrible enough to me when I'd gotten them straight just a few months before.

"But what if she screams? What then?"

"Men are stronger than women, you know that," one replied scornfully.

The fact that the information was delivered in such an offhand manner by cousins I admired enormously somehow made it even worse, and for a long time, the knowledge of this potential horror seemed to give the world a sickly, yellowish cast.

A step removed from the early stage of "just looking" or passing on information-or, as in my case, misinformation-is the kind of body contact play that older children often use with their cousins to find out more about sex, and to replace simple viewing. Said Dr. Fredland, "I distinctly recall a boy cousin a year-and-a-half older than I was with whom I used to wrestle all the time. We wrestled every time he visited, from about ages six to ten, and it had a definite sexual component. I always hoped he'd get me down on the ground and lie on top of me and I was never scared of him."

Similarly, Dr. Sager recalls an older girl cousin with whom he often wrestled when they were both about thirteen. "She'd entice me into wrestling, and I loved it, though I was certainly not aware of the sexual implications at the time."

A roughhousing game known simply as "Last One Through the House Has to Kiss Hester" also leads to cousins Johnny and Hester's first kiss, in *A Prayer for Owen Meany.* "We tried a small, close-lipped one, but Noah said, 'That wasn't on the lips!' And 'Open your mouths!' insists Simon." (Noah and Simon are Hester's boisterous brothers.)

> We opened our mouths. There was the problem of arranging the noses before we could enjoy the nervous exchange of saliva-the slithery contact of tongues, the surprising click of teeth. We were joined so long we had to breathe, and I was astonished at how sweet my cousin's breath was; to this day I hope mine wasn't too bad...
>
> They [the brothers] never marshaled as much enthusiasm for the many repeats of the game...Maybe they realized, later, that I began to intentionally lose...
>
> Did Noah and Simon ever consider the danger of the game? The

way they skied…-and later…drove their cars-suggested to me that they thought nothing was dangerous. But Hester and I were dangerous…

This kind of "hands on" early exploration is not the same as the crushes many younger cousins develop on much older ones, which are often at least as romantic as they are sexual and are often their first experience of sexual attraction. Wrote Jacqueline Adler, a journalist friend, "I remember well the mixture of fascination and repugnance with which I viewed my handsome cousin Wayne-twenty-three to my ten years-when I first saw him in a bathing suit at the beach. I could neither look-nor not look-at the very noticeable bulge in his swim trunks that I had never been aware of when, neatly clad in an open shirt and pants, he came to our house to visit my parents. I recall that day at the beach as a powerful memory of sexual awakening, and after that I became so flustered when he came to visit, to his bewilderment and my hideous embarrassment, that I'd run up to my room and hide."

And Greta Sawyer says: "I'll never forget the time I was sitting in the rumble seat of our car, and my cousin Arthur brought me an ice cream cone. After he gave it to me, he picked up my braid and kissed me on the back of the neck. I was probably no more than eight at the time, but I was in an absolute dream of unfocused erotic bliss for weeks afterwards, and I remember the feeling to this day."

Frances Kaufman Doft, who grew up in Toronto but saw her family in the U.S. a lot during the summers, recalls developing an intense crush on an older boy cousin when she first saw him in his army uniform. Sadly, he was killed in Korea, "so I always remember him as he was, my ideal first boyfriend." She also recalls still another cousin in the army on whom she had a crush. "But he came back, and of course I got over it. Now he and his wife are very good friends of ours," she said.

Romantic attachments to cousins, with or without a sexual component, are not confined to children. Coulter Ives, a curator at New York's Metropolitan Museum and an authority on Pierre Bonnard, told me that when Bonnard was a young man, he was romantically involved with his first cousin Berte Schaedlin for several years-in fact, until he met and married his wife Marthe. He used Berte as a model for his poster advertising Champagne; in a number of well-known paintings, including a portrait; in "Women with Dog" (1891); and in one of *Les Petits Scénes,* a book of piano music for children illustrating "La Danse."

Though the question of whether or not Pierre and Berte were involved sexually is open to speculation, when cousins grow older and their ages are close, the dawning sex attraction between them is often translated into action. "The combination of availability and a certain sense of connectedness often leads cousins to act upon their sexual feelings," says Dr. Donald Bloch. Lending further support to Professor Diamond's findings, he added, "There is a strong sense of familiarity; yet cousins are not seen as part of the strict incest taboo which brothers and sisters become aware of at an early age."

Dr. Sager put it this way: "In families where the aunts, uncles and cousins get together a lot, all the intimate relationships-including crushes-become accentuated. The interesting thing, though, is that though these people are 'family' and close, there's a loosening of the incest taboos. It seems all right to let feelings go in terms of crushes."

Jack Carter, an engineer who grew up in Florida, told me, "My cousin Susan and I had a thing going from the time we were kids and hid in the attic together while we were playing hide-and-seek. While we were up there, we got in the habit of checking out-frequently-what made boys boys and girls girls. Then when we were older, there was a period when she didn't seem interested in me anymore. But instead of discouraging me, that just seemed to fuel the fire. I'd look through the keyhole when she stayed over and slept in my sister's room, and catch glimpses of her half undressed that drove me crazy.

"Finally, when we were both about fifteen, there was a family party, and we got to talking about the attic and how we used to play hide-and-seek. We went up again, supposedly to revisit our childhood haunt, and there was an old mattress there that I never remembered from before. Anyway, whether it was the mattress, or whether it would have happened anyway I don't know, but we both lost our virginity that day, and we kept meeting up there whenever she came over for a few months after that. I don't have any regrets, and I don't think she does, either."

Elly, a former roommate, told me, "When my boy cousins came over, we always 'played doctor' or went behind the barn to compare notes. (Really there was a barn, because we lived in the country.) When we were older, the sexual interest was still there. In fact, when I was about seventeen, I had my first experience with my cousin Bill. It was very warm and comfortable. Our parents would probably have been shocked if they knew, but we were pretty clever about concealing it, and I guess they weren't suspicious the way they would have been if he were a boyfriend. Anyway, we stayed on intimate terms for three years, and then, when my parents moved, we finally drifted apart. He's married now, but we're still friends, though I don't see him very much."

Conrad Fernandez, the teacher whose large Hispanic family in New York was mentioned earlier, said, "The cousin relationship in Latin families tends to be particularly close-even more so with newcomers to the country who tend to cling together. You were encouraged to be close, and to try out all forms of social behavior with them, including sex. The attitude was, 'You shouldn't marry, but there's nothing wrong with dating, or even sometimes with having sexual experiences with a cousin.' And I certainly did."

Anthropologist Robin Fox, in his book *Kinship and Marriage*, discusses just such fine points in detail, distinguishing carefully between the difference between "incest'-which pertains to sexual relations, and 'exogamy' (the prohibition on marriage within the group, however the group is defined)-which pertains to conjugal relations. Of course, if one forbids two people to have sexual relations, this rather puts an end to chances of marriage between them. But one can forbid them to marry without necessarily forbidding them to have intercourse"-as Conrad's story clearly confirms. "This is doubly important," says Fox, "because many writers write 'incest taboo/exogamy' as though these were one and the same."

Several friends mentioned that the not-unusual phase of experimentation with their own sex that many girls and boys go through also took place with their cousins. "We used to play 'Fancy Pantsy' or some such nonsense, when we were twelve or thirteen," said my friend Sandra. "We'd get all dressed up in nutty costumes and pretend we were a boy and girl on a date. Then we'd usually end up on the bed taking turns 'being the boy' and just sort of stroking each other. I guess in retrospect it seems pretty tame, but it seemed very daring and exciting at the time. And I don't think I'd have had the nerve to try it out with any of my friends. I couldn't have faced them in school the next day."

Charles Le Grand of Rockville, Maryland, told two stories of sexual involvement with cousins, one of which spanned decades. "I didn't know Jody till I was in my teens," he said. "But when my mother left my father and moved in with another man, I went to live with my aunt and uncle, and Jody was one of their seven daughters. (They also had two sons.) Well, we were exactly the same age and were in the same class in school, too. Even though I thought she was pretty, she was very unsophisticated-I always thought of her as a 'country girl'-and she wasn't dating at all in high school, so I tried to fix her up. But nothing seemed to work. I felt kind of sorry for her, and one night I asked her to go to the drive-in with me. We started to neck and pet. I don't even remember how it got started, but it seemed perfectly natural at the time. But that was the only time we did anything, for a few years.

"After I graduated from high school, I was in the Navy for a while, and while I was away, she got married, moved to Key West, and had two little kids. Then I got stationed nearby and went to visit her and her husband Nick. This was about ten years after the first episode. It was the summer and fall of '63, and I'll always remember that I was at her house when Kennedy was assassinated. I guess we were both about twenty-five by then. Well, it turned out Nick was a real drunk. Anyway, soon after I got there, Nick started drinking one night and passed out. Jody and I decided to go skinny-dipping. When we got out of the water, we consummated what had started all those years ago.

"The odd part is that it was as though we'd been doing it all our lives, yet at the same time it was the most exciting sexual relationship I've ever had. (Oh, I forgot to tell you that I'd married a girl while I was in England. I didn't know it but she'd been molested as a child, and it had affected her in a way that made her really unresponsive. This made me appreciate Jody even more.)

"After that first time, I went up every weekend and we'd make love down by the water. Her husband knew, I think, but he ignored it. We could keep going all night, and the communication was terrific-like I've never had. We were completely open with each other. I always figured it had to do with our being cousins, and having been such good friends years before. We did everything-tried everything. It was all the things men fantasize. I just kept wondering, 'Is this going to last?'

"After we were separated and I went home, I got divorced (not because of Jody), but she stayed with her husband. Still, I'd call her a lot, and whenever I could I'd visit her, and we'd start all over again. She came to our twenty-fifth high school reunion without her husband and we had a great time. Honestly, this went on for years, and in fact it still does."

The other story had to do with the time before Charles moved to Jody's house, or in fact even knew her. "I was about twelve, and had this cousin Annie, who was sixteen or seventeen then. She was very attractive-looked like Elizabeth Taylor, I always thought. She stayed with us for a while so she could finish high school after her parents moved to another town. I used to watch her ironing clothes in her slip, and finally I realized she was watching me, too. Soon we were at the 'You show me and I'll show you' stage, and from then we went on to mutual masturbation.

"We never actually had intercourse, but I think I felt guiltier about what little we did do than I ever did with Jody. I was real scared of getting caught, and in fact once my mother did come home and caught us in the bathtub together. She talked to Alice and it cooled for a while. But then after a few months we started again. But it still never went past that first phase. I remember it as very exciting, especially because she had a driver's license and would take me for rides. But after she moved away, I didn't see her for years. She settled down and married a nice guy, and now we're on very friendly terms. We never talk about it, and I'm not even sure she remembers it."

None of this is to say that the incest taboo doesn't operate strongly for many cousins, or that sex attraction between cousins is either inevitable or indiscriminate.

Eduardo Riccio, the teacher who grew up in the Bronx, said, "Once we were playing spin the bottle-all the kids in the neighborhood-and when the bottle stopped, it was pointing at my cousin. Not only were we supposed to kiss, we were supposed to 'soul kiss.' Even though she was really pretty and I was kind of attracted to her, I was so embarrassed. After all, this was my cousin! I knew you weren't supposed to do things like that with a cousin, and I was pretty half-hearted about it, though I tried to go through with it."

When I asked Anna Quindlen if she'd ever been attracted to any of her cousins or had crushes on them, she said "Absolutely not! The boys in the family all looked and even talked like my father. They basically *are* my father. It would have felt like incest."

Said Carl Nyquist, a banker who grew up in Minnesota, "I had several girl cousins about my age, and all of them were pretty good-looking. But I was actually attracted to only one of them, Margie. Maybe it was because she spent the most time at our house, though I'm not really sure about that. I never acted on it in any way-I wouldn't have dared-but I certainly thought about it for years, and she was part of my first wet dream."

In our society, where the incest taboo extends to cousins in most groups, the attraction between cousins can also be a source of painful problems and guilt. Wrote one young girl in the "Relating" column of *Seventeen* magazine (subtitled "I have a forbidden crush"), "I've gotten myself into such a mess! A little over a month ago, my family moved to Nebraska, where almost all my relatives live. I was very lonely, and maybe that's why I developed a big crush on my cousin Andy. I kind of fell in love with him, and within a short time we were meeting secretly. Since we are first cousins, we decided that we couldn't continue, that our feelings would only grow deeper and our situation more painful.

"What really hurts is that now Andy barely speaks to me!...I'm also extremely nervous because my grandmother has noticed how Andy avoids me and wants to know why. How should I answer-and what about Andy?"

The columnist advised this unfortunate young woman not to worry about her grandmother, since "she probably doesn't suspect the reason," and that, as for Andy, "As you obviously realize, romantic relationships between cousins, unless they're very distant ones, are not sanctioned in our culture...Andy may feel that before the two of you can resume a more casual cousinly relationship, a period of exaggerated distance is necessary."

And it is important to note that, unless the attraction is mutual, sexual advances are usually unwelcome. A friend who preferred to remain anonymous told me of how frightened she was when an older boy cousin who was supposed to babysit with her used to open the door to the bathroom to try to see her naked. "And one time he came in and tried to kiss me! I was horrified. I screamed and told him to get out and he did, but I never really felt comfortable with him again. Somehow I persuaded my mother not to let him babysit anymore, though I didn't tell her why."

Oprah Winfrey's story had a far more dangerous ending. At the age of nine and for years afterwards, she was sexually abused by a teenage cousin, and then by other male relatives and friends. In an article in the *New York Times Magazine* (quoted from *People)*, she said that the experience wasn't a "horrible thing in my life," but only because she basically craved the attention, and found it pleasurable. She also claimed that it was extremely confusing because she tended to "blame myself for feeling good."

More often, when a child is sexually abused by a cousin, it is deeply traumatic. Said one of the psychiatrists I spoke to, who preferred to remain anonymous lest his patient feel he was indirectly betraying a confidence, "When there's sexual attraction that's one-sided, there is often sexual exploitation, too, because of the availability of the cousin. A young male patient of mine who had two boy cousins a few years older was forced to have anal intercourse with them for about three years-when he was ten, eleven, and twelve. He hated them, and finally threatened to tell his parents, at which point it ended. But it left him completely insecure about his masculinity. In fact, you could say it did to him what having incest with a father would do to a girl. But it left a terrible mark on him, and it took years to get over it, if in fact he has."

An interesting discovery I made was that for most people in our country the incest taboo in relation to cousins is so taken for granted that a good number of those I interviewed were startled when I even suggested the possibility that there might have been an element of sexual attraction. Upon reflection, however, a number acknowledged that in fact they had had such feelings, though they had never been aware of them before the question was posed directly, or had repressed them as unacceptable.

One case in point was Miriam Delson, a childhood friend of mine who now sells real estate on Long Island. Only after we'd had a long phone conversation about all her other cousins and hung up, did she call me back and say, "I've been thinking about your question on sexual attraction." (She'd denied any such feelings when we first talked.) "Now that I think about it, there was one cousin with whom that was undoubtedly a factor-my cousin Robbie, to whom I was very, very close. As children, we were inseparable, which is odd when you think about it, since he was four years younger than I was, and a boy.

"I remember so many things about our relationship that I now see as showing that attraction. He was really very handsome, with red hair and green eyes. And I remember that when he came out of the service-I was about twentyfive at the time-I said to him, 'You're so beautiful. Let me comb your hair.' And he let me. I got such pleasure out of doing that. I had a great desire to be near him physically, to take care of him. And I was so proud whenever he went out with my husband and me. Incidentally, he later told me he was very jealous when I got married-both times. But the funny thing is that my second husband was more than four years younger than I was and was named Robbie, too. What do you make of that?

"Another thing is that between my divorce and my second marriage he got very involved in the relationship with the Robbie I married. Even though he resented him, he would always drive me to see him, and things like that. As I look back, I can see that that created a vicarious connection between him and me. After the marriage, the two Robbies got very friendly, and my cousin was always at our house.

"When he got married, I was terribly jealous. I felt like he was leaving me. I found it so hard to handle that I basically withdrew from the relationship. His wife made me feel very inadequate. She was very glamourous and flirtatious, and even tried to come on to my husband. (We were still married then.) But then he got divorced, too, and I must admit I was delighted. But by the time I got my second divorce, he was already living with another woman, and somehow we've drifted apart. It does seem amazing to me that I hadn't thought about Robbie in such a long time. And as I say, in looking back I can see what I couldn't see then-the definite chemistry between us."

Lewis Frumkes, the humor writer, also said that until I asked him, it had never been in his consciousness that he had been attracted to a young cousin years before. "I saw Kathy often since I was very close to her older brother Donald," he said. "She was so cute and lovely, but much too young to have done anything about the attraction even if I had admitted to myself how I felt. I would have felt so awkward with her parents, to say nothing of her brother!"

In a tragic footnote, Lewis mentioned that this cousin had died of cancer while still in her 20's. "But Donald has a daughter who looks remarkably like her. And no, I'm *not* attracted to her, though I think she's a great kid."

Margot Levin, the librarian from Joliet who grew up on the same block as

four of her cousins, also said, "Until you mentioned it, I guess I never acknowledged it, but there was one of my boy cousins to whom I was especially close. As
I look back, I see that there was a definite attraction, and there easily could have
been sexual experimentation, but there wasn't. It would have been unthinkable
in our family!"

The longest and most complex story I heard directly-longest because it
involved a lifelong attraction that was never acted upon or even acknowledged
till my question provoked it-was that of Jean Allen, the Ohio-born artist, and her
cousin Paul. Jean had told me of the many summers she and Paul spent together, of his sister Betsy's jealousy, and of the things they had in common.

"But yes, as I look back, I see that there was also a strong sexual element,"
she said. "I think it first came out when we traveled to Greece together in our
late teens. We were trying to save money, so we were sharing rooms. And even
though we told everyone we were cousins, I don't think anyone believed us. We
just thought it was funny at the time, but as I look back and remember what happened, it seems more significant. Because we ended that trip furious with each
other. Barely talking! I think there was just too much physical proximity and
denial of sexuality for us to deal with. And the way it came out was in our beginning to bicker over every little thing. Once we got home and could separate out
again we made up, but as I say, I see now what was really going on.

"But that wasn't the end of it either. When he was finishing college, we wrote
each other all the time, and also when he was in the Air Force during World War
II. Then he moved to New York, and we saw each other constantly. I cooked dinner for him, we had a concert subscription together, we discussed his relationship
with his mother a lot. He always introduced me to whomever he was dating and
asked me what I thought of them. I had boyfriends, too, but all the women in
his life were always jealous of me. They all assumed we were lovers. Some said so
right out; others just sensed the competition. Paul and I laughed it off, but as I
say, in looking back, I can quite understand it.

"This was true right up to and during the time he got married. But then he was offered a job as dean of a private school in Vermont, and moved up there. His wife was so jealous that we actually had to sneak our phone calls to each other. But we stayed in touch as much as we could around that impediment known as his wife." I thought Jean's choice of words here said a lot.

"Well, that first marriage didn't last, and soon we were as friendly as before." (Jean never married, a fact that also seemed increasingly significant as she went on.) "He'd visit me in New York regularly, and we spent Christmas together for two or three years-just the two of us. Then he met a woman up in Vermont who was obsessed with him, and we had endless phone conversations about how to deal with her. She was always threatening to kill herself if he wouldn't marry her.

"She finally gave up, and he did meet a wonderful woman through his church. Now they live together, though they've never married. She's the first one he seems happy with. And the funny thing is that I began to withdraw from him after they moved in together. I don't know if it was jealousy or relief, though I tend to think now that maybe it was more of the former than the latter. But he does seem very happy with her. I feel he's in good hands. She kind of took over giving the support I'd been giving, and I guess that's all right. I just don't call him anymore, but I'll always be there for him. In fact, he's in my will."

Almost as an afterthought Jean added, "I guess I should mention that he's told me he had sexual problems with this woman. Whether they were physio-logical or psychological, I don't know. And what connection it might have with him and me I don't know either. But perhaps it is tied in somehow with our long-time bond."

A classic case of a longtime passionate cousinly attachment with sexual overtones is the one between Boris Pasternak, author of *Dr. Zhivago,* and his illustrious cousin, scholar and professor Olga Freidenberg. This fascinating relationship, documented in the many letters they exchanged over a 44-year period, certainly included sexual attraction on his part, though it was never acted upon nor in fact responded to by her. I learned about it through a 1982 article in the *New York Times Book Review* by Helen Muchnic, a professor of Russian literature at Smith College, in which she discussed a book entitled *The Correspondence of Boris Pasternak and Olga Freidenberg, 1910-1954,* edited and translated by Elliot Mossman and published by Harcourt Brace Jovanovich.

Ms. Muchnic writes: "Boris Pasternak and Olga Freidenberg were cousins. Their fathers, Leonid Pasternak and Mikhail Freidenberg, had known each other since their boyhood in Odessa. Leonid's sister, Ann, married Mikhail, and later, when the Freidenbergs settled in St. Petersburg and the Pasternaks in Moscow, they exchanged frequent visits and spent summers together. The children were playmates always; and Olga and Boris, who were born in the same year, were fast friends. Their correspondence begins in the spring of 1910, when they were 20.

That winter, as Olga recalled decades later, Boris came to see them 'in a new key.' She had become accustomed over the years to his 'appreciation, his exaggerated praise and hyperbolic feeling.' But this time 'he was more than attentive-he was infatuated,' following her, as they walked and rode to various places, 'as a lover,' whereas she took him with her 'as a brother.' She visited the Pasternaks that spring in Moscow, and in July, briefly, at their dacha...in a town called Merrekul on the shore of the Baltic Sea. There, according to her diary, she fell under the spell of 'the vistas opened up by his new, profound, meaningful words.' He talked for hours; she understood little of what he said but loved 'the unintelligible' that transported her 'out of the everyday world.'

He accompanied her back to St. Petersburg and then returned to Moscow. This memorable July was filled with a wonderful exchange of letters-long, passionate, tremulous and brilliant...

Olga had promised to come again to Moscow, but she put off her visit and finally did not go at all, sensing, as she subsequently put it in her diary, that hers was 'a passion of the fancy, not of the heart,' a sister's love, for however warmly and tenderly she loved Pasternak, she could never have fallen in love with him. And so, to avoid explanations, she broke with him, curtly and quite brutally. He was deeply hurt, but the year remained a vivid memory for them both.

There was a break-the only one-in their correspondence until 1921. During that time, Olga had become a Red Cross nurse, and afterwards she entered the University of St. Petersburg and embarked on a life of scholarship, attaining eminence in the fields of semantics, folklore and Greek literature.

Without getting into the sufferings of Olga and Boris during the Stalinist era-which, however interesting, are not relevant here-it must be noted that because of the repressive regime only one of her books was published during her lifetime. But Ms. Muchnic explains that she was a "witty and powerful writer" and that Pasternak "devoured" the learned articles she sent him. "How marvelously you write!' he exclaimed. 'If only I could do as well.' Her ideas, he said time and again, were very close to his own."

The essence of this ardent and enduring relationship between Boris and Olga is perhaps best expressed in these lines: "In this great story reaching deep into the past, still going on...' he wrote her in 1924, 'in this grim, this unendurable story that is our lives, you represent the best, the most profound, and my favorite chapters...Remember our coming back from Merrekul thirteen years ago? Remember the sound of the station names...? Remember?.... It's as if a recent gust of wind had swept it all away. Run after it and pick it up!"

And she, just the year before her death, wrote to him:

Have I ever told you what it means to a person to experience the singular joy of recognizing his *kinship* (literally that) to art?...It is of this I am speaking. I am, if you like, referring to those 'declarations' of our youth that we called 'our last will and testament,' remember? (oh, you do, you do!-your memory retains everything forever). Well then, that is the answer to our familial charades, the answer why I avoided you, withdrew from you, felt a distance between us of almost railroad dimensions, felt it well-nigh impossible to board the train and go to you in Moscow, to allow my fingers to touch your life, why

I loved you above all else in this world, why I found no words to convey how two-in-one you are to me-you who judged me in the light of integral calculus, expressing then and expressing always that part of me which is called my human self.

Concluded Ms. Muchnic: "It is on this level of deep affection and admiration that...they continued their correspondence for over forty years, helping, encouraging and inspiring each other, sympathizing, consoling, rejoicing."

Perhaps the account of this rare and beautiful love is a good point at which to move into stories where such relationships were consummated-not only physically, but with the rites of marriage.

5

WHEN COUSINS MARRY

I remember at four or five having already de-cided which of my male first cousins I would eventually marry.

-ELIZABETH STONE,
BLACK SHEEP AND KISSING COUSINS

IN AN IRANIAN film, *The Peddler*, a woman about to give birth to her fifth child tells the medics in the ambulance that she is already convinced her new baby will be crippled like the others. The medics suggest that either malnutrition or inbreeding might be the cause. "Why did you have to marry your cousin?" one of them asks. "Whose cousin should I have married then?" she answers.

This comment, with all that it implies about the acceptance of cousin marriages in her society, could easily be repeated in a number of other cultures and countries, even today. The doctor's question also implies a view of the risks of consanguineous marriages (marriages between relatives, especially cousins) which, except for special cases like that of the Iranian woman, is higher than current research has borne out.

Since the question of genetic risk to the children is often the first thing people think about when they hear of cousin marriages, I'll try to summarize recent findings on the subject, then provide some specific examples.

A recent paper by James S. Thompson, M.D., and Margaret W. Thompson, Ph.D., of the Departments of Medical Genetics and Pediatrics at the University of Toronto and The Hospital for Sick Children in Toronto, summed up the conclusions of work done by them and by researchers in Japan in a magazine entitled *Genetics in Medicine*. "Are cousin marriages unwise?" they ask. "There is considerable disagreement among geneticists as to whether the extra risk of defective offspring is significant," they report. The figure they quote, from comparative studies on inbred and outbred populations done for insurance companies, is that "the proportion of abnormal progeny is about 2 percent for random marriages, and about 3 percent for consanguineous marriages." Consequently, the insurance companies do not consider the offspring of cousins to have higher-than-normal insurance risks.

An in-depth study of the subject would involve dealing with genetic concepts too complex to deal with in a brief chapter, but in that risk increase from 2 to 3 percent, the following factors should be mentioned:

1. With minor exceptions, the increase in risk applies only to the first generation of offspring of related parents, not to subsequent generations.

2. The risk is higher when the parents are from a normally outbred population than when they are from a relatively inbred group. The reason for this seemingly inconsistent fact is that inbred populations have usually bred out the bad genes.

3. Consanguineous marriages more distant than those of first cousins have a correspondingly lower risk of producing affected offspring. And finally:

4. If, like the Iranian couple in the movie, the married cousins have a child who suffers from a recessively inherited disease

> [the result of having inherited a copy of a deleterious
> recessive gene from each parent] the parents are
> thereby proven to be carriers, with a much greater
> likelihood (one in four) of having a similarly affected
> child at a later pregnancy.

According to Audrey Heimler, the senior genetics counselor at Long Island Jewish Hospital and assistant professor at Albert Einstein Medical College, no testing of cousins can positively determine that there is no more than the 3 percent risk, but advice can be given on the basis of a thorough family history. "As a general rule," she said, "I would tell cousin couples with a known problem that the risk of their child inheriting the problem is up to 25 percent. If the first child is born with the problem, I'd tell them" (as would the Thompsons) "that the risk of a subsequent child having the same problem is still 25 percent for any subsequent pregnancy." The Iranian woman was apparently unusually unlucky.

According to Ms. Heimler, cousin marriages are especially common in cultures where people are still living in villages, as in Middle Eastern countries such as Iran, Jordan, and Lebanon, or even in remote villages in areas of Italy such as Calabria. Intermarriage is also still common in Latin countries, in Spain and Portugal, in Saudi Arabia, and in a few parts of India. Similarly, island communities-including some in America, like Vinalhaven, Maine-also have a high degree of cousin marriage, as do self-contained religious groups like the Amish and the Hutterites. The Amish, especially, have provided a rich and remarkably complete genealogical record, dating back to their immigration here in the mid-18th century. This wonderfully detailed record has enabled scientists to trace the genetic illnesses caused by generations of marriage between Amish cousins with great accuracy.

Though cousin marriage is discouraged or forbidden in many societies, both past and present, endogamy is not only accepted but encouraged in others-the Polynesian and Trobriand Islanders, among others. (Endogamy, the opposite of exogamy, means one must marry within the group.) But there are strict blood lines along which it is organized. In some groups, marriage between "cross cousins"-a son and a daughter of a brother and sister-is permitted, while that between "ortho" (sometimes called "parallel") cousins-children of two brothers, or of two sisters-is forbidden. Actual instances of such cross cousin marriages appear to be rare among the Trobrianders, however. On the other hand, it was reported that in a community of Kurds with similar rules, nearly 60 percent were of the preferred type-in this case with a father's brother's daughter.

The reasons such marriages make a lot of sense in these primitive societies are not hard to understand. There is a great belief that intermarriages strengthen family ties and prevent a weakening of the group. More importantly, if wives are in short supply, as they often are due to polygyny (having more than one wife or female mate at a time) or female infanticide, the difficulty of obtaining a wife is alleviated if it's recognized that a man has a preferential right to his cousin.

But most important of all are the rules governing property by which, in a matrilineal group, the man's heirs are not his own children but his sister's sons. A solution to the resulting impoverishment of his own children is clearly for the man's children to marry their cousins. (The very origin of the word "cousin" seems to hint at this female orientation, since it comes to us-via Middle English and the earlier Old French "cosin" or "cusin"-from the Latin "consobrinus," "a mother's sister's child.") The leap from cousin marriage in such far-off societies to the wealthy and powerful families of both today and yesterday is not as great as one might expect. Though the match never came to be, Tina Onassis at one time encouraged her daughter Christina to marry her cousin Phillipe, in order to unite the Niarchos family holdings. And marriage between royal cousins has been encouraged for centuries for basically similar property and inheritance reasons, though it is less common between first cousins than between more remote ones.

Ferdinand and Isabella of Spain were distant cousins, and it is appropriate that they head the royal list, since, as mentioned before, cousin marriage is common to this day in both Spain and Portugal. Queen Mary and King George V-the present Queen Elizabeth's grandparents-were second cousins once removed (their mothers were first cousins). As is fairly widely known, Queen Elizabeth and Prince Philip themselves are also second cousins once removed, since he is a second cousin of her father, George VI. Both are also descended from Queen Victoria, though on different sides; he, through the Mountbattens, she, through the royal family. And so the royal lines have twined and intertwined throughout history.

Examples of cousin marriage can be found in many famous families, too, especially in England. Among these are the Darwins, the Huxleys, the Wedgwoods, and the Mitfords. (The special reasons these were so common in Victorian times will be described later in more detail.)

For both social and economic reasons, there was a great deal of intermarriage in the so-called "Jewish aristocracy" of England as well-families such as the Cohens, the Rothschilds, the Goldsmids, the Montefiores, the Samuels, and the Sassoons. Chaim Bermant describes this graphically in his books *Troubled Eden* and *The Cousinhood*. In *The Mountain of Names,* anthropologist Alex Shoumatoff writes that "In 1875, 7.5 percent of all the marriages among Jews in England, who at that time constituted a closed, endogamous religious isolate, were between first cousins, about three times the rate among gentiles."

So accepted was the concept of cousin marriage in England in Gilbert and Sullivan's time that when poor Sir Joseph Porter (in *H.M.S. Pinafore)* lost the fair Josephine to Ralph Rackstraw, the humble sailor of noble birth, he quickly comforted himself by pledging to marry his long-suffering and patient cousin Hebe ("And we are his sisters and his cousins and his aunts.")

Among the most famous of other cousin marriages celebrated in fiction is that between Rose and Mac in *Rose in Bloom,* the sequel to *Eight Cousins,* with which I'd so closely identified as a child. And it was only a drop in the family fortunes that interfered with the planned marriage between Count Nikolai Rostov and Sonia, his beautiful cousin, in *War and Peace.* Similarly, in *David Copperfield,* only Steerforth's dastardly alienation of Little Emily's affections prevents her marriage to her devoted cousin Ham. Less well-known but powerfully portrayed is the ill-fated marriage of Simon and Mariella in Rosamond Lehmann's *Dusty Answer,* where again the setting is England, though the time is the 1920s. And in the film *My Beautiful Laundrette,* an Indian father encourages his nephew to marry his daughter, the young man's first cousin. Though the marriage never takes place, it's clear that all involved are comfortable with the idea of cousin marriage. (I learned, however, from an Indian friend who married her cousin, and whose story will be told later, that cousin marriage is by no means considered desirable in all or even most parts of India.)

In another literary footnote, an ongoing theme of *100 Years of Solitude,* by Gabriel Garcia Marquez is the fear that due to familial intermarriages-many between cousins-the children will be born with pig's tails, as one once was.

And while discussing South American writers, it should be noted that Peruvian novelist and presidential aspirant Mario Vargas Llosa married, first, his aunt, Julia, and then his 16-year-old first cousin. This intriguing story was told by writer Tim Golden in *Vanity Fair:* "In late 1961, Julia's sister Olga sent her…daughter Patricia (who was both Mario's first cousin and niece by marriage), to live with the Vargas Llosas in Paris and study French. Several years, lots of assertions about Julia's imagination, and one divorce later, Patricia and Uncle Mario were married."

In the plays of Shakespeare, marriage between cousins is also common, though not as common as people think. This is because many people are not aware that in Shakespeare's time the term "cousin" (more familiarly, "cos") was used by sovereigns as a general honorific for addressing persons of high, but not equal, rank. (The word "brother" in his plays is also confusing to modern audiences, since that term was used by one sovereign to address another of equal rank, even if they weren't related.)

It should also be mentioned that "kissing cousins"-a term often taken to mean cousins who are very close, or possibly even lovers-actually refers to non-cousins who are felt to be as close as real cousins. Hortense Calisher, in her memoir *Kissing Cousins,* defines them as "part of the family in every respect except blood." Schneider, on the other hand, defines the general term "kissin' kin" as "shirt-tail relations; wakes and weddings relatives" who are, however, related by blood.

Of course right here in the United States, there could be no more famous a real-life cousin marriage-albeit distant cousins-than that between Eleanor and Franklin D. Roosevelt. John Calhoun, the Confederate leader, returned home to marry his cousin, heiress of a well-to-do low-country planter, after graduating from Yale. And in 1885, Endicott Peabody, the founder and longtime headmaster of Groton, married his first cousin Fanny Peabody.

Harry Sedgwick, a Peabody grandson, told me the story. When Endicott fell madly in love with his beautiful cousin and wanted to marry her, his grandfather strongly opposed the idea, largely due to his fear of "mongrel" offspring. In line with the old tradition of travel abroad as a cure for unhappy affairs of the heart, Endicott was sent to England to "get over it." He didn't, and eventually returned to marry Fanny, with whom he had six healthy children.

Cousin marriage in America, however, continues to be held in some disrepute in many areas of the U.S., and according to Martin Ottenheimer, a professor of anthropology at Kansas State University and author of *Forbidden Relatives, The American Myth of Cousin Marriage,* first cousin marriage was still illegal in thirty-one states (62%) as recently as 1996. Among these, a few exceptions are made. Illinois, Indiana, and Arizona permit such marriages if the couple can't bear children, and in Maine first cousins can marry if they have had genetic counseling. North Carolina forbids marriage between double first cousins only. (When a sister and brother pair marry another brother and sister, or one set of twins marries another set, their children are called "double first cousins.")

In Europe, by contrast, not a single country has such prohibitions, though some churches or cultural groups may. Ottenheimer feels that inaccurately researched and wildly exaggerated health studies in America in the mid-to late 1800's (primarily the Bemiss report of 1858) led to both the adoption of such laws and the still prevalent prejudice against cousin marriage. He maintains that such laws are completely inappropriate and should be changed. While agreeing that it is certainly wise for cousin couples to have genetic counseling, so should everyone else, he says. "Forbidding cousin marriage works against this by providing a false sense of security and camouflaging the real issue that genes [from unrelated couples] can [also] be lethal or produce debilitating effects in offspring."

In this view-that supposedly unrelated couples also run a genetic risk-he is backed up by many experts, including Sir Julian Huxley. Their conclusions are fascinatingly outlined in Alex Shoumatoff's book, *A Mountain of Names* (already referred to in the discussion of intermarriage among late 19th century English Jews). Says Shoumatoff, quoting science writer Guy Murchie (*The Seven Mysteries of Life*):

> '...no human can be less closely related to any other human than approximately fiftieth cousin, and most of us are a lot closer...[In other words] the family trees of all of us, of whatever origin or trait, must meet and merge into one genetic tree of all humanity by the time they have spread into our ancestors for about fifty generations...'
>
> The 'family of man'...actually exists...Not that we are all descended from some common ancestors...rather, that each of us contains genetic contributions from practically everybody who ever lived. All it takes...for widely divergent populations to merge genealogically is migration by one person. 'A single indirect genetic contact between Africa and Asia in a thousand years can make every African closer than fiftieth cousin to every Chinese.'

Shoumatoff gives some surprising examples. Prince Charles and Diana Spencer are both descendants of Edward III, who ruled England from 1327 to 1377, and thus were definitely cousins, however remote; Presidents Jimmy Carter and Richard Nixon are sixth cousins, both being descendants of a New Jersey Quaker named Richard Morris, who lived before the American

Revolution; and Nixon, in turn, is a tenth cousin once removed of George Bush. Bush is also not only a seventh cousin of Elliot Richardson, attorney general during the Nixon Administration, but a kinsman of Ernest Hemingway as well. If not six degrees of separation, then fifty anyway.

But to return to Ottenheimer and his conclusions about American marriage laws: "…the results of recent scientific research into the potential physical dangers to the offspring of cousins recognizes that the risk has been much exaggerated…the laws against cousin marriage in the U.S.…symbolize an archaic view of the sociocultural aspects of marriage, reflect mistaken notions about the genetic impact of consanguineal [of the same blood] marriage, and work against society's best interests. The prohibitions against cousin marriage appear to be counterproductive."

Apparently, Edgar Kaufmann, the man who commissioned Frank Lloyd Wright to design Fallingwater and other buildings, was one of those affected by the U.S. prohibitions. According to an article by Brendan Gill in *Architectural Digest,* "His wife was his first cousin-not an unusual occurrence in the days when [as in England a generation earlier] Jewish families of prominence were accustomed, like royalty, to arranging marriages within a comparatively small circle. Still, it was against the law in Pennsylvania for first cousins to marry, and the young couple had to hold their wedding ceremony in New York."

Sheila, a doctor in Illinois, told me that when her two first cousins married in Chicago less than fifty years ago, the new groom was disbarred from practicing law there. An interesting and more recent footnote: in 1958, when the news that singer Jerry Lee Lewis had married his 13-year-old cousin Myra got out, it brought his career to a dead halt for years. In that case, however, the public outcry may very well have had as much to do with her age as with their blood relationship.

Returning to the genetic question, according to Lynn Godmilow, chief of genetics in the Department of Obstetrics and Gynecology at Pennsylvania

Hospital in Philadelphia, there is no reason, aside from the morals and mores of certain societies, why healthy cousins-even first cousins-cannot marry and produce perfectly healthy children. She agreed with the Thompson statement that the increased risk is slight, but added that, "People differ, and to some people, the increased risk seems enormous; to others, it's insignificant. The point is, people don't have numbers, they have babies, and if your baby has a problem or if you miscarry, it doesn't matter to you whether the risk was one in 100 or one in 1000."

My personal interviews produced some interesting and unexpected results. My friend Becky told me that her grandparents were first cousins and that her father's first cousin married *his* first cousin. The children of this later marriage between perfectly healthy cousins suffered from numerous ills, including bone deterioration, blindness, and deafness. And another friend told me of two friends from Brazil, cousins who married, who also had two children with problems-one was retarded, the other had severe tendon problems.

I of course accept the geneticists' word that the risks are slight, but I have to say that such disastrous reports, coming from the relatively limited circle of my interviewees, almost seemed to defy the laws of probability, and certainly make that "slight increase" very vivid.

One famous victim of that risk was Toulouse-Lautrec, whose mother and father were first cousins. He is thought to have suffered from pyknodysostosis, a degenerative form of dwarfism associated with familial inbreeding.

A fascinating addition to this disastrous list is Hedda Nussbaum, the woman whose adopted daughter Lisa died of the abuse and neglect she suffered at her parents hands in the mid-80's. Nussbaum's parents were also first cousins. What part, if any, this fact played in the physical or psychological make-up that made her capable of enduring Joel Steinberg's beatings herself and ignoring the violence done to little Lisa is certainly not known as yet. But when her early life and family history are studied in depth, as they surely will be-a childhood with a deep undercurrent of parental disapproval and brooding unhappiness has already been disclosed-the unusual cousin marriage will surely be an element that will bear close scrutiny.

On the other hand, it is also true that the vast majority of children of cousins are completely normal, and with the help of the genetic counseling now available, the risks can be greatly reduced-at least, in cases where there is a known problematic gene such as those for Tay-Sachs disease, sickle cell anemia, or hemophilia, the scourge of so many royal families. Mari, a brilliant medical student and the child of two doctors who are also first cousins, said, "When people find out my parents were cousins, they always look at me as though they expect me to have two heads. They don't seem to remember that the positive genes can combine, too."

Though this happens, the geneticists I spoke to said it would be foolish for musical cousins to marry expecting to produce a musical genius. The point is, birth defects are easy to prove and trace-much easier than, say, a jointly inherited talent for finger-painting, or foreign languages, or even for medicine. And separating out the environmental influences from the genes can also complicate the matter. But those positive combinations do occur-as in the case of Robert Moses' maternal grandparents, who were first cousins. In this case, the couple produced three brilliant daughters, one of whom was the mother of the "power broker." Whatever Moses' faults, he certainly lacked neither good health nor unusual intelligence.

Leaping back in time, one can cite Cleopatra as the superior offspring of an even more consanguineous marriage-not of cousins, but of brother and sister. Tryphanea, Cleopatra's mother, was thought to be Ptolemy XII's sister. Furthermore, Cleopatra herself was pledged at birth to be the sister-bride of her brother Ptolemy XIII, though in fact that marriage never took place. In the far off Inca civilization, as well, kings had to marry their sisters.

One final and related phenomenon is the one mentioned in the discussion of US. marriage laws: of brother and sister marrying sister and brother, or of twins marrying twins, a combination that produces what are called "double cousins" in the next generation. Said Hayes B. Jacobs, former director of the

Writing Workshops at New York's New School for Social Research, "Gretchen, my wife, who comes from the Northwest, has several double cousins, because in her family her mother and her mother's brother married another sister and brother. Genetically, these double cousins are almost as related to each other as they are to their own siblings, which is surprising until you think about it and realize it's true. I love looking at this group of people and observing their physical resemblances and psychological closeness, as well as contemplating the genetics. They were brought up across the road from one another, and in a way it was all one big family. They are still close-close-close. They all get along superbly with one another, and their family reunions are genuine love feasts."

Elizabeth Stone, whose childhood wish to marry a cousin opens this chapter, tells a story of even more complex intermarriages that to some extent explains her early wish. She says that when her grandfather, Gaetano Bongiorno, came to New York from the Lipari Islands near Sicily in 1890, he lived with his two married sisters, "who had married two brothers, and those brothers also happened to be their first cousins."

Fifteen years later, Gaetano was still not married. "One day in the mail, however, a letter came" with a picture of his cousin Annunziata, the youngest sister of Gaetano's sisters' husbands. Gaetano was taken with the picture, and to make a long story short, he ended up marrying Annunziata. "And thus it was that two sisters and a brother married two brothers and a sister and all lived right on top of each other on Union Street in Brooklyn."

Ms. Stone goes on to say that what this story said to her as a child "was that family was so important that one should even try to marry within the family...[and] that the essential unit was the extended family. The nuclear family-a couple and their children-tucked itself into the larger unit."

Before turning to some personal stories of cousin marriages today, there is one group, briefly mentioned before, in which the incidence of cousin marriage was so high that it bears further scrutiny. That group existed in the world of

Victorian England. In order to understand the evolution of this phenomenon-a phenomenon explored in depth by Nancy Fix Anderson in a paper for the *Journal ot Family History* (JAI Press) from which I gathered a great deal of information and which I will occasionally quote-it's useful to go back in history.

Cousin marriage, which had been forbidden by canon law, was legalized in the reign of Henry VIII. Its legality "was affirmed in common law court during the Restoration. [It] became accepted practice among the landed and wealthy merchant families in the eighteenth century, and continued among nineteenth century Victorians."

But here, a change took place, and instead of the economic reasons that had predominated before, romantic love became the prime factor. Why? The Victorian home was "relatively isolated from the outside world," and this led to the development of strong bonds between parents and children, and brothers and sisters. The sense of togetherness and exclusivity was made even stronger by the rigid Victorian restrictions on contacts with members of the opposite sex outside the family, which meant that sexual feelings tended to be contained within the family. "These attachments, with their strong, unconscious incestuous feelings, were so adhesive that many Victorians were unable to unattach themselves in adulthood, and their love for parents or siblings remained primary throughout their lives...Love for a cousin was a convenient and fitting displacement of love toward a nuclear family member." It was "a psychologically safe outlet for incestuous feelings, because it was an established marriage pattern and had functioned earlier to meet economic needs."

A second reason for the large number of such marriages was also an outgrowth of the social insularity of the Victorian home. Essentially, aside from their siblings, the only members of the opposite sex many young Victorians knew were cousins. "Anthony Trollope, in *The Vicar of Bullhampton*, praised cousinhood as an escape from the restriction on companionship between young men and young women. 'Cousins, perhaps, have romped with you, and scolded you, and teased you when you were young. Cousins are almost the same as brothers, and yet they may be lovers. There is certainly a great relief in cousinhood.' In an age in which sex was a source of great anxiety, a cousin could be a comfortable marriage partner, whose familiarity satisfied both conscious heterosexual inhibitions and unconscious incestuous wishes. The large size of Victorian families ensured, moreover, that there were usually a large number of cousins from whom to choose."

Examples abound, even if we exclude the marriage of Victoria and Albert, which, though undoubtedly a love match, was primarily a matter of state. When Charles Darwin chose his cousin Emma Wedgwood to marry, part of his reasons undoubtedly had to do with the fact that "after his five years' absence on the *Beagle,* she was one of the few women he knew, and he associated her with happy childhood memories at the Wedgwood family home."

But there were also the Oedipal associations. "Darwin's mother, Susannah Wedgwood, had died when he was eight. A beloved older sister, Caroline, whom Charles said had been a mother to him, married her cousin, Emma's brother, the same year Darwin decided to marry Emma." Emma, older than Charles, assumed the maternal role. "Emma for her part was devoted to her father Josiah, and wrote that 'one of the things that gave me the most happiness is Charles' thorough affection and value for Papa."

A second case in point is that of the novelist Margaret Oliphant Wilson Oliphant. She was raised, she said, "in a most singular secluded way. I was never at a dance till after my marriage, never went out, never saw anyone at home." Her much older brother Frank was the center of her childhood world-'my Frank, as I always called him.' When she married her older cousin Frank Oliphant, her brother Frank was so upset that he impulsively also married a cousin...After her husband's death abroad, Margaret returned to England with her two young children [both of them, incredibly, also named Frank] and eventually supported her bankrupt widower brother Frank."

William Makepeace Thackeray's daughter Anne was devoted to her father. Significantly, he called his daughters "little wives," and was especially devoted to "Annie," who took over running his home after his wife, incurably insane, was placed in custodial care. "After William's death Annie remained dedicated to her father's memory…She was therefore attracted to the young Richmond Ritchie, the son of her father's favorite cousin, with whose family William had lived as a boy. Annie enjoyed being with Richmond because she could talk to him about her father…Annie, at age 39, married her 23-year-old cousin in a generational reversal of oedipal feelings. Richmond's love…was a straightforward transference from his own mother, to whom he was so devoted that when she died, the 34-year-old Richmond nearly suffered a nervous breakdown."

Amazingly similar is the story of Sara Coleridge, daughter of "the restless Samuel Taylor Coleridge." Though Samuel was away during most of her youth, and Sara was raised "in the close isolated world of Great Hall in Keswick…which her family shared with her uncle Robert Southey," she did spend a short time with him at the Wordsworths' house in Grasmere when she was about five. "She remembered that he wanted 'to fasten my affection on him. I slept with him, and he would tell me fairy stories when he came to bed at twelve and one o'clock."

Sara didn't see her father during her teen years, "but carried an image of him as heroic and grand. She begged news of him from every visitor, and longed to go and join him. When she was age 20, she went to London to see him, and during that visit, she met her cousin Henry Nelson Coleridge, a dedicated disciple of her father. They fell in love almost immediately.

"Samuel Taylor Coleridge…was upset when he read a published account by his nephew in which Henry said that, 'I love a cousin; she is such an exquisite relation, just standing between me and the stranger to my name, drawing upon so many sources of love and tying them all up with every cord of human affection-almost my sister ere my wife." These last six words shocked Samuel, who disapproved of cousin marriage in any case, feeling it was too close to brother-sister marriage. But he finally accepted the situation, and the cousins married.

"Sara described Henry as her 'cousin-husband, certainly nearer and dearer to me for being cousin, as well as husband,' and said she loved him for his worship of her father. They lived in London near Samuel…and when her husband died, she had him buried with her father."

Edward Barrett, father of Elizabeth, and notoriously possessive of his children, "intensified incestuous feelings within his large family by his extreme restrictions on contacts outside the family. To his fury, cousins were able to slip through…His son Alfred married a cousin who had lived with the family as a ward for many years…and his daughter Henrietta married a cousin who had been able to visit the home under the guise of the family relationship. The father disinherited them both, as he did Elizabeth when she married Robert Browning." Though Browning of course, was not her cousin, Elizabeth created a cousin marriage in *Aurora Leigh* (1857), her most famous narrative poem, which has as its center the love between cousins Rodney and Aurora Leigh.

The list of famous Victorian families with cousin marriages and Oedipal attachments continues. The Christian socialist John Ludlow married his first cousin Maria soon after his sister Maria, to whom he was devoted, died. John Ruskin's parents were first cousins. Furthermore, if one discounts Ruskin's doomed relationships with two much younger women he met as children-first, "Effie," (their marriage was annulled for nonconsummation), and later, Rose La Touche, the object of his obsessional love who died insane at 27-it's easy to believe that "the only adult woman, other than his mother, with whom John was close was his second cousin Joan Severn, a relationship biographer John Dixon Hunt called 'curiously intense.' They talked baby talk with each other, and played the roles of mother/son and father/daughter. After his mother's death, Joan took over her role and mothered John through his final years of recurrent insanity."

Lewis Carroll, too, was the product of a cousin marriage. Neither he nor any of his siblings married until after their parents' death, "and then, only one of the seven daughters married, to a clergyman like her father, named Charles, which was the name of her father and oldest brother…Charles (Lewis Carroll)…remained, as Derek Hudson said, 'past fixated,' and handled his sexual obsession with young girls in the sublimated form of a 'love gift of a fairy tale.' "

The list goes on and on, both in well-known and less well-known families. Some final examples of prominent people who married their cousins in that era are Egyptologist George Glidden, scholar Alfred Henry Huth, artist Eliza Briddell Fox, and educator Maria Sherriff Grey, as did the daughters of Elizabeth Gaskell and Robert Southey, and the sisters of Thomas Carlyle, Elizabeth Fry, Charles Bosanquet, and Jane Brookfield.

Nor were such marriages confined to the real lives of the Victorians. Cousin marriages proliferated in the fiction of the day. Elizabeth Barrett's poem has already been mentioned. The novels of Dickens, Trollope, and Emily Brontë also provide examples. Jude, in Thomas Hardy's *Jude the Obscure,* marries his cousin Sue Bridehead.

According to Ms. Anderson, "Perhaps the most overtly incestuous cousin romance is to be found in Thackeray's *Henry Esmond...*The title character loved his cousin, to whom he referred in turn as 'cousin,' 'sister' and 'wife.' He also loved and eventually married his cousin's mother, who had been like a mother to him."

Along with all these romantic/Oedipal cousin marriages, the economic cousin marriage of convenience continued to thrive as well. By mid-century, however, especially after Darwin's theories became known, "consanguineous marriages became a hotly debated topic," as they were in America. Darwin disapproved strongly, believing "that inbreeding was harmful, not only because it intensified genetic traits, but because consanguinity itself causes degeneration."

His son George, who was the product of a first cousin marriage himself, did a statistical study to disprove his father's theory (there was undoubtedly an element of personal concern), and concluded that "the evil has been often much exaggerated." Nonetheless, Ms. Anderson tells us that, "within the inbred Darwin-Wedgwood clan...it became a joke to point to lazy or sickly members as examples of degeneracy due to consanguinity. They could also have pointed to the deafness of Julia Wedgwood and to Lewis Carroll's as well. On the other hand, defenders of cousin marriage used the remarkable achievements of Charles Darwin's sons as evidence that marriage between cousins of good stock was not injurious."

In the end, after much debate and numerous studies by eugenists, the general feeling in England was that in terms of having children, cousin marriage was dangerous. Consequently, as in America, it began to decline, though laws against it were never passed there. This change in attitude was also reflected in late-Victorian and early twentieth century literature. "In Trollope's *The Small House of Allington,* the disappointed Dr. Crofts says, when he hears that his beloved is going to marry her cousin: 'I'm not quite sure that it's a good thing for cousins to marry," and it was "the foreboding motif in *Jude the Obscure* (1895), in which Sue told Jude 'it is bad for cousins to marry." In Galsworthy's *The Forsyte Saga,* of 1922, though cousins Holly and Val marry, they decide not to have children. And a 1911 biographer of John Ruskin attributed his mental illness to his parents' cousin marriage.

Ms. Anderson concludes that "the concern about the harm of inbreeding was an important reason for the decline of cousin marriage, so that in contemporary England it is very rare." Moreover, there is of course much greater social mixing and freedom now. Nonetheless, she stresses that "The choice of a marriage partner is still often determined to some extent by resemblance to an early familial love."

Which brings us back to our quails, to their fascination with "unfamiliar first cousins," and to cousins who marry today. Remarkably, almost every story of cousin marriage that I found among cousins who married today or in the recent past fit this picture of no or little early familiarity and later discovery, attraction, and decision to wed. (In a fascinating addendum, I learned from psychologist Linda Brown, who counsels relatives who fall in love, that sisters and brothers who are separated at birth, adopted by different families, and later reunited follow the same pattern of "unconscious drawing towards that unfound relative. There's a need to reconnect with what has been torn asunder that often becomes a sexual obsession.")

Sita Kapadia, a teacher at New York's City University who is currently working on a biography of Mahatma Gandhi's wife, is married to her first cousin
Naren, now a realtor but formerly a company executive in the foreign department of an international insurance company. When I spoke with her, I was
already aware of the usual pattern (early familiarity, separation, rediscovery and
attraction) but didn't want to put any such notions in her head just to prove the
point. Sure enough, within minutes, it turned out that her story was completely
typical in that sense, even though it took place thousands of miles away in the
Indian state of Gujarat, north of Bombay.

"I saw Naren, my father's sister's son, who by the way is nine years older than
I am, fairly often until I was about seven," she said. "Then there were about seven
years when he was not visible because he went away to college in another town.
Meanwhile I was at a girls school. He was doing his masters degree when he came
back to Bombay and we began to see him again. I think we liked each other right
away, though I think he understood the feeling much sooner than I did. I was
really so innocent!

"Now I have to tell you that in India there is no distinction made by the parents between their own children and between nephews and nieces, so much so
that if someone introduces you at a party as a 'cousin brother' instead of just a
'brother,' even though you are really only cousins, that is considered a let-down.
It's looked on as an insult-a diluting of the relationship. Naren's family, which
was all boys, especially considered me a sister.

"I tell you all this to explain that in India there is a special Brother and Sister
Day-it's usually around August 15-where brothers and sisters (or cousins, since
as I mentioned they're considered brothers and sisters, too) who are especially
fond of each other have a special custom. The sister ties a kind of bon-bon, called
a 'rakhi' on the brother's wrist. This is especially done in times of war, but in general the 'rakhi' is supposed to be a guardian or protector for the brother. The
brother in turn pledges to take care of his sister all her life.

"Well, I went to Naren's house to tie on this thing, but he never turned up, even though he knew I was coming to do it. I waited and waited for hours, but he never came, so I finally went home. And the next time we met, he never said a word about it! I was quite surprised, and finally I brought it up to him. I told him how I'd waited and waited, and then I asked him, 'Don't you like me?' He said, 'You're an idiot!' but he said it in a nice way, so I knew he was just teasing. Then he said, 'Don't you see that the problem is not that I like you, but that I like you a little too much!'

"After that, I think we both knew how we felt. But you have to know that cousin marriage is not approved in most parts of India. Yes, it's common among certain groups, like the Parsis, but on the whole it is not encouraged or quickly accepted. So we had a little problem. But I was lucky. My grandmother and my father and my mother-in-law to be were very flexible and forward-looking, and I remember my grandmother saying, 'I'm not going to produce any thunder.'

"Still, at eighteen, my father thought we should stay apart for a while and try to clarify our feelings for each other, and that worked out because by then Naren was working as an executive in Singapore. But we corresponded the whole time he was away, until I was twenty-one, and when he got back we were engaged for just a few days, and then married. But it was the first case of cousin marriage in our family."

The marriage has been a very happy one, and Sita gave birth to a boy and girl-"healthy, bright, and good-looking."

I asked Sita if there had been any problems of acceptance by others, and she said, "Sometimes people are shocked when they find out. They ask me, 'How did you meet him?' and when I say 'He was my cousin,' there's a bit of a chill. But it passes quickly."

I also wanted to know if she had had the mystical feeling of familiarity described by so many other cousins who were attracted to each other at the time of their re-meeting. "Strangely," she said, "I actually thought he was very differ-ent from my father at the time. Yet what I've found out over the years is that actually they are very much alike-in terms of values and even of personality. I suppose the similarities were there all the time, but I wasn't aware of them then."

Gina Riccio, sister of Eduardo, the teacher from the Bronx, also married a first cousin. Since she is now living in Italy, I relied on Eduardo as my source for the story, and while I couldn't confirm the basis of the attraction with a personal interview, it seemed to fit the cousin marriage pattern perfectly. "For years Gina had heard about this family in Italy-my father's sister's family-and about the land and the farm and the town, Santa Carmela, where they all lived," said Eduardo. "But she never met them till she was about eighteen. She was studying art when she went for a visit and met Elio, her first cousin. She was immediately attracted to him, and they began to correspond. Sure enough, about two years later, they were married. She moved to Santa Carmela, has two very healthy children, and has adapted happily to a completely different way of life."

A story with a less happy ending, but one that fits the cousin marriage pattern in every other way, is that of Tom Burstein, a lawyer who grew up in New York City but is now living in California. He, too, was eighteen when he met his first cousin Doris, the daughter of his mother's brother. "I'd met her father many times, when he came in from Detroit on visits, but somehow Doris and I had never met. Then my parents and I went out for a visit, and I was immediately attracted to Doris, who was the same age I am. We started going out together within a day or two, and in fact we went out every night of the two or three weeks I was there. When I went back to New York we started corresponding"-letters seem to have played a large part in many of these romances-"and then she moved to New York and stayed with my family for a year.

"When we decided to marry, my parents were shocked at first, but they didn't put up any serious opposition. But we did have some trouble at the marriage bureau. The clerk we went to first, who it turned out was new on the job, seemed very startled when he realized we were cousins and said, 'You can't get married.' But another clerk who was standing nearby and had worked there a long time overheard the whole thing and said, 'Of course they can. It's perfectly legal in New York and it happens all the time.'

"We were very happy for a number of years. She worked and put me through law school during the first two years we were married, and then I supported her while she finished school. But after our second child was born, she began to have mental problems, and they became so severe that eventually she had to be institutionalized. At the same time, she became very hostile to me, and we were finally divorced. But the marriage did last seventeen years, and in many ways I still love her.

"As far as our children go, they've had their problems, but I'm not sure they're any worse than they would have been if we weren't cousins. My boy is very stable, but the girl has had a number of breakdowns. I later found out that there was some insanity on both sides of the family, and I would encourage anyone planning to marry a cousin to check out in detail the family history before having kids. We thought we'd done it, but of course when you're in love and want to get married you don't want anything to stop you, and consciously or unconsciously you're probably not probing as much as you should. All our doctor said was, 'If there are no major diseases that you know of on both sides, you're OK,' and of course that's what we wanted to hear."

Esther Blau, an 82-year-old from Oklahoma City, Oklahoma, is a widow now, but she fondly recalled the first time she met her first cousin John. "I had just graduated from college and was driving east with a friend," she said. "I decided to visit an aunt and uncle I had never met who lived in Indianapolis. I don't know why we'd never met; I guess it was just a matter of distance. Our fathers were brothers; there were five boys and eight girls in their generation-but some moved to Oklahoma and some to Georgia, so I guess that explains it. His family had recently moved from Georgia to Indiana.

"Anyway, there was John, two years older than I was, and I thought he was great. He thought the same of me, and we did have a brief romance then-just a few days, mind you-but actually, I didn't see him again for twelve years. We wrote for a while, but then it faded.

"If he hadn't been in the army and stationed near us, I'd never have met him again. But he was going through Oklahoma City in order to get to paratroop camp, and he stopped off to see me. He said later that he fell in love with me the minute he saw me again. I can't say exactly the same thing, but I was intrigued. After eight dates-not on consecutive nights, but close enough-we decided to get married. And I have to say it was a beautiful love affair. We were very happily married-in fact, if he'd lived [John had died eight years ago] we'd have been celebrating our forty-seventh anniversary.

"John was a doctor, and insisted we check out the medical books, as well as our own doctors, before we got married, and I went to the library to do some research. But we finally went along with the doctor who said it was perfectly all right as long as both sides were well. We thought we were, and nothing I've found out since has given me reason to think otherwise.

"Because we married late, we had children late. My first boy was born when I was thirty-eight, the other when I was forty. And everyone thinks that's something new-having children late in life. I must have been a pioneer! But anyway, we have two brilliant sons-one's a TV producer in Boston who makes films for *Nova* and *Discovery*-and the only problem we encountered was that we couldn't be married in Oklahoma, because it was against the law there to marry your cousin. We had to get married in Texas. That was a shock, but it didn't seem so terrible. Besides, my parents were thrilled. They adored John and completely approved of our marriage.

"As far as other people were concerned, if they were bothered I never knew about it. I think they had a chance to get over it because in those days the wedding announcements in the paper were very detailed. And that big headline, 'Esther Blau married to Captain John Blau' with all the details of what I wore, gave them a chance to get used to the idea."

World War II also brought together Adele Mills and Bernard Schweid, who are third cousins. Bernard was passing through Nashville in 1942 on Army maneuvers and had no place to stay. He remembered that he had relatives there, and called and arranged to stay with them. In order to get the key, he had to stop at the R.M. Mills Bookstore, where Adele was working. Kiddingly, he quotes her "warm" first greeting: "Here's the key. I'm terribly busy." Despite this unpromising beginning, they were married five dates later, and in fact became business partners. (Adele Schweid was honored in 1987 by the Women's National Book Association for her role as one of the seventy most influential women in publishing.) Again-a case of late meeting and instant attraction.

Lest these final stories give the impression that cousin marriages are common in our society, however frequent in others, I should mention that this is by no means the case. Anthropologist Robin Fox estimates the present rate at less than 1 percent, except in some fairly endogamous rural areas.

From cousins who marry we move on to the very different but often surprisingly strong connections many people form with cousins who "marry in"-those seeming intruders who often became as close as those related by blood-or with their more remote cousins: second, third, once or twice "removed," who for numerous reasons are sometimes closer than first cousins.

6

THE OUTER
INNER CIRCLE

COUSINS BY MARRIAGE;
2ND, 3RD, AND 4TH COUSINS;
COUSINS ONCE
OR MORE REMOVED

[In America] there is no formal, clear categorical limit to the range of kinsmen...The decision as to whether a particular person is or is not to be counted as a relative is not given in any simple categorical sense.

-DAVID SCHNEIDER,
AMERICAN KINSHIP: A CULTURAL ACCOUNT

Guido Morris and Vincent Cardworthy were third cousins. No one remembered which Morris had married which Cardworthy, and no one cared except at large family gatherings when this topic was introduced and subjected to the benign opinions of all.

-LAURIE COLWIN, *HAPPY ALL THE TIME*

ONE DAY WHEN I was about 14 years old, my mother told me that my cousin Saul-middle of the oldest set of three brilliant Jaffe boys-had taken a house near us in Hewlett for the summer. A few years earlier, he had married a girl I knew only vaguely as Selma, and they would be bringing their newly born baby boy so that he could benefit from the country air. I received this news indifferently, being an overweight and depressed teenager at the time, but having nothing better to do, I agreed to go over with her one late afternoon to welcome the new arrivals to the community.

My first shock was at the sight of Selma, who to this day I regard as one of the most beautiful women I have ever met. Why her beauty hadn't registered on me before, since I was inordinately preoccupied with people's appearances (especially my own inadequate one) I don't know, but somehow it hadn't. She had naturally platinum blonde hair done in a shining pompadour, a slim graceful figure, despite her recent pregnancy, and dazzling aquamarine eyes.

Usually, such a combination of attributes would have awed me into total silence, but Selma would have none of this. She was as warm and welcoming as she was beautiful, and after showing us the new baby, confessed that she and Saul had so far been unable to decide on a name for the now three-week-old child. She appealed to us for help, and I took the appeal seriously enough to go to the library the next day and get out a book of names.

After reading it over and over, I decided that "Jonathan"-which meant "son of Saul"-would be a good recommendation. I felt-and later in the day told Selma-that it could easily be shortened to "Jon," yet the spelling would be different enough to distinguish it from the usual run of "Johns." To strengthen my case, I pointed out that it also went both alliteratively and rhythmically with "Jaffe."

Secretly, I'd thought perhaps Selma hadn't really meant what she said, and had actually had a name picked out or under serious consideration already. But no, she was delighted with my suggestion and promised to talk it over with Saul that evening.

The next day she called and announced that the baby would indeed be named "Jonathan," and that she was thrilled at the work I'd done to help. While I can't say that this small triumph was enough to eliminate my other problems, it was certainly an encouraging moment, and after that Selma and I always had a special feeling for each other. She always joked that she was my "halfway" cousin (she was exactly fifteen years older than me and fifteen years younger than my mother) and to this day, though my cousin Saul is long gone and Selma lives far away for most of the year, I love to talk with her.

More to the point-even when Saul was alive I had a closer relationship with Selma. He was an unusually quiet and often depressed person himself, and though he intrigued me-as did his brothers Henry and Bernie-his brooding silences made conversation difficult. On those rare occasions when we were alone for a few minutes, I never knew what to say to him. Furthermore, like Selma, he was considerably older than I was, and while this seemed to present no problem to Selma and me, at the time it seemed to put a huge distance between Saul and me. As with my other older cousins, the distance later became far less difficult to bridge, but by then Selma's and my relationship was definitely the primary one.

So, as it had been from the start, it was the surprisingly close nature of this and other of my own "cousin by marriage" relationships that made me begin to think about "the outer inner circle" of cousins. (I should emphasize that I am not referring here to the mates of "best friend" cousins, whose arrival on the scene often provokes intense jealousy. That is a topic by itself and will be dealt with in the next chapter.) What I am talking about here is the category of spouses of cousins with whom one has a less proprietary relationship.

I realized that in almost every case not only was I at least as close or closer to the cousin who'd "married in" as I was to my "real" cousin, but that in my own mind I made no distinction between them. Nor was this because I'd always known them as couples. Until I was age 11 or 12, all the cousins I grew up with except Saul were single. Yet in looking back, I see that I'd accepted the new mates almost immediately. Perhaps even more surprisingly, they did the same to me.

And I've heard similar stories from many others.

I can truly say that many of these cousins by marriage-the first group in the "outer inner circle"-have been at least as supportive and involved as their mates. Why? Perhaps some of the same family characteristics that attracted them to their wives or husbands were present in me. Or perhaps my cousins were automatically drawn-as the quails have proven-to people who in some curious way resembled their family. And undoubtedly most people start off wanting to establish good connections with their new extended families. Still, I have to say that I think some of the same magic felt between real cousins rubs off when cousins marry. Otherwise, why should these relative (or rather *non*-relative) strangers, introduced into a family as adults, take such an interest? And in my case, they certainly did.

The questions of "Why, indeed?" and "What in fact is a relative?" runs through anthropologist David Schneider's *American Kinship: A Cultural Account*. You may recall that he was the one who stressed the "blood" relationship as "unalterable...a state of almost mystical commonalty and identity" and also analyzed the different ways in which blood related cousins were "distant" (through lack of proximity, socio-emotional distance, or genealogical distance).

Since cousins by marriage are not related by blood (what he calls the *order of nature)* what is, or should be, their relationship to us? he asks. "The feature which alone distinguishes [such relatives] is their pattern for behavior, the code for their conduct. I suggest this is a special instance of the other general order in American culture, the *order of law.* "

In discussing who does or does not belong on the family tree, he says, "Assuming the tree is shaped like a pyramid or Christmas tree," with the Ancestor at the top, those who are related by marriage "constitute a major source of additional numbers for the bottom rather than the wider spread which could be obtained by tracing back further..."

The point is, "there is a choice among kinds of links, so some require blood connection, while others permit the addition of members *through* spouses as well as *to* spouses." He concludes that, in America, in keeping with the spirit of individuality and personal choice, "The decision as to who is a relative is made by and about a person-that is, an individual as opposed to a group. Sometimes the decision is common and usual, and informants agree that it is the 'right' decision...others may regard it as eccentric or 'wrong.'"

In a chapter on "kinship terms," Schneider makes the ambiguity of these relationships even clearer (if that's not in itself a contradiction in terms).

> Some said that a cousin's spouse is a cousin and should be called 'cousin.' But some said that a cousin's spouse is a cousin's spouse and nothing else and...should not be called 'cousin' since they are not cousin or even relatives. But others...said that although a cousin's spouse is a relative by marriage, there is no proper kinship term for them and they are most appropriately called by their first name of whatever may be polite under the circumstances...
>
> We can now see that each of these informants is correct, each in his own way...For some, but by no means all...it is possible to append the suffix 'by marriage' or 'in-law' to any kinship term, so that the constructions 'cousin-in-law' or 'cousin by marriage' are held to be proper kinship terms.

It should be mentioned that anthropologist Robin Fox does differentiate such relatives with special terms. *"Consanguinity* has long been distinguished from affinity-relatives by blood from relatives by marriage," he says. *"Affines,* then, are people married to our *consanguines."* However, aside from their presence in books by and for specialists in the field, I for one have never heard those terms used in ordinary conversation.

Personally, I clearly made the choice-eccentric or otherwise-to consider my cousins by marriage or remarriage relatives, to call them cousins and to introduce them to others as cousins. Or perhaps they chose me. Probably a little of both. So did many people I've talked to.

I should mention that the argument for doing so presented here will be largely personal and anecdotal; that is, my own stories and those of others. The reason: aside from Schneider's interesting psycho-social-anthropological analysis, none of the experts I spoke to had ever done any research on the subject, except in those rare cases of therapy where the total extended family was being treated. Even in such cases, few therapists had thought to go beyond the blood-related cousins or the first cousin level, if they went that far, and even more so because these less directly connected cousin relationships were rarely troublesome ones. Quite the opposite, in fact, as is shown by a few more stories of my own:

A few years before the summer of Selma and Saul, Saul's brother Henry, the eldest cousin and already a precociously successful theatrical lawyer, became engaged to the actress Jean Muir. Jean, whom I had seen as Helena in the 1935 film of *A Midsummer Night's Dream,* was also a classic blonde beauty. Starstruck, I couldn't believe she was actually going to be my relative.

Furthermore, though I was already a chubby and selfconscious pre-adolescent, I hadn't yet entirely abandoned my fantasy of being "discovered"-the talent hidden beneath my unpromising exterior miraculously catching the attention of some unusually perceptive Broadway or Hollywood scout. Perhaps Jean would be the one to alert them.

When Henry brought her to our house to meet my parents-an accepted ritual for nieces and nephews in our family-I was mute with adulation. For some reason, shortly after they arrived, my parents disappeared with Henry. For an awkward and thrilling moment, Jean and I were alone. Suddenly, she looked at me searchingly, and-almost as though she could read my insecurities-said, "Someday you'll be a lovely and successful woman, Jo. I can see great character in your face."

I clung to those words throughout the turbulent adolescence to follow and long after the marriage dissolved. They didn't lead to a movie contract, but they did give me a lasting and comforting sense of future possibilities.

Fast forward to me at age 15. My cousin Elliot D. had married a girl named Sylvia, and they bought a house not far from us in East Rockaway. Today, Sylvia- a brilliant, energetic Cornell graduate-would have no doubt been a lawyer, a doc- tor, an account executive. But it was the 50's, and instead she was tending their small house on Margaret Lane and expecting a baby.

It was summer. There was no school, and I was still too depressed and self- conscious to go to camp, as I'd done every summer until the previous one.

Either out of her own loneliness and boredom or an instinctive empathy for my friendless situation, Sylvia asked me to her house one day, and I spent that afternoon and a large part of every day that followed with her; and eventually with her and Ellen, the baby she had that July. Sylvia and Elliot-who was also friendly, but busy all day and a bit more preoccupied-were invariably kind and cordial. They had me to dinner a few times a week, invited me to the opera when winter came, and often took me with them when they went to New York on Saturday nights to meet friends and listen to jazz at Nick's in Greenwich Village. I still have a photo of a group of us-all the others smiling couples in their early 20's-and me, a fat, gawky, insecure 15-year-old wearing a heavy coat in August to cover my fat. I can't imagine what their friends thought about my cousins dragging along this awkward and withdrawn teenager week after week, but I don't recall any sense of being unwelcome. Without my knowing, Sylvia must have somehow prepared them in advance.

The friendship lasted. I have a packet of letters Sylvia wrote to me in col- lege, telling me in lively style of the doings of their (by then) three children (eventually to be four), and I visited them regularly on vacations until I moved to another city for a number of years.

When I moved back to New York, I lived in the city, was married myself (they were of course at my wedding), and soon had children of my own. Somehow, it worked out that I only saw them for a few visits when I was out vis- iting at my parents' and on family occasions-as always, the adhesive that helps keep cousins in touch. Still, on those brief visits we always picked up just where we'd left off.

Sadly, Sylvia and Elliot were also eventually divorced, and the question of divided loyalties definitely came into play, especially since at the time of the divorce my cousin Elliot D. made a real effort to reach out to me and his other cousins in order to explain his actions and how they were intertwined with certain long-standing feelings he had about his parents, especially his mother. (This reaching out will also be discussed in the next chapter.) For the first time, he and I began to talk on a meaningful level.

Still, though I began to understand where he was coming from, I've always had-and always will have-feelings of love and gratitude towards Sylvia, with whom I've tried to stay in touch. On looking back, her generosity of spirit and interest in me seems even more remarkable than it did at the time.

David Schneider again moves beyond science to make acute observations about such situations: He begins by reminding us that "Substance or blood…is a fact of life nothing can change…It is *involuntary.* " Then, using the example of divorced or widowed spouses of such blood relatives, he says,

> The code-for-conduct element [toward such spouses] is quite the opposite. It is *voluntary.*…As informants said so clearly, 'It all depends on the relationship'…If the relationship, the code for conduct, the pattern for behavior is such that the family wants to maintain a relationship, then it does so…But if by mutual consent they would heartily like to see the last of each other, then they have ample grounds for doing so…A relationship that lacks such a substantive base lacks the binding permanency which substance entails…
>
> These are relatives because they *choose* to follow that code for conduct…not because they are *bound* to follow it.

In my own family, however, divorce so far has been rare, and most of my cousins by marriage have remained so. My other cousin Elliot, always called "Elliot R.," married a girl named Claire, who'd grown up in our community and who in fact my brother had dated briefly. Still, I didn't know her very well till she married El. It turned out that she was a gifted pianist and like my mother an amateur singer of unusual talent. Because she had so much in common with my music-loving parents, she and El began to spend a lot of time at our house at musicales. I began to get to know her then and was always attracted to her warm, ebullient personality.

But we really became friends a few years later. I was in my early 20's, single, and living in New York, and she and El were renting a garden apartment on East 31st Street. They, too, often had me to dinner or to parties. Claire encouraged me to play the piano and sing, though unlike hers, my voice was completely untrained-more in the jazz or pop tradition-and tried many times to fix me up with male musical friends of hers she thought I'd like. Though I didn't marry any of them, when I did marry someone else we stayed friends, and remain so to this day.

Furthermore, their daughter Nan and my daughter Clare (the similar names are coincidental, since my daughter, Clare without an "i," was named for the cousin Clare I grew up with) are very close. This is due at least in part to the fact that as they were growing up Claire and I made a real effort to get them togeth-er-alone or on family visits. (When I get to second and third cousin relationships, I will quote from a letter from Nan in which she discusses her relationship with my daughter and with other second cousins.) Again, my "real" cousin El was a willing participant in keeping the connections going, but I would have to give a great deal of the credit to Claire.

Though the scales seem weighted in terms of friendships with the female cousins who "married in," this may well be due to the fact that all but one of my older cousins were boys. To the one male "cousin by marriage" in that group, I became, if not quite as close as to his wife, then almost so. This was Arthur Cohen, who married my much admired cousin Phyllis, the pianist who had also been my one-time camp counselor.

Arthur and Phyllis met at our house-that is, the house where I grew up in

Cedarhurst. In fact, I clearly remember the night they met. I was about 12 at the time, and had heard that something of a matchmaking venture was afoot, though at the time I had only a vague grasp of the concept. Arthur worked in my father's textile firm and had earned my dad's admiration not only because he was conscientious and shrewd but also because he was an intellectual with an interest in music. To my parents, it certainly seemed worth a try.

I have no idea what else happened that night, but I have a clear picture of Phyllis and Arthur at the piano, Phyllis accompanying while Arthur-an elfin, slim, charmer with a reedy, slightly off-key voice-plaintively sang "The Foggy, Foggy, Dew" while looking at Phyllis adoringly. Clearly, the match had "taken," and only months later they were married. It was the first wedding I ever attended.

By then, World War II was on, and Arthur was stationed with the Navy in Washington, so I didn't see them much for a number of years. But after the war, when they moved back to the city and had their first child, I began to visit often, and Arthur and I became fast friends. He introduced me to the work of Saul Bellow and to folk songs, and always took a great interest in anything I was doing. When I married, and they moved to Westchester, we kept up the four-way friendship and again, our daughters were good friends. (Their last child, a "caboose" baby, was only a few years older than my first.)

When Arthur died a few years ago, I certainly felt no less sorrow than I would have if he'd been a blood cousin. As I said of my cousins by marriage in general, all such distinctions had vanished years before.

Even more obscure cousins by marriage often become friends and in some cases can be surprisingly helpful. Nora, a lawyer, told me the following story: "When I was three or four, I had an aunt, Pauline, who married Sidney, an Englishman who'd moved to the States to go into the jewelry business, but whose family was still in England.

"When the war broke out and the blitz began, Sidney's two sisters, Bette and Irene, and their children moved to Sheepshead Bay to stay with relatives till the war was over. Since my parents and Pauline and Sidney were very friendly, they went out together from the city frequently to visit, and several times they took me along. I was about eight then. I was absolutely fascinated with Marian, Irene's daughter, who was about two years younger than I was, but seemed to me very grown up for her age.

"First of all, she was absolutely beautiful. By then, *Gone With the Wind* had opened, and I thought Marian looked like a miniature Vivien Leigh; same green eyes, black hair, and white skin. And she had the most beautiful clothes. I particularly remember a beige wool princess style coat with a velvet collar. Amazingly, though I hated wearing dress-up clothes like that and usually disliked kids I knew in America who wore them, on Marian I thought they were perfect. My mother couldn't believe it. 'When I try to get you to dress like that, you absolutely refuse,' she said.

"Most of all, I admired Marian's English accent. I thought it sounded so charming-elegant without being affected-and only wished I had grown up in England so I could talk like that, too. In fact, now that I think of it, Marian probably had a lot to do with my eventually becoming an incurable Anglophile.

"Actually, I don't think Marian and I met more than five or six times over the three years they were here, but it was always for long visits, and once Marian came to spend a day at my school with me. I was thrilled to have such a pretty and friendly 'cousin' to show off to my friends!

"After the war, Marian went back to London, and I completely lost touch with her, though I'd hear news about the family through my Uncle Sidney. I heard that she'd married 'the boy next door' at nineteen, and was living in Hampstead, and that after a few years she'd had a son.

"Many years later, at least twenty, my husband and I went to London for the first time. Before we left, I got Marian's address and phone number from my Uncle Sidney. When we got there, with great trepidation I called her up. At first, she wasn't even sure who I was, but when I reminded her of the visit to my school, it all came back to her and she insisted we come to tea. And what a tea! Roast beef, salad, cakes, cookies-an amazing repast.

"But the best part of it was that we felt completely at home right away, and I even felt that way with her husband Stanley, who turned out to have a great sense of humor.

"We saw them at least two more times on that short visit, and several times on every subsequent trip, which turned out to be often, since my daughter Heidi went to boarding school in England for two years. I guess we had infected her with our Anglomania!

"Since Heidi was still young then, Marian insisted on meeting her at Heathrow every time she went back to London after vacations and on keeping her overnight before the bus left for Gloucestershire the next morning. She also insisted on putting her on the plane to return.

"We've stayed in touch and I can't tell you how close we've become. And to think, she's really not even a blood cousin; she's an uncle-by-marriage's niece! Yet that tenuous connection was obviously very meaningful to both of us."

Not that this is always the case. In his chapter "A Relative is a Person" (meaning, as it did with the cousins by marriage, that the decision is based on individuals-persons-rather than group rules) Schneider includes an amusing exchange he had with a woman during the course of his interviews. In this dialogue, Schneider (S) was asking the questions of the woman interviewee (W):

S: Do you have to be close to someone to have them
      related to you?
W: Yes…When it drifts away you are no more related.
      You see, I went to one of my husband's cousin's bridal showers.
      It was for a first cousin's bride-to-be. You only meet all these
      people there, You meet them like at weddings or showers or
      funerals. For those things they call on you and I answer the
      roll call.
S: So are these people related to you?
W: They are when you meet them like that, but when
      you leave them, they're not anymore.

S: Have they ever been related to you except at things
       like weddings and funerals?

W: Oh sure, but they aren't now. You see this business of
       being Related to someone has to do with sociability.
       There are social cousins.

S: Can you give me any kind of rule for the person who
       is related to you?

W: Well, they got to be sociable with you or they're not
       related.

S: Do any of your female first cousins have husbands?

W: Yes.

S: Are they your cousins?

W: I never see them.

S: Are their children related to you?

W: No, because I never saw them.

The woman's comment, "When it drifts away you are no more related," brings us back to the question of distance-genealogical and otherwise, but for now limited to genealogy.

Never one to sidestep taking a stand, Schneider refers back to the *order of law,* and states that in foster homes or Cinderella situations, for instance, where there is no blood connection *[order of nature]* between the stepmother and the stepchild, "The cruel stepmother...should rise above the literal definition of her relationship to her stepchild, and have the kind of relationship-affection, concern, care, and so forth-which a [natural] mother has for her child." If not, he says, thanks to the *order of law,* one "who fails to care properly for a child can be brought to court." But ideally another kind of "law" will prevail-"law in its most general sense: law and order, custom, the rule of order, the government of action by morality and the self-restraint of human reason."

Which brings us to another sub-group of the "outer inner cincle"-a small but special category known as stepcousins. Fortunately, most of the stories I heard about these relationships belied the "wicked" steprelative image.

"Erica was the daughter of my uncle's second wife," said Mandy Roberts, a Columbia Business School student who also works in real estate. "I guess that makes her a stepcousin. Certainly we're not related by blood. Yet, even though we're ten years apart in age-she's thirty-four now and I'm twenty-four-we've been like sisters really. When I came to Choate [a boarding school in Connecticut] from Cleveland, Erica was living in New York. I was kind of homesick and had nowhere to go on weekends, and she invited me to visit her many, many times. I think that's when we really started getting close. I idealized her life in New York. She had her own small apartment and a job as a mortgage broken, and it all seemed very glamorous to me. We'd go out to dinner and the movies, and she really became sort of my New York family.

"Then, when I went to the University of Pennsylvania, I'd still come to visit a lot. By that time, we were always comparing boyfriend stories. Aften I graduated, she became not just a friend but kind of a mentor. She got me the job interview that led to my first job as a commercial real estate broker, and while I was there I called her all the time asking for professional advice. She also set me up with clients.

"About two years ago she got married and moved to Connecticut, and I'd go up to visit her there, too. She had a horse, and I loved to go riding. But the marriage didn't work, and even though I'm so much younger, I know my moral support has helped her a lot since she separated from her husband. In fact, in general, there's always been a funny kind of age reversal, in that Erica's very emotional and has a lot of problems and has been in therapy for years, and I've been the more stable, settled, 'mature' one who gives her support.

"In many ways, she always wished she was me. She wished she had my parents, because they supported me financially and emotionally, and hers really didn't. Her father was kind of a playboy, and her mother's a cold fish. This year, I was especially aware of the reversals. I'm getting married, and she's getting divorced. I'm working while I go to school, and she's looking for a job.

"But I can tell you one thing. I'll always be there for her, and I know she will be for me. In fact, even though I do have a real sister, I think in many ways Erica and I are closer. We certainly have more in common. My real sister and I are completely different-she's very homey and domestic. Erica and I are interested in fashion and things like that. She's going to be a bridesmaid at my wedding, and I guess that tells you how important she is in my life, even though we're not related by blood."

I must admit that I thought Mandy's "stepcousin by marriage" relationship almost unique until I began to think about my Aunt Lil's stepson Richard. Just as Mandy had known Erica all her life, I'd known Richard from childhood, since my aunt and uncle were best friends with his parents and I spent a lot of time with my aunt. Though Richard is a few years younger than I am, we always connected in some special way, recognizing each other as troubled soulmates from an early age.

When I was about twenty, Richard's mother and Lil's husband died within a few years of each other, and several years after that my aunt and Richard's father married. The marriage gave even more substance to the bond between Richard and me. Eventually, he became a gifted psychotherapist, and as a friend with considerable expertise, he has often given me sage and insightful advice.

Yet, not until we drove out to the airport recently to meet my aunt, who was returning from a trip, and discussing my "cousins" project did I realize that I was face-to-face with my very own "stepcousin by marriage," and a very dear one at that.

Undoubtedly, in today's world of frequent divorces and remarriages, this still rare non-blood relationship will become more common. In fact, Susan Newman, in her book on raising only children, suggests actively encouraging such connections. "Your only child will bear the burden of decision making when you grow old, but she can have a strong network for emotional support. You can lay the groundwork now for that future support system. Seek out family beyond the obvious immediate relatives. *Strike up links with second and third cousins, aunts, uncles, and cousins of stepparents. A remarriage can provide additional supportive connections for your child* [my italics]."

Most often, though, there is a blood connection, however remote, that brings and keeps together the other members of the "outer inner cincle"-the second, third, and fourth cousins, the first and second cousins "once removed." Over and over, I heard stories of how these cousins, tied by only the slightest blood relationship befriended, supported, and helped each other.

Just such a relationship is at the core of Laurie Colwin's novel *Happy All the Time,* and in fact the opening paragraph (quoted at the start of the chapter) begins: "Guido Morris and Vincent Cardworthy were third cousins. No one remembered which Morris had married which Cardwonthy, and no one cared except at large family gatherings when this topic was introduced and subjected to the benign opinions of all." The boys are best friends from childhood, and their individual but intertwined lives and loves-with which each tries to help the other-are the subject of the rest of the book.

David Schneider has interesting things to say about third-and all the other less-directly related-cousins *in nature* as well. "[The immediate family, including first cousins], are all genealogically close even if physically distant," he says. "But if we go out...to second or third cousins, many possibilities present themselves. One person may say they're relatives simply because they're related by blood. Or he may say with equal propriety that they are too distant, so...he does not know how to count them. He may say, 'What is a second cousin anyway? And what does 'removed' mean?'...One cannot say that all second cousins are relatives, but all third cousins are not. An American can, if he wishes, count a third cousin as a kinsman while a second cousin is actually alive but unknown, or known to be alive but nevertheless not counted as a relative."

Which again brings up the interesting topic of kinship terms. "'Second cousin' is an example of a derivative term," Schneider tells us, "'cousin' being the basic term, 'second' the particular modifier." And he brought to my attention the fact that the "removed" modifier is reserved to cousins alone. Furthermore, he points out that in discussing "Who is Called What and By Whom," there is a wide variety of alternates. "Cousins are addressed by their first name, nickname, a diminutive or other personal form of designation, or as cousin-plus-first-name ['Cousin Jill']." And Robin Fox tells us that in Hawaii, "the rogue term 'cousin' is applied promiscuously to all relatives outside a narrowly defined group bounded by uncles, aunts, nephews and nieces."

To sum up, says Schneider, "By one definition, there is no option: those related by blood…no matter how distantly, are relatives." But in America, as with cousins by marriage, the rule is completely "ambiguous, and full of logical inconsistencies."

The word "ambiguity" would certainly apply to a large group of cousins in my husband Leslie's family, whose actual blood connection (as with Guido and Vincent) has been the subject of conjecture for years. However, the most popular theory has it that his paternal great-grandfather and the grandfather of Agnes Gertsacov, a marvelous matriarch of 90-plus who rules over a teeming, three-generation family in Providence, Rhode Island, were first cousins. And thereby was added to Leslie, my own, and my children's lives, a fascinating group of people who have given our family a whole new dimension.

As a child, Leslie, who lived in New York City, was taken often to visit these relatives, and remembers being fascinated by the large house on Benefit Street where the cousins congregated. Even then, he recalls Agnes as a force to be reckoned with. A woman who ran a jewelry business after her husband deserted her, she dispensed advice and lox with cream cheese with equal generosity. Her daughter Joan, who inherited much of her mother's forceful personality, was a contemporary of my husband's and she, along with all the other "Providence group" were at our wedding.

A few years later, Joan, whom we hadn't seen since our marriage, called to invite us for a visit. What I didn't know was that, like me, she had had three children within three years, though hers were a few years older. Unlike me, she was quite unfazed by it. Joan became a role model for me in terms of raising my kids.

She and her husband had a camper, and we went on camping trips with her, her children, and our kids, the basis of a lifetime interest in the outdoors and coping with nature for all my children. When my daughter Clare was going through a difficult phase, Joan invited her to spend an indefinite time camping out in Canada with her, her own children and the children of all the other Providence relatives as well. It was enormously helpful-for Clare and for us.

Some misfortunes have struck. Joan's husband, like her father, eventually bolted. Joan's response: a return to law school at age 40, and a successful law career. Her brother was killed in a car crash. Still, the Providence connection goes on. We attend weddings and bar mitzvahs and look forward to words of wisdom and lox and bagels from Agnes on our visits to Providence. How much these cousins, "however remote," have added to our lives!

But then, so have the other members of the "outer inner circle." The extraordinary interest taken by many older "first cousins once removed," in their younger counterparts, for instance, has already been touched on in the context of other themes. One example: in describing "Cousins Who Love," the lifelong friendship between Lew Brackley and his cousin Ellen (a friendship that grew to include their husbands and wives), Ellen's extraordinary interest in both Lew's and his sister Sally's children, her "first cousins once removed," has been cited.

Using my own family as a source once again, I see the same dynamics at work. I am deeply involved not only in the lives of a number of my first cousins once removed-especially two who are the daughters of my close cousins Clare and Helen Louise-but also with the sons and especially the daughters of a number of others.

Why? Of course there are individual reasons in every case, and I start out with the great advantage of having known them all their lives. Still, the same could be said for the children of a number of good friends. What is different here? Once again, I have to conclude that it's the powerful sense of familial familiarity. In my cousin Katie, my cousin Clare's daughter, I hear echoes of her mother-so much so that even when she was in her teens I found myself confiding in her as though she were an adult; almost as though she were my cousin Clare herself. (Katie was, in fact, unusually mature.) In Jan (an updated contraction of my name), I see Helen's wistful charm and keen intelligence, and I play duets with her brother Michael. In Nan, Claire and Elliot R.'s daughter, whose letter will conclude this chapter, I see a lack of pretense and common sense that were strong traits of my father and, I like to think, of me as well. She also bears an unusual resemblance to my daughter Clare, with whom, as mentioned earlier, she is close friends. Like many of the other cousins, she is extremely musical, and played the harp in a young people's orchestra of which my mother was a founder and in which the entire family has taken an interest.

In Alice, Ira's daughter, I see the actress I'd like to have been, and in her and her equally artistic sister Madeline the dry take on life that is a family trait. In Dr. Andy Plager, Helen's older son, I see his mother's warmth and caring, and when Andy was married, he was thrilled that my son Jed came in from across the country for the event. Despite the proliferation of relatives on my father's side, there were few on my mother's, and my children (their second cousins) were basically the only cousins Helen's children knew. I grew to love Andy's wife Lori as well, and their three daughters (my first cousins twice removed) became my beloved goddaughters, Jessica, Hanna, and Sara.

And what am I to them-these young first cousins once removed? In many ways, more of a mentor and friend than I've been able to be to my own children. To some, like Katie and Alice, a role model as a writer. To them and others, a confidant to whom they can often speak more freely than to their parents. Just as the cousin relationship is not a "hot" one for cousins of the same generation, so is that between my generation and the generation "once removed" unthreatening. Free of the intensity of the parent-child bond, yet closely connected across the years, we definitely click in some special way.

And speaking of cousinly mentors and supporters, no one could have been more helpful to one of my sons when he was applying to a particular college than his first cousin once removed Bernard Jaffe, the third of the Jaffe brothers who have cropped up from time to time throughout the book and twice in this chapter. He had a close friend who was a professor at the school, and though he hadn't seen a lot of my son Jed over the years, Bernie took it upon himself not only to write a letter of recommendation but to make sure Jed was in touch with his friend in case he needed any help once he was accepted.

His wife Fern, another cousin by marriage, was equally supportive. (In an irrelevant but, I think, entertaining aside, I have always been amazed at how many of my married cousins' or friends' names rhyme or are alliterative with their mates: Bern and Fern, Saul and Selma, Lew and Sue. My cousin Phyllis Cohen married an Arthur Cohen. My cousin Clare, *née* Weinbaum, was married twice and on both occasions to men whose names begin with "W," though it's one of the shortest sections of the phone book.)

Others say the same about the mentor members of their own "outer inner circles," psychiatrist Veva Zimmerman noting that, "When something is needed, a cousin always sort of rises to the surface. Like when the kids are applying to college, there's one who's identified with that process and sort of takes over and helps with the whole thing."

Of course, all the personal stories I've told are within the context of a large family and a cafeteria of cousins to choose from. How much more important can the "outer inner circle" be to small families with few remaining relatives. Said Iseult Froelicher, "I think because my mother's family here in America is small, we particularly treasure every cousin-first, second, once removed, on whatever. We celebrate every single cousin's birthday every single year, and [as was mentioned in an earlier chapter] everyone writes poems and songs for the occasion. Age makes no difference, and my first cousin once removed, Ira Palestin, [an art dealer in New York] is especially important to me and my mother."

Similarly, though the cousins I grew up with were almost all first cousins and there were many of them, due to the large families of my parents' generation, in this era of smaller families there is considerable connecting between the second cousins. I mentioned several times the letter sent to me by Nan Rosengarten, my own first cousin once removed (she is the daughter of Claire and Elliot R.) and my children's second cousin. I had written her in Denmark, where she is currently working, and mentioned in passing that if she had time, I'd like to know how she felt about her cousins. Her reply, I think, sums up the role that these "outer inner circle" relatives can play for her generation.

> About cousins. Let's see…Cousins have been very important to me, maybe more than they are to people that have siblings. I remember we spent a lot of time with you and your kids when I was growing up and I probably fantasized that they were my siblings. I distinctly remember that one time we were on vacation together and I hoped that other people thought all four of us were brothers and sisters. It's funny because for me, I don't know why, I have always felt closer to my second cousins (or whatever you call your kids and Frank's) than I have to my first cousins…Most of my first cousins are too far away in age to have meant much to me, but I remember really enjoying being with Clare, Jed, Cory [my children], Phil, Dan and Lydia [my brother Frank's children], as well as Shari [Phyllis' daughter]…For me, I guess they were the closest thing to siblings I ever had, but in a way it was even better because we were close enough in age to be friends, and didn't fight like siblings tend to do, but (for me, anyway) there was a closeness from being family.
>
> I realize I talk about the extended family a lot, and my boyfriend Søren recently asked me how many cousins I had because it sounded like there were so many. So I started explaining and he was surprised that I would call you or your children my cousins. He only counts first cousins. Even in New York I can remember a lot of

people having trouble keeping straight all the different family members I talked about, also because "cousin" included so many different people and generations. It's funny, because I've never thought of our family as being particularly close, but when I started to explain the whole thing to Søren the other day, I realized it is rather unusual, how our extended family holds contact.

About people in your generation, it varies. I have enjoyed the contact I've had with them, and at different times I've felt closer to different people, but I think all of the attention and interest in my accomplishments and activities meant a lot to me, and I only regret that in my childish mind I never thought to ask about "your" activities, work, vacations, etc., after answering all the same questions posed to me. You and Les, Phyllis Cohen, your parents, Bern and Fern, your brother Frank, Charles and Marilyn, Fran and Gerald [Fran's husband], and I'm sure others that don't come to mind right now have had an influence in one way or another at one point or another, and certainly in a different way than my parents' friends have, but it's rather hard to explain how. Maybe because friends come and go more than family does.

Jo…I hope this is something like what you wanted.

Yes, exactly.

7

THE TEST OF TIME
WITNESSES AND WORKERS

The older I get, the less the age differences matter...After all, [my cousins] are the only witnesses who share with me the memories of that wonderful family that disappeared. The past draws us close-the past more than the present, although of course we talk of current things as well. But the past is the subtext.

-GISELA MARKS,
WORLD WAR II REFUGEE.

I like my cousin Claire, though I used to hate her when we were kids-she was one of those skinny perfect-looking blond brats so ladylike you wanted most of all to push her into a large stinking mud puddle. I was fat, sloppy [and] smart...I had spent a lot of my life avoiding Claire (we exert a magnetic force on each other-alternately fascinated and repelled, we have been through whole cycles of bumping together and fleeing apart...)

-URSULA PERRIN,
THE LOOKING-GLASS LOVER

LIKE ALL RELATIONSHIPS, those between cousins are not static, though the family tie does seem to give them more ballast than is usual between "just friends." As Dr. Richard Schuman said earlier, "Unless there's been a rupture in the parents' generation or you live so far apart that you just can't get together, you're likely to meet and re-meet over and over again, even if you don't like each other. With friends you can easily drift apart, but because of the family tie, you're almost forced to stay in touch with cousins-especially while you're kids, and often, even afterwards."

What happens over the years, then, when cousins who have been best friends marry and the new mates dislike their spouse's cousins, or vice versa? Or when, even if objectively the cousin's new mate is liked as an individual, he or she is perceived as in some sense a rival? Certainly, the same problems can exist when a close friend marries, but there is an added poignance that the cousin relationship can engender. As people develop and change, how do cousin relationships alter in other ways, and what special role can cousins play as we grow older? What happens when adult cousins begin to work together-either in already established family businesses or as founders of new ones? I wanted to find out how and why some cousin relationships endure, though often painful changes occur in the process.

Certainly, in my own case, while I was maid of honor at both Helen's and Clare's weddings, and genuinely liked their husbands, I felt, deep down, an intense sense of betrayal and isolation for a long time after they married. Only when I realized that I could still see them alone sometimes and continue the relationship on a one-to-one basis was that feeling modified.

And when I, still single at age 28, visited Helen and her first baby, I felt a much keener sense of being behind in life's timetable (girls were marrying earlier then) than I had ever felt visiting friends in similar circumstances. This was my cousin-my almost sister, my pal-sworn at age 8 to lifelong fealty in blood, and the same blood at that. If she was married and a mother at this stage of her life, why wasn't I? Our lives had been so parallel before that my sense of disorientation was extreme.

And my friend Carla Schwartz, who had re-met her cousin Harry when they were both single and living in New York, and palled around with him for several years ("All those shared memories…put us totally at ease") said that when she married, everything changed. "My husband didn't take to Harry, so we began to see each other a lot less often. But I still feel a bond to him. I mean, a friend can stop being a friend, but you can't stop being a cousin," she said, unconsciously validating David Schneider's earlier point about the differences between friends and relatives.

The alienation caused when one's mate dislikes a close cousin was also described as a problem by Karen, an executive secretary living in downtown New York with Gordon, her fiancé. "Gordon detested my cousin Arthur," she said, "so I hadn't seen much of him for several years. It was easy to drift apart because he lives in the suburbs and I had almost no chance to see him on my own-which I certainly would have tried to do otherwise.

"But during the transit strike a few years ago, when he needed a place to stay, I completely ignored Gordon's feelings and insisted on offering Arthur a place with us," she said. "I knew I just had to do it, even if Gordon walked out on me. I don't know, I had this really primitive feeling about blood being thicker than water. And I'd never even realized I felt that way.

"As it turned out, once Arthur arrived, Gordon found out he wasn't so bad after all, and while they never became really friendly, he was able to tolerate him. Also I think Arthur suspected he wasn't Gordon's favorite person, so he ended up going out most evenings with his friends, which took a lot of the pressure off. So in the end it worked out better than I'd thought it would. I really don't know what I'd have done if it hadn't."

In saying what she did about "blood being thicker than water," Ann, like Carla, was spontaneously confirming two previously mentioned theories: Schneider's (the *order of nature* will prevail) and Robin Fox's (we do indeed feel an obligation towards cousins).

But the marriage of Eduardo Riccio's best friend and favorite cousin Tony to a woman neither he nor the other members of the family on their street in the Bronx liked (the feeling was decidedly mutual) created a rift the years have not healed. "Forget it, it was over," he said sadly, referring to the relationship he'd had with Tony from boyhood and all through college."Tony was the key cousin," he explained. "He was a leader of both the girl and boy cousins. As a kid, he was always the organizer of all of us. But she didn't want that. She wanted to separate out, and even though I was best man at their wedding, it's never been the same. She definitely has influenced him against us. In fact, now she's trying to get him to move to Florida, so they can be farther away. 'You people do everything together,' she always says, as though it's some kind of insult. When Tony and I re-meet now, I'm still so aware of our shared history, and we can go on and on with the stories, but there are no new ones, and I know he's as sad about it as I am."

Flow and change over the years, quite apart from the pressures of outside interference from competing relationships, was also described by Eduardo and many others. Now affirming Schneider's earlier comments on how socio-economic differences can create distance, he said, "I feel that the fact that I have a college education and a masters degree and have become an educator has been something that has separated me somewhat from the others, none of whom went much beyond high school. I feel sometimes that there's a world that I've lost. The feelings are there, but there are just certain subjects we can't discuss."

A happier end to the experience of lifelong flow and change was told by Gloria Hochman, the Philadelphia writer whose cousins came to her rescue after she broke her arm in a snowstorm. "As teenagers, we were all very close," she said. "Then, during our 20's and 30's, I guess we were all very busy establishing our own lives-going in different directions. But at around forty, we started to know each other all over again. Our lives had taken shape, and we weren't so busy trying to prove ourselves. That continuity and the safety of those relationships became even more important to me then than it had been earlier."

A similar pattern of early closeness, separation, and reunion was described by my brother, Dr. Frank Rosengarten, a language professor at Queens College, who had shared with me a childhood of multi-cousin visits and much togetherness. "When I was a kid, my cousins occupied a particular place in my life, and I always looked forward to seeing them-even the ones I wasn't especially close to. I felt a special bond between them and me, and also a lack of rivalry. There was an acceptance of my cousins 'as they were' which wasn't true of other relationships. And I thought they felt that way about me, too. In a few cases, I felt they were really interested in me, and I enormously admired a few of my older male cousins who were good-looking, were excellent musicians, and whom I considered very witty.

"But as I grew into adulthood, the bonds weren't strong enough to overcome the alienation of later life. Ideologically, I was completely separated from them and I started to see them as part of a conventional world I didn't belong to or accept. Interestingly enough, though," he concluded, "as I entered my mid-fifties and re-met them at some family gatherings, I began to appreciate them all over again. But I had to put things in my own life in perspective before I could do that."

Then there's the phenomenon of certain cousins playing different roles at different times in one's life. Said Anna Quindlen, "There were particular cousins I felt an affinity for as my life changed, depending on whether I was looking for a friend, a role model, or someone I could be a role model for."

And Berneice Lunday, the North Dakota woman who collected "cousin stories-funny things, crazy things that happened to us over the years" for a cousins' directory, said the same thing. "At different times, I've been close to different cousins," she said. "As a child, I was close to my cousin Raymond, who was one year older. My sister had a girl cousin closer to her age, so Raymond became my special friend. We played cops and robbers a lot, had foot races and so forth-my parents were so proud when I won. But as I grew older we grew apart-I don't know if it was because he was a boy or what the reason was-and now I'm closer to one of my older girl cousins."

The process of change over the years within a single relationship was made especially vivid to me by two of my interviewees. The first of these was Jean Allen, the Ohio artist whose lifelong attraction to and friendship with her cousin Paul was told earlier. That was in its own way a story of drawings together and pullings apart, of times of intense mutual need and eventual distancing. But another cousin has become even more important in her life-central to it, in fact- a cousin she wasn't even friendly with as a child.

"Annette is two years older than I am-fifty-nine now, unbelievable as it seems to me," said Jean. "If you had told me when we were children that one day we'd be each other's main support and greatest friend, I'd have told you you were crazy. Well, to go back…we lived in adjoining suburbs of Columbus, Ohio, ours being Bexley, the preppy, WASP-y one, with old money, Annette's being the one for those with so-called 'new' money. But we were close enough for our families to get together quite a bit.

"Annette's mother was very rigid, intolerant and hostile-I remember she wouldn't even let her husband have a drink in the house-but she was also an intellectual, and had formed an alliance with her younger daughter Lynn that left Annette out, since Annette wasn't an especially good student and didn't have the same interests. But I did have those interests-playing the piano, reading (some of which I see now as sublimation, but that's another story). At any rate, because of the common interests, I actually liked Lynn better as we were growing up.

"I was afraid of Annette, especially when we were in junior high and high school, because I thought she was all the things I wasn't: not just that she was very popular, but that because she dated a lot she somehow represented the possibility of sex. You have to know that by that time my own mother had instilled in me such a fear of sex that I actually never got over it. Again, I was considered a brain, and though guys did sometimes ask me out, I was so frightened of what it might lead to that I'd never go out with them. Also, because of my mother's attitudes, she completely disapproved of Annette and certainly didn't encourage me to be her friend. What I didn't know then, but found out later, was that

Annette was miserable in those days, too.

"We went to different colleges-she to Cornell, I to Swarthmore. Well, she never finished. She got married (she had to) to this real preppy guy, and ended up pregnant in a Westchester suburb. I don't know why, but I called her up one day and went up to visit, and found she was either completely different than I'd remembered her or had changed completely. She'd become a kind of mother figure, catering to everybody, really-not just to the three kids she eventually had, and to her husband, but also, in time, to me. I'd never seen this subjugating side of her, and I must admit that her being so giving filled a great need for me. At the same time I realized we had this enormous similarity of idiom-it had to be, given our same family upbringing-and I discovered she could do a hilarious imitation of her mother, who I found out she really hated, even though the two of us would go out to Columbus together to visit. That made the visits out there tolerable. So we started to be very close then.

"What I was ignoring, though, was that there was a third part of Annette, a part she was repressing by locking herself into the same kind of background she grew up in. Slowly, she began to rebel. The first thing that happened was that she divorced her husband and married a Jewish man. That shocked the family. Of course I backed her up, though I soon saw that this man was really no different from the first, except for his religion. He expected her to cater to him, too. But the more we talked, the more I realized that she wasn't at all happy with the role she'd stuck herself with, and I was able to recommend a wonderful woman psychiatrist to her who has been helping her really find out who she is.

"I found some of the changes in her hard to take! Here I'd had this loving, giving, selfless cousin whom I relied on completely to be 'there for me' as that obnoxious phrase goes. And I'd certainly needed her, having had all kinds of problems and tried all kinds of therapies myself-drug and otherwise. (They finally found out I had a chemical imbalance, and found a drug to help.) And now I had to adjust to a changing woman who was beginning to recognize that she didn't always want to be so available to everyone else. I began to see that unconsciously

I'd been taking advantage of her myself.

"But pretty soon I realized that she really had no support for this emerging self besides me and her psychiatrist. So I decided to back her completely in her breakaway efforts-taking baby steps, then umbrella steps, then giant steps. And if she doesn't stand up for herself when her husband puts her down in public, which she's beginning to do, I speak up for her. It's not that he and her kids don't appreciate her at all, but I'm afraid it's for a lot of the wrong reasons-the times when she's reverting to her old compliant self.

"We're closer than ever now. We often have lunch and talk on the phone, and I have to say she's an incredible person. She's been able to maintain her intrinsic generosity of spirit during this really agonizing transition. And she's not just generous in spirit. Over the years she's helped me enormously, giving me checks and presents, and she even arranged things so that my mother set up a trust for me, besides leaving me some money of her own.

"So in looking back I see that we've gone through three completely different phases in our relationship, and have ended in a place I'd never have believed possible when we were little girls in Columbus with nothing to say to each other."

The other case history-and in speaking of the test of time the full evolution of a relationship seems of special relevance-is that of Tom Harwood, a gay man in his fifties who is financial manager for a well-known international magazine.

"My cousin Mara and I are a year apart," he said. "She was born in 1935 and I in 1936. We were very close, even as infants," he said. "Our mothers were sisters who were very close, and we spent two weeks every summer together all through our childhoods. All the family movies and snapshots show us playing together, even though she had an older brother. We lived near each other-I in Raleigh, North Carolina; she in a small town nearby where her family was prominent. Actually, I loved her whole family. They were my favorite family among the relatives, and her mother, whom I idolized, was my favorite aunt.

"I followed behind her in school by two years (she was very smart and had skipped) and we always laughed a lot. In fact, on family visits, we were always being sent from the table for giggling. But what I didn't know then was that I had the picture of her family all wrong-at least, as she saw it. She later told me she was very unhappy then. She thought of her mother as domineering and of her father as weak. But she said my being around had been a great help to her. And she was terrific for me. I hadn't admitted even to myself that I was gay-though I realize now that I was attracted to her brother-but somehow I knew I was different, and I didn't have that many friends besides her.

"We went to the same college to start-though I entered behind her-and both transferred to the University of North Carolina in the same year. She became a big influence on me intellectually then. There are so many authors I'd never have read if it wasn't for Mara-Ring Lardner, Eudora Welty, Thomas Wolfe, and one famous writer I won't even mention since Mara has done a book on her, and it would give away who she is. She also has a wonderful position at a well-known Southern school, but I won't name that one either.

"So to get back, we were in touch all through college. Then I moved to New York, and of course it made the times we could get together rarer, but we managed. As the years went by, and she didn't marry, I began to suspect that she might be gay, too, but we never talked about it. In fact, I still hadn't completely acknowledged that I was gay to myself, and I certainly hadn't admitted it to anyone else, though I was having a lot of conflict over my sexuality. Then I heard about a group called 'The Advocate Experience,' which is a little like what EST is for straight people, but not as harsh. Part of their program is that you have to come out to a person you're close to-a mother, a father, whoever. And right away I knew it was going to be Mara for me, both because we were so close and because I was assuming she was gay, too. I wrote her about it, and she wrote back immediately. I was shocked! She was completely understanding about *my* being gay, but said I was all wrong about her. Of course, it was embarrassing, but we kept on as before and were even closer as a result. At that point we were spending every Christmas together.

"About twelve years ago, she wrote me and said she'd met a woman she was in love with. Not that I was surprised. She was forty-five at the time-late to come out. They bought a house together and for a couple of years she was very happy. But then suddenly the woman left her for a younger woman, and she's been depressed and distraught ever since. And basically I've been her only confidant. In fact, when she was working on one of her books, she came up and stayed in my apartment for six weeks. That at least was a happy time for both of us. She even dedicated her book to me. We also arranged for each other to be our beneficiaries in our wills.

"But now there's been a whole earthquake in our relationship. Because a woman I'd known many years ago in grade school called me up one day, and said she wanted to see me. She told me she'd moved to New York for a new job but also to get away from a very unhappy marriage of thirty years. She told me straight out (no pun intended) that she'd always been in love with me, and wanted to get to know me again. I couldn't get over how she'd changed when we met. I hardly remembered her, but what I did recall was a very unattractive and overweight little girl with terribly crooked buck teeth. She'd lost all the extra weight, and had had all kinds of work done on herself-teeth fixed and so forth, and was really good-looking. I couldn't believe what was happening, but within a few dates I was in love with her, and now we're living together, and I've never had a better love relationship in my life.

"That part of course is wonderful for me. But Mara is furious. And of course terribly jealous. She absolutely hates Peggy, and says, 'That's just the kind of girl I hated in high school!' She thinks Peggy was always pretty and the cheerleader type all her life, and I can't seem to convince her that she's really not like that at all and has had to struggle to become who she is. But I'm really terribly upset about the situation. I don't want to lose Mara, and yet I can't get her to accept Peg. I even dream about it. My friends think Mara will come around, but I don't know. I think it would be the greatest blow of my life if we were never reconciled-or rather, if at this late date in our lives-after having meant so much to each other all our lives-there was a permanent rift."

Stories of permanent later alienation weren't common, but there were a few. One came from my own cousin Clare, with whom I've remained very close, though even with her there was a ten-year period when she and I were separated not only geographically but by our completely unsynchronized schedules for marriage and child-rearing. She had this to say: "I guess I was always at one remove, growing up in Philadelphia. And because even in my adult life I've lived so far away from everyone else for so many years [in Wisconsin, Australia, Ohio] the geography alone became really difficult. It felt like a tremendous job to stay in touch, and I had to say to myself, Well, you have to live without them, so select which ones to keep up with.

"And then also, there's such a mass of feeling attached to each and every one of them that it's almost easier to leave it alone. I continue to buy into the family myth that these are really unusual people, but every contact is so loaded with memory and emotion that it's almost more than I can handle."

My high school friend Miriam, who had been half in love with her handsome younger cousin Robbie, had become even more cut off from the aunt and same-age girl cousin with whom she'd been very close as a child. "I loved Betty and her mother for years, but as my aunt got older she became very critical of me, and Betty always backed her up. Even so, when she was sick and in the hospital, I called her and sent flowers every day. But no matter what I did, it was never enough. She'd become hostile and bitter, and she even told my mother, 'You know, neither of your girls even sent me a card!' I was terribly hurt, but after a while I became more assertive, and didn't take it anymore. I said, 'You've no right to call me up and berate me or complain to my mother. I've always tried to do everything I could for you.' And we never spoke again. Of course that meant the end of my relationship with Betty, too. So you're talking to the wrong one if it's continuity you want. But I have to say that I miss the family enormously as I've grown older. I wish I had a circle of cousins like you do, and like some others I know."

But for the most part, the stories of changing relationships were positive ones, many people describing the increased importance their cousins had taken on as they grew older. Said Paula Silver, a psychiatric social worker of fifty who specializes in the care of the elderly, and has given a great deal of thought to the role of cousins in her clients' lives and more recently in her own, "I find that these relationships often are an important support group for many of my clients," she said. "But even to me, my cousins have become more and more important in the past few years. After all, there aren't that many people left who knew me as a child, and I think people who've known you that long really know you better in certain ways than even very close friends you make later in life. These are people who know things about me that nobody else would-not just how I was afraid of the dark, or cried a lot, but the good things, too-how I was good at ping-pong, or always talked to the kids who didn't have any friends.

"Even more, as nieces and nephews to your parents, they knew and remember your parents when your mom and dad were younger. They can confirm some of the memories of your parents as active, vital people, which can be a real comfort when newer friends or even your own children see and will remember only the sick old person who's left. [Paula's mother had died after a long, debilitating illness.] They can also straighten you out on your own perceptions of how your parents seemed to other people, and sometimes give you a fuller picture of what they were really like. They had enough distance as children to be able to view them more objectively than you could, while at the same time they were more closely involved than your friends and had a lot of chances to observe them at close range. They can let you know how they appeared to others-sometimes better, sometimes worse than you might have thought."

I myself was shocked to learn recently from Helen, who I'd thought admired and loved my mother unqualifiedly as a child, that this was not the case at all. She had often found my mother's moodiness and short temper frightening, and resented her control over her own mother, my aunt. Though these aspects of my mother had caused me problems as well, I was fascinated to learn that she hadn't been as successful at covering them up with other family members as I'd thought.

Coming at it as the observer myself, I've often disputed my cousin Elliot D.'s picture of his mother, my Aunt Madeline, as a willful and domineering woman who attempted to run the lives not only of her own two sons, with disastrous results, but of everyone else with whom she came into contact. I, on the other hand, found her wonderful-one of my favorite aunts, in fact. What he saw as an unbending nature I saw as unusual strength. The sharp tongue he dreaded I saw as a delightfully dry sense of humor. The attempts to control his life he described as the horror of his childhood I took, when applied to me, as signs of unusual interest and of an effort to give me good advice.

She bought me books I remember to this day-*Understood Betsy*, a tonic for a time in my childhood when I was feeling a little too sorry for myself, and the copy of *Eight Cousins* that had such an influence on my life. Her domination of a social situation I took as a tribute to her rare charm-and God knows she was charming. I particularly remember the way she greeted me and others. Instead of just saying hello, or giving me a perfunctory aunt kiss, she'd reach out, clasp both my hands in hers, look at me with what I took as rare warmth, and say, "Jo, darling. How wonderful to see you." I was sure she meant every word, and Elliot has never convinced me that my picture of her is a false one.

Needless to say, the reverse is even more true, but I do know that the results of our discussions (no one, even our respective spouses, can understand the passion Elliot and I bring to these talks) are that we both have a broader and more accurate picture of what Aunt Madeline was really like.

Anna Quindlen related the phenomenon of such completely different viewpoints to an old Indian folk tale she'd heard. "It's like the story of the guys with the elephant," she said. "Three blind men are feeling the different parts of the elephant, and the one who's feeling the trunk says, 'The elephant is like a snake.' The guy who's feeling the leg says, 'The elephant is like a tree.' The guy who's feeling the tail says, 'The elephant is like a switch.' Everybody's feeling a different part. And with cousins, everybody's positioned in a different place and has a different sense of what's going on in the family."

Still, a lot of these different viewpoints can only come out when enough time has passed to give some perspective-in other words, when we're not only grown up, but moving onwards from there. Paula, the psychiatric social worker, explained how she'd come to her conclusions about the important role cousins can play in the lives of older people. "I guess I'm particularly aware of this aspect because for so many years I didn't see mine at all," she said. "When my mother was alive, I knew she had a grudge against her sister. She'd never tell my brother or me what it was about, swearing that she couldn't remember, which drove us crazy as kids. Still, we saw my cousins pretty often till I was about eight, when we began to see less and less of them, and finally stopped seeing them at all.

"Even when I was older and married, and could have sought them out on my own, I didn't, out of loyalty to my mother. When my children were born, she did say it was OK for them to come over once in a while, and she let them visit once when she was so ill. (They'd have come more often, but Mom didn't want them to.) Otherwise, that was it.

"But when my mother died two years ago, one of the first things I did was re-contact those cousins, and I've been seeing them ever since. I guess I feel it puts me back in touch with who I really am. And of course the continuity is great. They knew me, my parents, and my own children, too. You might say they have both a broad view, and at the same time a more intense and intimate one, of who I am and where I come from than anyone else I know. And I have the same view of them. This means we can talk for hours about all the other cousins and their peculiarities-no need to hide skeletons, they know about them already-and about my parents and their parents. [I was reminded of my discussions with Elliot D.]

"Sometimes we even talk about grandparents we never met, speculating about how the stories we know about them would explain things about the family. We're all equally fascinated. Because directly or indirectly, it all involves and explains us, and how we got to be who we are," she said, unconsciously voicing what Elizabeth Stone (in *Black Sheep and Kissing Cousins*) had said earlier about how family stories shape us.

But the speculation and family mythology, even the fresh take on one's parents, usually take second place to the all-important aspect of cousins as witnesses to one's own life. This was mentioned over and over as people tried to define the special role cousins had come to play in their lives.

The memories about oneself may not always be the ones you'd like to be remembered for. Though Paula Silver said earlier that "These are people who know the good things, too," the opposite is at least as true. My cousin Clare often reminds me of how my chewing on lamb chop or chicken bones horrified her as a child. And in Ursula Perrin's novel *The Looking-Glass Lover* (quoted at the start of the chapter), Barbara says of *her* cousin Claire, "Sometimes, someone you have known since early childhood becomes a kind of mirror and, looking at her, what you see is yourself as she must see you: aged six, sad and dumpy, or at fourteen-an angry adolescent with a rash of pimples on your forehead, or an overweight college girl, teary and morose, recovering from a first love affair. You know that this mirror has recorded all your hideous vulnerabilities and worse, it has a memory that is deep, unforgiving, inconvenient."

But most people take even such embarrassing or unhappy memories as interesting reminders of where they've come from and who they were. And of course there's the enormous compensation of discussing the shared experiences-pleasant or otherwise. Barbara Lindeman, who you will recall had spent every Sunday as a child visiting her grandmother with her twelve cousins, says, "When we remeet now, we tell 'grandma stories.' That's our family lore."

Cynthia Levin adds, "When we get together, we tell 'mother stories' about our mothers that have us rolling on the floor. Nobody else would believe how nutty our mothers were. But at least when we're together we can laugh about it."

I can recall "in" jokes myself. After all, who else would burst out laughing at the mere question, "And how is Spike?"-the secret name Clare and I gave a dod-dering and absentee uncle about whose failing health older family members were forever inquiring?

Which brings up the family secrets you can share and maybe even laugh about that you'd hate to share with a stranger (the skeletons Paula said there was no need to hide). One friend who requested anonymity told me that only with his cousins did he feel comfortable discussing a strain of mental illness that had cropped up at least once in almost every generation and branch of the family. "Only with them could we talk about the fear we had that it would affect us or the kids. It even got so we could joke about it in a black humor kind of way. I was ashamed to mention it to anyone else-especially potential girlfriends. But what a relief to be able to talk about it with my cousins!"

Dr. Martha Gibbons, a family therapist, put it this way: "The fact of your shared yet somewhat separate history with cousins is what makes the big differ-ence. It's something you don't have with anyone else, not even your siblings, because your siblings are much more likely to see things as you do and to know the same parts of the family history you do. There's not the same dynamic. With the cousins, you can catch up and fill in ancient family history. They'll bring in facts and secrets they learned from their parents about your grandparents you couldn't find out any other way-and sometimes things about your parents, too."

This was new-not the already shared myths, history, and memories, or even the different opinions, but the unknown facts you can discover. A case in point is that of David Forman, the art dealer whose artist cousin Peter had been a role model for him as he was growing up, and later, when he visited him in Italy. "Everything I know about my parents' meeting and marriage I owe to my cousin Ruthie," he said. "She's a very Brooklyn-y type, kind of like Barbra Streisand, only a lot more so. Still, I'll always be grateful to her for filling me in about my parents. My parents were very closed about their own childhoods and their own relationship, and until I was thirty I knew absolutely nothing about how they'd met or married. Of course, I'd asked questions as a child, but when I never got answers, I guess I gave up.

"Then, long after I was out of college, my older brother was getting married, and I re-met Ruthie, whom I hadn't seen in a long time, at the wedding. I think I said something about, 'Well, do you think there's any great passion here?' And she said, 'Well, there may be passion, but I don't think they're great lovers, like your parents were.' I was absolutely floored, especially since I'd hardly ever seen my parents so much as embrace, and I begged her to tell me what she meant.

"My mother [my aunt, who had died years before] told me they were quite an item,' she said. 'Your dad was living in Baltimore, and one summer when he was about nineteen or twenty he got a summer job as a cabana boy in Atlantic City. Well, it happens that your mother's father took his three daughters and his son to Atlantic City every summer. So the rich girl from Brooklyn met the cabana boy from Baltimore, and they had a big romance. When the summer ended, they wrote to each other all the time, and he came to New York to visit, and finally to live-so he could be near her. They knew her father wouldn't approve, so the next winter they eloped. And for two years they kept their marriage a secret. Finally, when your dad was getting established, they told her father about it, and I guess by then he had to accept it. But he insisted they be remarried by a rabbi.'"

"To say that I was dumbfounded by this information would be a wild understatement," said David. "It made me think of my parents and their relationship in an entirely different way, and also of them as individuals in a different way. Suddenly they seemed much more mysterious and interesting. I just couldn't get over it. And if Ruthie hadn't told me the story, I'd never have known about it."

Sometimes cousins can remind you of incidents from your own childhood you've forgotten. Artist Jasper Johns, who grew up feeling somewhat detached from most of his cousins in Allendale, South Carolina, mentioned that there was one cousin, an older girl named Mary, he'd been close to-and still is. Only recently she had reminded him of a childhood adventure he hadn't thought of in years. "It began when I saw a poster from the Library of Congress-a poster with a photograph by Walker Evans of a sign that said 'Silas Green from New Orleans," he said. "Seeing that ad for a minstrel show made me recall how I'd loved to go to those shows as a kid. I'd go with the whites on the 'white day' and with our cook, who was black, on the 'black day.'

"The next time I talked to Mary I mentioned it to her, and she reminded me of the time we'd gone over on the day they were setting up for the show, and of how they'd let us dance on the platform. It was a very happy memory that I'd completely forgotten till she mentioned it."

Gisela Marks, the jewelry designer who had come to the United States as a refugee when she was only 9 years old, had very definite ideas on the subject of cousins as "witnesses." In fact, it was she who first used the term to me. "Who else knows what it was like in Europe then, or what my mother looked like, or remembers all the relatives? My cousins are my only link to that past."

Her story was in many ways a tragic one, despite its idyllic beginnings. "As a child growing up in Berlin, I had a host of cousins," she said. "My grandparents on both sides were from families of five or six, and they all had five or six children. So you can imagine the ramifications. Strangely, though, in our generation each of the five or six had only one child, and these were my contemporaries.

"Every summer, all of us-cousins, aunts, and uncles-would go to the Baltic Sea, where our grandparents (who incidentally included two sisters married to two brothers) had houses, and we had the most wonderful time. My concept was of cousins as friendly people who played with you no matter what your age, which to a little girl made them just wonderful. In fact, I had a crush on a much older boy cousin who used to play cards with us.

"When the trouble in Europe started, my parents decided to get out quickly. But unfortunately, most of the others didn't. The cousin I had the crush on, by the way, was the first to get caught." She sighed sadly. "Of those who remained, only one of them, a girl cousin, escaped the camps and lived. She had lost her child, but after the war she came to the United States and miraculously discovered her husband. She lives in Chicago and we talk often.

"There were only three who came over at the same time we did, and with those I'm especially friendly, even though one of them is four years younger than I am, one is ten years older, and one is fifteen years older and living in Palestine-a fabulous woman.

"But the older I get, the less the age differences matter. After all, as I said, they are the only witnesses who share with me the memories of that wonderful family that disappeared. The past draws us close-the past more than the present, although of course we talk of other things as well. But the past is the subtext."

Perhaps one of the hardest tests of time any relationship can be called upon to pass is that of working together in a business. The same, of course, applies to cousins. Nor did I have to go farther than my friend Emily's family to find an example of the disastrous consequences that can occur-directly or indirectly.

Though her father and his brother had had a good working relationship running a sporting goods business for years, when the possibility of their sons entering the firm came up (her father had one son, her uncle two), the atmosphere became tense and competitive-actually, more between the fathers than the sons. Each father feared that his son/sons would somehow be outmaneuvered by his cousins-although, ironically, Emily's brother actually had little interest in becoming part of the business at all, and, I recently found out, the other two were ambivalent as well. The upshot was that the two fathers' hostility reached the point where, though they remained in business for a few years, they never spoke again. Even more ironically, all three sons ended up in different fields anyway.

Fortunately, since they had been more or less uninvolved in the bitterest quarreling, the cousins were able to rescue their relationships, and as discussed in an earlier chapter, their fathers didn't make them feel they were being disloyal if they saw each other. But the fact that the two brothers themselves never spoke again always seemed to me a tragic aftermath of the feud.

Perhaps if David Bork, author of *Family Business, Risky Business,* and president of Coda Corporation, a consulting firm that specializes in in-depth counseling and planning for family businesses, had been around at the time, the conflicts could have been avoided. He concedes in his preface that, "There is a strong popular myth that nothing good can come out of working with one's family. This attitude is so ingrained in the public mind by television, film, and print media that family members themselves have come to accept it." But he was determined to do something to change the myth-and the reality.

In his attempts to get to the roots of the complex and seemingly insoluble situations with which he was often confronted in his work, Bork found the psychological theories of Murray Bowen, a pioneer of family therapy, of great use. Briefly mentioned before, it is often called a "systems approach," and is "based on the premise that we are who we are because of our family system. Each generation in a family repeats the patterns of the preceding generation. Such a theory diffuses blame backward over the generations...It says none of us asked to be who we are...and sees what is going on in the individual as inseparable from the family network."

While emphasizing that a person can exercise free will and change his behavior, "'in the clutch'-when they are under stress or pressure-people revert to the 'messages' (behaviors) from the family of origin" and must learn to "short-circuit that reversion and behave according to patterns learned elsewhere."

Furthermore, a person must be properly "differentiated"-i.e., be sure of the boundaries that separate him or her from another emotionally, since "when anxiety builds up in people or organizations it pours over into other relationships. Two people can manage only so much anxiety. Enter a third person to whom the anxiety can be shifted. This does not resolve issues, but does slough off anxiety by involving another in the issue. With the involvement of the third person, the system is temporarily stabilized. Bowen calls this predictable emotional pattern among three people *triangling.* "The less well-differentiated people are, the more likely they are to become involved in triangles, but "Only when triangles are eliminated can two people resolve their conflict with each other."

I asked Mr. Bork if there was anything different in the way cousins relate in business to the way siblings do. He began by repeating almost word for word what Dr. James Framo had said about the factors contributing to good relationships between cousins in general. "A lot depends on the relationship between the cousins' parents. Often when there were dramatic differences between the parents, those animosities got played out through the children, to the detriment of the business, and almost invariably were also very destructive personally."

"One of the assumptions among cousins who are entering a family firm is: we're all in this together and we're all the same. But they're not the same. They didn't grow up with the exact same ancestry, family system and rules. After all, only half of them is the same; the other half (brought in by the parental mate who married in) is different. So you end up with a lot of false assumptions. The cousins are often less similar than people expect."

I also asked him if he felt cousins were more or less likely than siblings to succeed as business partners, and he said, "I'd be reluctant to make any predictions of better or worse. It all depends on the premises they start out with and the kinds of communication in the family. I do think that one of the advantages of the cousin connection is that there's a lower level of interpersonal exposure, so often there's a higher level of differentiation. [Dr. Donald Bloch's comment earlier in the book that the cousin relationship is not a "hot" one, applies.] Cousins who are well-differentiated will do very well together."

He cited as a success story the Rockefellers, who even referred to themselves as "The Cousins." "For instance," he said, "they made decisions two to three years ago about what they wanted to do and how they wanted to do it that are directly connected to the sale of Rockefeller Center."

Bork addresses a number of the special problems inherent in cousins joining a family firm (as opposed to siblings only) in a section of his book entitled "Succession by Multiple Heirs."

In one business, four cousins each managed a different division. Each was capable and successful in his own way. But when it came to overall business planning or sticky financial planning, they engaged an outside business consultant to keep them on target. If one of the four cousins disagreed with a decision, he could call for review by an outside arbitrator. The heirs agreed in advance to be bound by the arbitrator's decision. However, if one of the four called for arbitration three times in five years and was decided against by the arbitrator each time, he was required to sell his interest to the other three members at a price arrived at by a predetermined formula...It forced each [partner] to take a reasoned position that would stand the review of an outsider. Also, each heir knew in advance the full consequences of being unwilling to work out a compromise. As a result, petty arguments were reduced and the professionalism of the management was enhanced.

He added that, of course, "The arbitrator...must be completely free of any profit from the decision." He then went on to say that

Multiple-heir successions often work surprisingly well. The Bass brothers, the four nephews of Texas oil billionaire Sid Richardson, have continued to build a business dynasty on their uncle's old fortune. Ranging in age from twenty-eight to forty-two, [the cousins] are sophisticated, ambitious, and well-trained businessmen who have a social conscience. Each works hard to ensure the continued success of the family's far-reaching financial enterprises. Without their professional attitude toward management and willingness to call in expert advice, this family empire could easily have crumbled under incredible business strife. On the contrary, the Basses are considered the modern-day heirs to the Morgan and Rockefeller family business tradition.

As are the Bronfmans and the Tisches, among others. A recent article in *Vanity Fair* said that "the Tisch family has begun to emerge as America's newest dynasty, with a $19 billion empire that includes 25 percent of CBS, the Loew's Hotels, CNA Financial Corporation, Lorillard tobacco, and the Bulova Watch Co.

Even those who have gone off on their own, like Steve Tisch, nephew of Lawrence Tisch, the head of CBS, and son of Preston Tisch, who served as postmaster general, acknowledge their debt to their training in the family business. Steve, producer of such movies as *Risky Business* and *Big Business* and such TV dramas as *The Burning Bed,* worked as a film booker for the family's movie chain while in college, and said, "I was the oldest of seven cousins. I watched my father and uncle put it all together, so I never took any of it for granted…After watching my father and my uncle, I felt I could do it on my own."

On a smaller scale, though also a second generation business that has gone from founding brothers to sons (in this case a son and a son-in-law) there is the example of Andrew Fier, who, together with his cousin-by-marriage Mortimer Jaffe (no relation to my own Jaffe relatives), runs the Plaza Funeral Home on New York City's west side. "I was an only child, and I grew up right near my cousin Blanche, who was actually a first cousin once removed, though we were the same age. I felt about her exactly as I think I would have about a sister, except without the hassles. Our parents ran the business together, and even though I was already in my early 20's when she married Mort, I felt immediately that he, too, was my cousin. It seemed completely logical and natural that we'd become partners. I never had any doubts that the partnership would work out. And it has."

I can also cite a case in point from my own family. Since the original edition of this book, my niece Lydia has joined my husband's small but very active real estate firm, Leslie J. Garfield and Co., and the arrangement has worked out surprisingly well. Her closest associate in the business: our son and her first cousin, Jed. In spite of the fact that they've had to share a small office, they've been able to work together (and separately) with a remarkable lack of friction. Though as children they rarely played together when our families shared weekends in the country-typically, Jed hung out with his same-sex cousins Dan and Phil, Lydia with my daughter Clare-there were things all the kids did as a group: baseball games, long walks, a truncated but ambitious production of *A Midsummer Night's Dream*. (The bucolic setting, at least, was perfect.) I like to think that that early contact lent an immediate ease to their association so many years later.

But so far only well-and often long-established family businesses have come up. What about the businesses being set up by cousins today? Bork was optimistic. "The stereotype of the family business as a cauldron of unresolved personal tension and eccentric behavior is yielding to a new image in the 1980s [and 90's]," he says, in a section of his book entitled "The Future of Family Business." "Newspapers and popular magazines are featuring articles on families who chose to go into business together. Many of these families will not fall into the traps that previous family businesses fell into. Better educational opportunities, increased sexual equality in the job market, and enlightened social conditions that allow families to seek help for their business problems are paving the way for a business atmosphere and increased communication among families who work together."

One example-albeit a fictional one-of this new style of cousinly business relationship can be found in Mary Gordon's novel, *The Other Side*. Cam and her cousin Dan, who were raised together and have been close all their lives (they were mentioned in the section on substitute siblings), form the law firm of McNamara and McNamara. Theirs is the kind of partnership forged between cousins who feel that, besides their lifelong affection for each other, their complementary abilities and personalities will help them work well together. And in fact, such is the case.

> He's been happy, working beside Cam, but working differently from her; they split the practice, their strengths and weaknesses make a coherent whole...
>
> She sees the people she defends as part of a long parade, leading to something. She likes to stand back from them; she likes them best after they leave her...For Dan, each case...exists by itself in the

world. She reckons he spends three times longer talking to the clients than she does. He gives them his phone number at home. They call him at all hours…'Don't worry, things will be all right,' he says. And they believe him…She says, 'Don't worry, we'll win.' She would never think of promising that things will be all right.

Though Cam and Dan's is a fictional partnership, I heard some of the same comments about having complementary qualities from real-life cousins who had gone into business together.

Linda Laventhall and her cousin Enid Harris recently founded Celebrations Ink, a business that handles specialized invitations, announcements, stationery, and gifts. I talked to Linda, whose voice on the phone, incidentally, is impossible to distinguish from Enid's. "Our mothers were sisters," Linda said, "but when we were growing up, the eight-year difference in age between Enid and me meant a lot. We liked each other, but we only really got friendly as adults.

"A few years ago we were both at a point in our lives where we were ready to try something new. We looked into different kinds of businesses for about a year and a half, and at the same time we did a lot of soul-searching into our personalities, and into what, in fact, we would be comfortable doing together. I was very adamant about a lot of things I didn't want to do; Enid had things she didn't want to do. We were really coming from very different directions. I'm much more social service oriented; Enid is much more product oriented. We both knew we didn't want to go out and pound on doors trying to sell products because neither of us wanted to deal with that kind of rejection. We knew we needed a business where people came to us. So it was really an ongoing process.

"Even though we're different in the ways I mentioned, Enid and I are very similar in disposition, and we sort of compensate for each other in whatever our weaknesses are. Certain things one doesn't like to do, the other does. Because of our similarities, we can sort of understand what's happening very quickly. If I'm uptight, she backs off, and if she's uptight, I back off. But the important parts of our personalities are similar. We have similar values and I feel that's very important."

Haki Morai grew up in Osaka, Japan, and never met his cousin Cathy till he came to the United States at 18 to go to Temple University. Cathy was working as the manager of a restaurant in Atlanta, but they met on several vacations, and got along "amazingly well"-as newly discovered cousins so often do. When Haki was graduated, they decided to start a Japanese restaurant together, and Haki, too, mentioned both their easy communication and their compensatory qualities. "When I get hotheaded, she's cool, and vice versa. I'm good at the food angle, she's good at the bookkeeping. It's worked out fine." As it has for Arnie and the cousin who founded the Cousins Color Laboratory in downtown New York, or the group of cousins who run the Cousins Taxi Service in Queens.

In concluding his study of Bowen's theories as related to business, Bork says, "Family behavior patterns stem from family rules...The goal of family systems therapy is to bring hidden rules to the surface and to loosen rigid rules so that patterns that create pain and keep family members from establishing themselves as individuals can be eliminated. Families can then be flexible as they move from one stage to another."

Not that all cousins who enter new or long-established businesses necessarily need therapy. But they do need flexibility as they move from the personal into the working relationship. In fact, it is that trait-flexibility-that is probably central to passing the many and varied tests of time that confront the lifelong cousin relationship.

8

COUSINS TODAY

Based on all visible signs, those who talk of weakening family ties could have concluded that family was not one of my major concerns and that wherever it was I had come from, I had left it far behind. But they would have been wrong, as wrong about me as they may be about others. Those who say that America is a land of rootless nomads who travel light, uninstructed by memory and family ties, have missed part of the evidence.

-ELIZABETH STONE,
BLACK SHEEP AND KISSING COUSINS

WHAT, THEN, *IS* the evidence?

For my research I relied on interviews, articles, books, and personal experience. The only formal study I'm aware of on the subject is "Best-Known Cousin and Secondary Kin," in Bert N. Adams' already quoted book, *Kinship in an Urban Setting*. (The "best-known cousin" was the one his respondents felt he or she knew best, though they didn't necessarily have to like them best. "Secondary kin" are cousins, aunts, uncles, and grandparents.) Although his findings differ from mine, they are worth looking at.

Adams takes a dim view of the prospects for intimacy between cousins in the urban United States, which he says are "obviously slim unless relations between their parents are close, or some common interest or activity draws the cousins closer together, or they live in close proximity to each other. That is, the conditions must be just right for a cousin to become an important 'other' in the individual's world." He follows this with the even more extreme statement that "Secondary kinship [in America] is basically superficial regardless of stratum"-conclusions with which I heartily disagree.

He bases this gloomy judgment on interviews with 799 people in the city of Greensboro, North Carolina. The criteria were valid enough. He counted as important: "home visits, including emergencies, social activities, engagement in the same organization, ritual occasions, working together, communication by phone and letter, and mutual aid."

The results? Over one-fourth of both the men and women in the sample either knew no cousin or else didn't feel well enough acquainted to assess the extent of their similarity in values or opinions. Another 50 percent felt they had little in common with their cousins. In short only about 25 percent "expressed close feelings for their cousins."

Since such a large proportion of the population lives in cities, I feel compelled to point out the main problem with conclusions based on those figures, and it's not that the study was done in 1963-64. I have no reason to think his statistics would be much different now. But the makeup of the group was very narrowly focused: "All of the respondents were to be white, married, married only once, and married for twenty years or less."

Such a group of respondents is simply not representative of all groups of cousins. Not that it wasn't necessary to have controls. Any study must. But how could one exclude the entire body of older and younger cousins, to say nothing of other ethnic groups, singles of all kinds, and divorced people?

Adams' conclusions, then, may be valid for that particular group of young adults *at that point in their lives,* but the overall picture is only one-third painted. As Ms. Stone so aptly said at the head of this chapter, "Part of the evidence" is missing. This is because, as previously shown, cousins so often are important to people as they're growing up and then become important again later in life, frequently being eclipsed in importance during the years in which families are being started and careers built-the very years Adams was studying.

Dr. Bernard Farber, professor of sociology at Arizona State University gets to the heart of the problem in an article for the *Journal of Marriage and the Family:* "With the passage of time and with sampling of different population segments, one finds that *the accumulated results of studies yield weak and/or contradictory tendencies* [my italics]," he says. He also notes "much chance variation in sampling," and concludes, "the position taken here opposes the view that either (a) kinship structure is slowly disintegrating in American society; (b) lower-class kinship exists in a highly disorganized state, or (c) changes in domestic arrangements represent a demoralization of American society."

Certainly, nothing in my wide range of interviews-and I spoke or corresponded with over 300 people over the years-indicated the degree of remoteness Adams found, be they cousins raised in the city or in the country. In fact, I can think of only about twenty of these people who said they had no interest in or contact with one or more of their cousins. As we've already seen, proximity, parental closeness, and common interests are important, but as we've also seen, cousin relationships often thrive even when few of these factors are present.

Still, however mistaken in its overall conclusions, the study is certainly interesting in its parts. Adams has intriguing things to say about how class differences are reflected *within* cousin groups, not just *between* them in today's world, and cousin mavens will certainly want to know about some of them:

"Those from a working-class background tend to live closer to their best-known cousin," for instance, "and the young adult females...interact with somewhat greater frequency." (Eduardo Riccio's close-knit Bronx family fit this profile remarkably well.)

Not only did Adams find more interaction between females in the working classes. "Female contact at all levels was…more frequent," he says, and close cousins tended to be the children of sisters, with the daughters of sisters closest of all. This is not surprising considering that Adams also found that most sisters were more in touch with each other in adult life than were brothers or brothers and sisters.

There was, however, one exception to the "best cousin" as the child of sisters: "The young adult males whose parents are blue-collar [mostly chose] as their best-known cousin one to whom they are related through their father." He adds that, in blue-collar families, males and females were separated "not only in marital and parental roles but in leisure and kin contacts more completely than in white-collar networks."

Like David Schneider, Adams found that class differences tend to create distance between cousins, noting "a fundamental tendency to keep in more frequent touch with cousins…of one's current occupational [and economic] stratum." In addition, he says that "though almost any kin network will cover a wide range of occupational statuses…there is likely to be clustering at a particular level."

Surprisingly, in spite of their struggles up the ladder of success, he says that the upwardly mobile are as much in touch with cousins as stable white- and blue-collar workers (and more so than the downwardly mobile), though they do "tend to claim as best-known cousin [someone] of their current stratum, even if he or she lives much farther away."

An example that supports and explains the occupational and economic cousin alliances, but refutes their shallowness (typically, more in his early and later life than in the middle) is that of Dr. Michael Fellner, the dermatologist in New York City who had mentioned the important role his cousins played in his life as an only child. "When I grew up, I didn't exactly lose touch, but I saw my cousins less often. Now, as I've grown older, I've felt that my world is shrinking and I've deliberately sought them out-and vice versa. I knew they knew me from way back, which of course was great. But what also happened was that I decided I could trust them more than most people. *They had all become very successful so I had nothing to fear from them.*"

The section in italics at first sounds a little odd, but actually is an honest statement that explains to some extent why cousins of the same status may feel closest (and safest) with their peers. Of course, where the wealthy are concerned, there is always the possibility-often joked about in movies or TV-of the indigent relative coming around for a handout. But there are other, more benign, reasons, too, and these were expressed to me by both humorist Lewis Frumkes and lawyer Larry Levine, who mentioned with pleasure the success and prosperity of their close cousins as a link between them. Not because they were snobbish and only wanted to mix with the successful or well-to-do, but simply because it made for fewer differences and less cause for envy. I also picked up on a sense of family pride. ("That we have all done well must say something about us as a family.")

On the other end of the spectrum, it would logically follow that cousins in lower economic and status groups tend to be closer, too. In other words, the "birds of a feather" phenomenon. Cousins do, and surely will continue to, flock together, frequently within-but also across-class lines. And this despite the naysayers and the assaults of modern life. Nor am I alone in disagreeing with Adams' negative analysis of cousinly togetherness today or in the future. Other prominent analysts of society also see things differently. Says Robin Fox: "Kinship is tenacious…But why should it be? When the demands of our industrial civilization drive us towards an impersonal, bureaucratic, rational social structure, why should these irrational sentiments of kinship still have a hold?" He reviews aristocratic and Mediterranean codes of honor and loyalty between kinsmen, and notes that in the latter they are still a force. "Whence their strength?" he asks. "Could it be the hangover of centuries, not to say millennia, of kinship-centered experience? In [earlier] societies it was clearly…important to have support in a dispute…People lived in kinship-based groups and a 'kinless' man was at best a man without social position, at worst…a dead man. Thus, even our relatively kinless society cannot throw off this slowly accumulated, almost innate wisdom of the blood. If it is basic in our natures to trust the familiar and fear the strange, then those who share our blood share part of ourselves, and so are by definition the most familiar of all."

Though a theorist and scientist, David Schneider has already been shown to be a man who is not afraid to go out on a moral and philosophical limb about how it should be between cousins or other secondary relatives. Not only is it true that, as he said in analyzing what was special about cousins, "the relationship cannot be ended or altered and…is a state of almost mystical commonalty and identity…of diffuse, enduring solidarity" but, including both those related *in nature* and *in law,* he states outright that "love is what American kinship is all about."

Finally, Adams himself indicates some room for questioning his conclusions about the shallowness of cousin relationships when he says that some of his colleagues have noted that "in the large metropolis there are now being reborn-or may still be found-the meaningful secondary kin networks of earlier rural-agricultural days. The ghetto, the ethnic mutual aid kin association, and other megalopolitan kin groups-these may be important, if not emerging-phenomena."

There is no doubt that this generation of cousins will differ in some important ways from those in the past, even a past as recent as mine, if for no other reason than that people are having fewer children than the generations that spawned families like the Kennedys, the Quindlens, my own-the Rosengartens-and countless others. The increasing dispersion of families has already been noted. Rainie and Quinn, in *Growing Up Kennedy,* say of that family's cohesiveness, "It cannot last. The logistics will not allow it."

In the final paragraph of his chapter on cousins, Adams quotes the wife of a bus terminal clerk as saying, "It's distressing that distance is pulling families apart so. Seeing relatives was very important when I was young and I miss it now. It bothers me that my children don't know their cousins and play with them like I did."

And Anna Quindlen remarked about her own childhood with many cousins nearby, "I think in an odd way they were vestiges of a childhood people don't have anymore."

This is certainly true. Yet there is reason to believe that when cousins today do make the effort to stay in touch, to absorb family history, become friends with the ones they have and stay that way, it has more than just pleasurable benefits. In fact, according to Dr. Murray Bowen, the aforementioned founder of the "family systems" concept of psychotherapy, one ignores the extended family of aunts, uncles, and cousins at some risk to mental health.

In *Family Evaluation,* by Bowen and Dr. Michael E. Kerr, Director of Training at the Georgetown University Family Center, the authors say, "The person who is less cut off [from his extended family] has a more reliable emotional support system than the person who is more cut off." And furthermore, "A person who stays away from his family completely is vulnerable to developing serious symptoms should his 'substitute' relationships crumble...In fact, such a person is also cut off from other emotionally significant relationships."

In dealing with families already in trouble, the point is reiterated and developed. "If a therapist is dealing with two people who are fairly cut off emotionally from their extended families and who have little motivation to bridge the cutoffs, it is very important that he be aware of it...People who do not bridge cutoffs with the past can get some improvement in the present, but they usually get less improvement and it generally occurs more slowly and is less durable." Most importantly, "Although it may not appear so to a nuclear family, an extended family is almost always a potential resource to the nuclear family."

Supporting the role of cousins and other members of the extended family as witnesses, they state, "The family of origin becomes a resource when a person goes back to it, not to get something from the family such as support, approval, or acceptance, but to learn more about himself or herself in that context."

In terms of prognosis for the troubled family, "The more stable and intact an extended family system that surrounds a nuclear family, the more likely the extended system will be a supportive influence on the nuclear family." The result will be a "less intense emotional process" in that family. "A less intense process appears to favor a more benign clinical course for whatever dysfunction exists."

Their conclusion: "The degree of emotional cutoff may be the most significant family variable that influences prognosis. When a major symptom occurs in a highly cutoff nuclear family…the prognosis is less favorable than when a major symptom occurs in a nuclear family that is in good emotional contact with extended family."

Since cousins are probably the most numerous, and certainly the most likely to be around for a long time, of the extended family members (which of course also includes aunts, uncles, and grandparents), they can clearly be an important and continuing asset to a healthy person, and especially to those experiencing difficulties. And here my findings are again in conflict with those of Adams, who comments that, "After the death of the older generation there is likely to be a loss of interest on the part of young adults in their secondary kin"-i.e., their cousins, since they are all that is left.

First of all, many of my interviewees stated quite the opposite, among them psychiatrist Veva Zimmerman, who said, "When the aunts, uncles, and grandparents are gone, the cousins are the only remaining relatives, and you really try to hold onto them." And Georgia Miller, a lawyer in New York, mentioned that "Even though we weren't that close as children, after all the aunts and uncles died, we formed a club so we wouldn't lose touch. And I must say we keep it up, and I really enjoy it." Elizabeth Stone put it neatly. "If the extended family has any meaning as an institution, then cousins are to [that group] what siblings are to the nuclear family."

But even if this loss of a focus (the grandparent or others of the older generation) and consequent alienation does occur for a time, as it may during the young adult stage of life Adams was studying, all the evidence I collected shows that as that stage draws to a close, enormous interest in redeveloping such ties occurs, even in people who previously had little or no interest in their cousins, or who had never known them at all, or who rediscover them, by chance or by design.

It seems fitting to end with a number of such stories of discovery and redis-covery. Not just the events, but what they meant to those involved. And while certain sections of the book called for the input of experts, this is one that can't be proven or validated by doctors or psychologists or sociologists. Some are miraculous discoveries of long-lost cousins; others have to do with a develop-ing awareness of cousins who have been there all along-a psychic rediscovery, so to speak.

Inevitably, the stories overlap in some ways with what has gone before, because it is at just such times that all the elements-the sense of clan, the mysti-cal/magical sense of kinship, the peculiar attraction, the inexplicable similarities and ease of communication-begin to fuse. Still, because of the added excitement of discovery or rediscovery, they have a special significance in the story of cousins.

"Magical" was in fact the word used, without any prompting from me, by Dr. Girard Franklin, a psychoanalyst in New York as he told a story of discovery. "The older generation of cousins on my wife Gloria's side, to whom I've become very close as well, call ourselves the 'family circle,' and for years we've been get-ting together the first Saturday of every month for a family meeting. We also had an annual picnic, but our kids were never especially interested-I guess they thought it was just for the older generation-and only a few of them even knew each other.

"Well, this year was to be the fiftieth anniversary of the family circle, and we thought of it as kind of a farewell party, since a lot of the old-timers have been dying off. Because we thought it was going to be the last reunion, instead of just having a day picnic, we decided to live it up and go to a hotel in the Catskills for a few days. We also decided to really try to include all the generations this time, although we weren't too optimistic. By now, most of the kids were all grown up, and some of them have kids of their own. Also, they're spread all over the country and would have to come in by plane, and we felt that would get really expensive. Besides, as I said, they'd never seemed very interested.

"I for one was amazed at the response. Everyone wanted to come! We all gathered together at a hotel where there's swimming and tennis and all kinds of other things to do, and spent three days together. By the end of the weekend, the kids were exchanging phone numbers, planning to visit each other, and insisting on another reunion next year. They suddenly felt such a strong sense of kinship! Really, this magical thing happened. They absolutely bonded to each other. So now, there's a whole new lease on life for the family circle."

Dr. Franklin is one who feels, based simply on his own observations and experience, that there is an ethnic or religious/cultural factor involved. "I'm a Protestant; Gloria is Jewish, as are most of the relatives we've been in touch with. I always felt more distance with my cousins. We were rarely brought together as kids. Anyway, I feel there are certain kinds of ties between certain groups, like the Italians, Jewish, Greeks or Indians, that don't exist for us WASPS. In any case, it all goes back to the strength of that family bond. Of course, our kids hadn't met either, but they knew of the connection between all of us as first cousin parents, and that must have played a part in the quick sense of family they all felt."

Though I could find no studies officially confirming Dr. Franklin's opinion, my word of mouth indicates that many people-both members or non-members of these groups-perceive them as having closer ties with their cousins. I have to add, however, that when I brought this up with a number of other (for want of a better term) "WASP" friends and acquaintances, they didn't agree at all.

When Arnett Stokes, a Canadian in his late fifties who is gay and has lived in New York for many years, received an invitation to a family party in Alberta last year, he made a sudden decision to go, even though he hadn't been in touch with five of his cousins for years, and didn't know the other two at all. "I realized I'd been thinking about them, and about my childhood, a lot recently-more than I ever had before I stopped working. [He had retired from his job as a graphic artist a few years earlier.] That was what was behind the decision, I guess.'

"In meeting even the much younger cousins I'd never met, I felt that I knew them. There was an automatic community of interests. After all, most of us had been born and brought up on a family farm-it was a land grant-and in or around the very house where my mother was born. So we all know where we're coming from-literally, the place we were coming from. And I loved it.

"One in particular-my cousin Charlotte, whom I'd only met once, at my dad's funeral, wanted to know what I thought of her dad, my uncle. Actually, he was a terrific uncle, very warm. I used to hang onto his coattails and follow him all around the farm. Well, Charlotte was fascinated. She couldn't hear enough. And another cousin's wife wanted to hear all about the family history so she could tell it to her four kids.

"They were all terribly impressed that I'd made the effort to fly up from New York, and then drive the one hundred twenty miles to the party. They assumed I had other business reasons for being there, and when I said I didn't, they couldn't get over it. I can't tell you how much it meant to me-and apparently to them. And now we've pledged to stay in touch. I feel that there's a whole new dimension in my life. And I have to add that I think cousins can be especially important to gay people who don't have nuclear families of their own, as they grow older."

Carole Klein, the author of *Aline, Gramercy Park,* and most recently, a biography of Doris Lessing, among other books, told me the following story. "When I was a child we spent summers at the Jersey shore, and I had two boy cousins-one my age, one two years older—that I played with. The older one I considered kind of nerdy, so I'd ally myself with Barry, and we stayed friends till he got married. Well, Barry married a terrible woman, and she really alienated him from the family. Meanwhile, I got friendly with the older brother, who married a wonderful woman, with whom I've formed a deep bond, and with their two kids, too.

"I didn't see Barry for twenty years, and then I heard that his wife had died, so I sent him a condolence note in which I mentioned that I was coming to Philadelphia, where he lived, on a book tour. When I got there, he called and said he wanted to see me, and he came over to the hotel right away. I couldn't get over seeing the eleven-year-old I still remembered from so long ago transformed into this plump, middle-aged dentist. But we started talking and didn't stop till 4:30 A.M., and by the time we were through I felt closer to him than I do to my own brother, who's much older than I am, and towards whom I feel a lot of guilt for various reasons. For the next year and a half Barry and I were incredibly close. Tragically, he died then, of leukemia, and I miss him terribly. It seems so tragic that just as we'd rediscovered each other he died. But I've always been so glad that at least we reconnected for a while, and that the bond remained so powerful."

A book tour also reunited Blanche Wiesen Cook, author of the acclaimed three-part biography of Eleanor Roosevelt, with a longlost cousin. Though she'd been close to a number of her cousins as a child, when a rift between the parents occurred, all contact was cut off, as is so often the case. Decades passed. Then, "I was in Seattle one night, and at the end of my talk, this man came up to me and told me he was my cousin, Alan Wiesen. I couldn't believe it. When we were kids growing up in Brooklyn, the two of us played together all the time, but of course I hadn't seen him in years. It turned out that he'd moved to Seattle a long time ago, but I didn't know it. I also found out that he was a writer, too, and a psychologist as well. He'd heard I would be there promoting the book, and he and his wife decided to come and hear me talk. Afterwards, we went out to dinner together and it was a big affectionate reunion. We talked for hours, and we'll definitely stay in touch."

From the newspapers, I uncovered some extraordinary stories of discovery, in two cases through the combination of chance and the direct efforts of cousins in America to make contact with relatives thousands of miles away.

On June 14, 1989, the *New York Times* reported:

> This is the story of a baby who lost her mother to the Holocaust a half century ago, grew up in Britain as a Baptist thinking she had no family of her own and journeyed here last month at the age of 53 to find herself part of a large and loving Jewish family.
>
> The lesson perhaps is that happy endings are not entirely extinct in New York City. During a three-week visit that began May 18 [1989], Susi Stocken met six first cousins. She discovered she resembles her mother and shares her love of bright colors…'It's as though I'm having the most extraordinary dream and I'm going to wake up in the morning,' she said.

The article goes on to recount how Mrs. Stocken, then Susi Bechofer, had been part of the Kindertransport campaign to rescue Jewish children from Hitler. She and her twin sister, only two years old, became foster children of a Baptist minister and his wife. She was renamed Grace, and her twin sister Lotte (who died of a brain tumor at only 35) was named Eunice.

At age 7, having heard rumors that she was adopted, she confronted the minister, who admitted she was from a Munich orphanage, but said that all the records had been burned in a fire. At 15, she began to suspect there was more that was known when, for an exam, she was told to sit with the B's. The minister's name began with L. Only then did she find out that her legal name was Bechofer.

From that time on, Susi was troubled by questions about her identity, but didn't think there was any way to find out more. She became a nurse, married, and gave birth to a son. The child became a choir boy and wanted to be a conductor. But Mrs. Stocken knew of no musical ancestors. 'He's got such talent,' she thought. 'What's it all about?'

One day [several months later], a friend interested in genealogy urged Mrs. Stocken to pursue her obsession about her past. A recent change in British law allowed adopted children to see their records. These established that Mrs. Stocken's name was Susi Bechofer...She then wrote the West German consulate...

Destiny piled upon coincidence. Mrs. Stocken happened to hear about a reunion of Kindertransport children and became friendly with the woman organizing it. In her travels, the organizer inquired about Susi. She struck gold when she had a tape played on Israeli radio asking about Susi. Girard Bechofer soon wrote from Manhattan. "Are not you one of the twins?" he asked his first cousin.

So the orphan known as Susi came to New York City and discovered she wasn't alone. There were family barbecues, the Empire State Building, the Statue of Liberty...Family stories, like the one about a great-great-great-grandfather taking the family name from a little town in Bavaria in 1813...Most important were the hugs, the smiles and the beginnings of a new faith.

And if her cousin Jerry hadn't been alert (he and the others had been looking for their twin cousins all along) all this would never have come to pass: a history, a family, the beginnings of a new faith.

According to the New York *Daily News,* cousins were also instrumental in enabling Jewish activist Josef Begun to win his freedom from the Soviet Union in 1987. Begun, a Ph.D. in electrical engineering, was exiled from Moscow for eighteen months after applying for a visa in 1977, went on a 100-day hunger strike, was convicted of being a "parasite," exiled to Siberia for three years, and in 1983 was imprisoned in Chistopol prison, where Anatoly Scharansky was also a prisoner. But due at least in part to the efforts of his cousins, his ordeal finally came to an end. According to the *News* story of Sept. 8, 1987:

The jubilant voice of…Joseph Begun leaped over the wires from Moscow yesterday telling relatives, "Wonderful, wonderful! It's the happiest day of my life!…"

Begun's cousin, Zelda Tepper…said she put a call in to Moscow as soon as she heard Begun had been told he would be given an exit visa after a 16-year struggle…"We confirmed he has the visas," she said…

"It's been a long, hard fight," said Rabbi Chaim Wassermann of Passaic, N.J., whose wife Leah-Tepper's sister-is also a cousin. The two sisters and Wassermann were among 14 protesters [insisting on the release of Begun and other refuseniks] arrested outside the Soviet Mission.

And it was these protests that directly or indirectly brought about Begun's release.

Sometimes people will seek out even the remotest cousins in order to compensate for what they perceive as a real lack in their family lives, or to provide a larger family circle for their children. Someone who did just that is Dr. Mark Shulkin, a psychiatrist specializing in family therapy in Philadelphia, who grew up thinking he had only a few cousins in his native Milwaukee.

As a young man, he regularly checked out "Shulkins" in the telephone book whenever he visited a different city. Aware of the possibilities for spelling changes, he had even checked out those with slightly different spellings that sounded alike. But either there were none, or they turned out not to be related.

When his own children were growing up and expressed curiosity about their cousins, he became even more determined to research his roots in Europe many generations back and to try to track down every branch of his family and every cousin, however distantly related, in the United States and abroad. He did this by insisting that one cousin, who he knew was privy to some family secrets he wasn't in on, "tell all."

What he found out was that during Prohibition, a cousin from Cleveland had been mixed up with the Mob, a fact no one in the family liked to discuss, even though the cousin was a kindly fellow who, when hiding out in Milwaukee, liked to take kiddies to the zoo. But along with suppressing that interesting bit of news, the genealogy had been suppressed as well.

Once things were out in the open, Dr. Shulkin was able to track down the locations of a number of relatives. The final result: literally hundreds of cousins found and contacted (when possible) and a real sense of continuity and family history established. Not surprisingly, his collaborator on the venture, which resulted in a book, *Search for the Family*, was the very cousin from whom he had extracted the family secret, clinical psychologist Dr. Sallyann Amdur Sack.

Interestingly, in my research on the internet, though I uncovered little professional writing on the topic, I did find numerous listings of other privately published cousins' histories written by family members. *Some Martin Cousins*, by Goldie Sweet Martin and Dorothy Martin Bayless (publisher G. S. Martin) and *Among Cousins*, the Bland Family Newsletter (C.L. Bland publisher, and editor) were only two of the many listed.

The decision by one of her cousins to do just such a family genealogy led to yet another happy case of cousins newly discovered-that of Lucie Mellert, the daughter of noted Provincetown artist Grace Martin Taylor, both of whom now reside in their home town of Charleston, West Virginia. Lucie is the only child of Ms. Taylor's early marriage to George Frame, from whom she had a bitter divorce which completely alienated Lucie from her father's side of the family when she was very young. As a result, since her mother had no sisters or brothers, she grew up thinking she had no first cousins on either side, though an older second cousin on her mother's side was Blanche Lazzell, probably the best known of the Provincetown artists. Blanche actually taught painting and printmaking to her talented cousin Grace-another example of shared cousinly talent.

A few years before her father's death, a Frame cousin who, it turned out, had been living in Charleston all along, called from out of the blue. She said she was doing a family genealogy, had discovered Lucie's existence or been reminded of it, and invited Lucie to lunch. "That alone was fascinating," said Lucie, "and I loved the idea of having cousins at last." (There were three, all approximate contemporaries of Lucie, to whom she was especially drawn.)

But it was upon her father's death just a few years later that the relationship really began to develop. Her eyes sparkling with enthusiasm, Lucie recalled, "They were unbelievably friendly and warm, and I felt completely at home with them right away. I just don't know how to explain that sense of being immediately at ease, but there it was. Now I talk to them almost every day. They call me 'Hon,' tell me their secrets, and one of them told me just recently that she feels closer to me than to her own brothers and sisters. And this all developed within months! I certainly wish they'd been around during my childhood, when I felt so isolated."

But even if they'd been around, the real connection might have had to wait many years to take place. Such a case was one from my own family, and the one that to me most pulls together the interweaving strands of discovery and rediscovery. This is the story of my cousin Elliot D., one of the older boy cousins I so admired, but whom I'd later learned had had very mixed feelings about the family togetherness I so accepted and took for granted.

It was a crisis-a divorce and remarriage very late in his life-that almost forced Elliot both to rethink his feelings about his cousins, and to make a real effort to set up new lines of communication with them. Certainly, partly due to our differences in both age and sex, we had never been especially close-though as described in an earlier chapter, he and his first wife Sylvia had been enormously supportive of me during a very low point in my teens. So I was somewhat surprised when Elliot called me one day not long after his separation and invited me to lunch.

Though he focused on the reasons behind his recent decision that day, the conversation was remarkably frank, and it was then that I began to see how simplistically I had perceived many things about both him and his parents. And that day, too, we began a kind of ongoing dialogue about the whole "cousins scene" we were part of as we grew up, and especially the evolution in Elliot's feelings that had put us face-to-face across a lunch table five decades later.

Elliot's feeling that his cousins were "thrust upon you as children, unlike friends you pick," his resentment of the weekly visits and the constant comparisons-always negative-between himself and his cousin Ira ("He was always displayed to me as 'This is the way children should be' "), his overall sense that "everything stemmed from my feeling that these weren't *my* relationships, they were an extension of my mother's [my Aunt Madeline]" have been mentioned in different contexts. Even the family orchestra, which I'd always considered the symbol of our family unity, he acknowledged as "very positive and vital" in some ways, but not from the family point of view, because again it was all so forced.

The only other positive thing he recalled, aside from the visits to my house, which, though also obligatory, were pleasant because "your mother would really let you be yourself," was his friendship with Elliot R., "who was the closest to me in age, and definitely my best friend in the family.

"But otherwise, I seem to jump from the rest of you as youngsters right up to late adulthood," he said. "It's almost as though I've unconsciously blocked all of you out until very recently, when all this happened and made me reevaluate my whole life." This was especially surprising, at least to me, because Elliot had in no way lost touch with everyone, and was a regular at family parties, often being the one to take all the candid photos. But as I was finding out, he was there in body only.

"Now, though, because of this crisis, I've rediscovered my cousins, and they're very important to me. I've found a tremendous support system. But it's not only support I've gained, because as you know, I've also encountered some strong opposition to what I've done. As long as the opposition is honest, though-and it is-I can handle it. Anyway, I'm not looking to have everyone agree with my actions, I'm looking to establish-or maybe I mean dig down to-the roots that exist in our family, so cousins were absolutely vital to me.

"I was probing deep under the surface. For instance, about eight years ago I began to find that I have a lot in common with Ira. Now isn't that strange, after all the negative comparisons? In fact, I found out the same thing was happening to him as a child; he was being compared to me. But I'd never permitted myself to think of him as a person or a friend. Yet maybe all of us had this in common-the inability to communicate.

"As for Bernie, Henry, and Saul-the brilliant Jaffe boys [he said this with a wry smile]-I never had a relationship with them either. In the early days, we'd visit Aunt Rebecca [their mother] in Borough Park, and I remember Bern had electric trains, and my brother Frank [Frank D.] had a close friendship with him as they were growing up. But all I ever heard about was their wonderful scholastic achievements. Only recently I've established some relationship with Henry. Perhaps the problem was that I was younger. Certainly when we all went to Camp Modin, I felt like an outsider-not exactly an outcast, but not a member of the group. I was five and a half then, in the "midget" group, along with Elliot R. The older cousins had their own group, to which I definitely didn't belong.

"To me, the connection always came back to domineering parents." And here Elliot amazed me once again by saying that in fact, with the exception of a gentle and funny uncle who died young, he saw all his aunts and uncles on my father's/his mother's side as dictatorial and domineering-another instance of cousins as witnesses affording a different perspective, whether or not you agree with them. My own father, who I knew could be stern, but who I thought of as possessing a marvelous dry sense of humor and being a great raconteur, Elliot recalled as being not the least bit amusing-ever. "My perception of your father is of someone very purposeful, a person with an agenda, with a goal, and God help you if you got in the way. And the ones who weren't so tough got cast into roles by him and the other strong ones: 'poor Jessie,' 'poor Leah' as though they were helpless."

I too had been aware of this pigeonholing, and had come to see it as unduly condescending, but I'd had no idea how troubled Elliot had been by it.

He continued. "This is what I learned in rediscovering my cousins. I no longer accepted the stereotypes of them or my aunts that I'd automatically accepted. There was no more 'poor Jessie'-but I only found that out through this whole process of rediscovery. I began to realize that these nonentities had personalities of their own; that they were interesting people with positive assets. And I was saddened that I'd excluded enjoying the benefits of these relationships in a different way for all those years.

"Still, there's something to be said for starting, or rediscovering, a relationship at a more mature age, when you're in a better position to understand and absorb. My relationship with you, for instance, wouldn't be the same if we had had a long-term close relationship. I view it as one that has just started.

"But now we come to something else important," he continued. "Maybe we all had to go through the obligatory visits and the camp summers together to reach this point, because it's that familiarity, that common denominator that started when we were kids, that gives the relationships I'm reestablishing now a kind of looseness and taking for granted that one that only started recently with a friend could never have. The end result has got to be something deeper. In fact, even my relationships with the cousins I've been closest to-Elliot R. all my life, and Ira for the past eight years-have a different quality now, from as recently as this year. It's as though all the pieces-the aunts, the uncles, all the cousins, fit together and add up to something important for me.

"I think it's because in our family before-even all during my first marriage-I never felt that I was my own person, which I desperately wanted to be. I feel it was made especially hard for me by all the family involvement and by the role I felt I had to play in response to my mother's demands, which somehow got to be a part of my marriage, too.

"So now I have to say that in looking back on how I raised my own kids in terms of their cousins, I have begun to feel a lot of regret. I was so upset at having been forced to visit as a child that I think I went too far in the other direction. I thought it would be a positive approach for me to have the kids completely decide for themselves who they wanted to see. On my side, it was easy, since I had no brothers. [As mentioned earlier, his brother Frank D. died during World War II.] But Sylvia had brothers and they had kids. In our house, though, I saw to it that it was never 'Today is Sunday so we'll go to Jim and Sandy's house to see the cousins.' And I guess it didn't occur to the kids to ask very much, since they didn't know the alternative. As a result, little developed in the way of cousin relationships between them.

"But interestingly, the pendulum is swinging right back. My daughter Ellen is actively trying to see that cousin relationships develop for her children on her husband's side." He added that, to his regret, the divorce has made her chances of developing much with her second cousins on his side somewhat problematic, since the situation is so strained. (Here I have to add that I for one have tried to stay in touch with Ellen, whom I remember so well from her birth the summer I spent so much time with Elliot and Sylvia.)

Elliott continued. "I also see and envy what I see being fostered and developed among my Uncle Emanuel's [a paternal uncle] grandchildren. His kids are mostly grown up, and have a very positive and close relationship with their cousins. When I see that closeness, I now think, 'Maybe my way was not the right way."

The evidence certainly seems to indicate that Elliot's was indeed not the right way. But at least he had the choice, as does his daughter.

Increasingly, this may not be the case. As has been pointed out, with many young couples in the United States and elsewhere delaying parenthood and/or deciding to have smaller families when-and if-they do have children, a cousinless childhood (and adulthood) may be more and more common both here and abroad. That invaluable resource, that multi-cousin pool of which a number of psychiatrists spoke so favorably, would appear to be in danger of reaching a very low level, if not drying up completely. Those of us lucky enough to have grown up with many cousins (and cousins within a reasonable distance, at that) may have been the last American generation to have the luxury of picking and choosing among these quasi-siblings, separate enough to have an exotic appeal, yet bound to us through powerful bonds of heredity and heritage.

How does it feel to be without these friend-relations? A little lonely and envious, say cousinless friends. "When the girl who shares my apartment went to London on business last month, she ran into her cousin in the lobby of the Hilton," said Linda, a magazine editor. "They went out to dinner that night, and spent all their free time together after that, even though they hadn't seen each other in years. I was fascinated," she said, then added wistfully, "My parents were both only children, and I didn't have even one cousin when I was growing up. I always wished I did, and wondered what it would be like."

And Clive Driver, curator and director of the Provincetown Monument Museum, said emphatically, "I felt terribly deprived. My father was an only child, but he'd had forty cousins when he grew up in England, and I heard a lot about them. Even though I had a sister, I had no cousins, and I so envied the extended family he talked about or others I'd read or heard about in movies and books."

Some people will continue to ignore the cousins they have, though as has been pointed out, they may pay a psychological price for it. In today's fragmented, rootless world, turning one's back on this resource-their importance as substitute siblings to only children or children widely separated in age, to gay men and women, as witnesses to one's own and one's parents' lives, keepers of the family history and mythology, sharers of family secrets, supporters, best friends, teachers, and role models-may cost dearly.

To come full circle, I can't imagine my life without my cousins. It would seem to me to have been sadly diminished, to have lost a richness and variety no number of unrelated friends could supply. After all, what would've happened to Rose without her cousins? Or by extension, to me? I doubt we'd ever have budded, let alone bloomed.

HOW YOU AND YOUR CHILDREN CAN CONNECT, RECONNECT, AND STAY CONNECTED WITH COUSINS

THE COUSIN CONNECTION may indeed be magical-but there's no spell needed to establish or reestablish these relationships. In fact, the guidelines are all implied or even stated in the chapters that tell why some cousins love and others don't, or why some remain close and others drift apart.

Still, looking at a list is undoubtedly easier than going back and trying to ferret out clues. So herewith are some of the ways you can make cousins an important and valuable part of your own and your children's lives:

DO'S:

IN GENERAL

- Search out cousins you haven't seen in years, even if you once didn't get along. People change. Write or call them up. Better yet, arrange to see them. Chances are, they'll be genuinely happy to hear from you, to see you, and to stay in touch. (The internet can be an invaluable tool for locating those with whom you've completely lost contact.)
- Don't limit your outreach to first cousins. The "outer inner circle" can enrich your and your family's life enormously. If

you had a specific problem, try talking it out. Family ties are stronger than you may realize, and most people are only too happy to make peace and reestablish contact.

- Search out cousins you've never seen. You'll probably be amazed at how much you have in common.
- If years ago there was a divorce or business rift in the older generation, get back in touch with your own generation of cousins anyway. Nine times out of ten, they'll be delighted to see you and to forget the whole thing.
- Discuss common ancestors, history, or family characteristics with them and/or with your children.
- Work together on a family tree, history, or directory with them and/or with your children. Again, the internet can be a great aid.
- Compile a "memories" book of stories from all the cousins and send it to all the contributors and whoever else is interested.
- Start a cousins newsletter.
- Spend holidays or other special days with them.
- Form a club (or if you prefer, "affinity group") that meets on a regular basis.
- Have yearly reunions, at the very least.
- Try to plan trips, vacations, summers, or parts of summers together. If your children go to camp, send them to the same one.
- If at all possible, try to locate within reasonable visiting distances. If not, plan on regular visits. Don't leave it to chance, because more than likely, it just won't happen.
- If you're planning to get married or enter any other kind of serious relationship, make a point of bringing your cousins into the picture early on, so they can get to know the newcomer-and vice versa.

- If you marry or remarry, be open to your new mate's cousin network. You may suddenly find yourself part of a whole new family circle, who can supply friendship and support.

BUILDING GOOD RELATIONSHIPS
BETWEEN THE KIDS (ALSO SEE ABOVE)

- Explain the cousin relationship to your children, and why it's special.
- Be sure they understand the particular way they're related to each cousin. They like to know.
- When children are small, if they're the same age, get them together to play as often as possible. Steady exposure on a regular basis is often the foundation of the closest cousin friendships. Even if their ages are different, see that they have some kind of regular contact.
- Try to mix the cousins from both sides of the family together as often as possible. This can create a very cohesive family feeling, and help extend the friendship/support system. Also, if this is done from an early age, children will accept both sides equally when they're older.
- If there's a divorce or business rift, try to keep the kids and their relationships out of it. Children are the losers if they're cut off from their cousins.
- Especially when there's a divorce, help and encourage children to keep the cousin connection going. Have them write or call, and keep photographs around.
- If one of a divorced pair moves far away with the children, or feels hostile to the whole family of his or her "ex," point out the importance of their kids staying connected to their cousins. (It can supply much needed continuity and help buffer the sense of loss all around.)

- In cases of remarriage, encourage the kids to consider their stepcousins "real" cousins. It helps create a sense of belonging and can be the basis for important friendships and an additional support system. This applies equally to teenagers.

DONT'S:

IN GENERAL
- Don't keep reminding them of the time you were both in third grade and…[to be filled in].
- If there was a family quarrel between your parents years before, don't try to win it for your mother or father now. The less said the better. (This doesn't apply to your own individual differences. In such cases, talking it out is probably a good idea.)

THE KIDS
- Don't tell nasty stories about parents who may have been difficult as children in front of their kids or yours.
- Don't make invidious comparisons-about looks, clothes, grades, or anything else-about them or their children in front of them or their children.
- Don't foster undue competition between young cousins about looks, grades, clothes, or anything else.
- Try not to pass on any long-term competitive feelings with grownup cousins to your kids.
- Don't try to get grandparents or other relatives to play favorites.

WHAT THE KIDS THINK

WHILE I WAS working on this book, I was also involved in a project sponsored by the National Arts Club to bring writers into the New York City public schools. The object: to encourage the students to write. By great good luck, I connected with Suzanne Davis, a talented teacher at the Clinton School, an exciting junior high in Manhattan.

On my second visit, when I was almost finished with the book, I was stuck for a topic to work on with the children. It suddenly occurred to me that I had a great potential resource for some spontaneous reactions to cousin relationships today. I went into the seventh grade class and talked with the kids about how they felt about their cousins. Then we worked up a few general questions to be answered, and I asked them if they'd write personal essays on the topic. The results were delightful, enlightening, and *very* refreshing. Furthermore, they support a lot of what I'd already found out about why some cousins get along and others don't.

When I go back, we'll polish the essays, but for now I've copied them almost exactly as they appeared. All the students were twelve or thirteen years old.

Hilberto Ramos

I quoted Hilberto earlier in the book (in a section on cousin rivalry) as saying that his relatives were "serious bragers" [sic] *He had a lot more to say, too. He finished that essay:*

...But the part I like is the food and when my cousin comes. We eat pork and cake, pie, soda. After we eat, my cousin who's in the navy and I play poker and he always catches me cheating. But then we play movies, eat popcorn and candy. We love watching horror movies but then he has to go and I have to clean up. There is always good and bad things in life.

Hilberto was so interested in the topic that, since he'd finished his first essay quickly, he decided to do another-again about his navy cousin:

My cousin is one person I must respect or he'll beat me to a pulp. He is eighteen, his name is Pablo Cintron. He's in the navy and he has one sister. I like it when he comes over and fool around, especially in the summer. We go outside and he would attack my brother and I with a hose until we catch it. But what's more fun is when we go bike riding. He and my brother always runs away and leave me behind. Then I get tricky. I take a short cut and then they say, "how did you get here so fast?" Then I say magic and then we go home and go to sleep till the next day. Then he has to go. He's six years older than me and I hate that, but we're still friends.

Mizuo Peck

I have a lot of cousins. They live in: Connecticut, Long Island, Japan and California. I love going to my cousins house in Long Island because my aunt never had a daughter and treats me really nice. She takes me shopping and stands up for me. I also *don't* like it because my two older boy cousins are always at their job and my boy cousin who's my age (13) is always bugging me or only plays with my brother.

I get along well with my oldest cousins in Connecticut. Since I'm younger than them they treat me like a young sister. They are in their 20s and 30s. Some are even married. None of them bug me or make fun of me because they are too mature for that.

I never see my cousins in Japan anymore and I don't even know how many I have over there. I see my cousins on Long Island the most. I see my cousins in Connecticut on Thanksgiving because my dad, brother and I go to

Connecticut and visit them then.

Kien-shi Chen

I have around over 20 cousins. I have six cousins that are smaller than me. The baddest of my little cousins is the biggest of them. He always gets into trouble. In school he is baddest. He is only 8 and he is 5 feet 1 inch tall and he is the strongest 8 year old I ever seen. In class, when the teacher is not there he line every one up and slap them. He still lives in China with my uncle.

One day the Principle found out that he is causing lots of trouble and took him to a high stage and every one stare at him. He does not care and starts laughing and said look at all those people.

He gets along with older cousins like me and my other older cousins, but he always gets into fights with my younger cousins. When he visits my six year old girl cousin he gets into a fight with her because she's a girl.

My girl cousin is very smart. When she was four she got into acting school and her mother is planning to let her become an Actor. I get along with her nicely. She listen to me whatever I say. All my cousins are very nice but the 8-year-old one.

One more cousin I haven't met. He's in China and was born four years ago. When I visit four years ago he was not born. After I came back, my grandfather died of a heart attack in China just a few days after my cousin was born. I sort of believe that my grandfather was reborn as my cousin. I sure miss my grandfather and sure want to meet my cousin to see if we get along. I hope we do.

Jennifer McCloskey

My favorite cousin is 28 years of age. I have alot of cousins. I mean alot. My favorite cousins name is Carla. She's married and has two children. She's a college teacher. She's my favorite cousin because she always would think of me before any of my other cousins. She invited me over her house every Saturday to stay over till Sunday. We would bake cookies, go shopping and rent movies.

One year my cousin Carla invited me to travel to Cyprus and my mother said yes but the day when I was leaving for the flight to Cyprus (it's in Europe)

I was crying, but then I thought how lucky I was that I was invited out of all my cousins so I stopped crying. So we left and my cousin and I visited Greece where my younger cousin (by four months) Angela lives. She use to live in Queens but her father is Greek so they went there and lived for two years. When I returned to Kenedy Air Port I saw my mother. I thanked my cousin for inviting me.

The sad thing that happen was August 14, 1989 my cousin Carla and her children and her husband moved to Cyprus and I really miss her. On Christmas eve I talked to her on the phone. That's why she's my favorite cousin.

Jon Abrahams

I have six cousins. I will start with the ones I know the best, Patrick and Courtney. Patrick is 16, and Courtney is 20. They are brother and sister. I usually see them on vacations or on birthdays, but occasionally they stop by to go to the movies or something. They live on 90th and Madison and I live on Hudson and Franklin.

Patrick is the type that hates his mother and then loves her, sort of an on off relationship. When he's with me alone he's the nicest person, but when he's around a friend, he's the meanest, most horrible person I ever met. He pinches me, spits, etc.

Courtney could never be mean but she tends to have to stick to a plan. For instance once we were going to go ice skating but I got sick and canceled. She insisted we go the day I got better at the same time, same place. Although it sounds funny they've always been my role models-especially Patrick who I'm still trying to figure out why.

Luis Nuñez

Good: 1) I'm the only child so my cousin is like my brother.
2) He's funny and he likes to have fun.
3) He's my family best friend.
4) Sometimes he's nice and thoughtful.

Bad: 1) He's younger than me and he gets on my nerve.
2) He always wants to play some stupid game most of the time. Everything to him is playing.
3) He's very spoiled and gets away with everything.
4) Sometimes he's a *Brat*.

Sherrie Jubiler

One of my favorite cousins is Cecil. He is very cute and I like to bring him around my neighborhood to show him off and I think he knows that I've been doing that.

My other two cousins are very spoiled by my grandmother and I hate the way she treats me and my sister because she has heard bad rumors about us from other aunts. I hate when that happens. I'm thirteen and one of my cousins is twelve. We're alike in a way but they live in the south Bronx so I don't see her too much.

Olga Mendez

Hello, I'm Olga and I'm 13 years old. My favorite cousins are Katie (who's 9) and Lizzie (who's 5). I like Katie a little better then Lizzie because Lizzie always has to have her own way. Lizzie can be nice and cute in her own way. Katie is artistic like me, and I get along with her a lot better than Lizzie.

The reason their my favorite cousins is because their the only ones I get to see, and they look up to me (but mostly Katie does)!! I'm sort of a role modle to them.

One incident happened while I was up at their house in upstate New York. Katie and I were playing games, then Lizzie wanted to play so we let her. Then we meaning Katie and I were getting sick of playing the game. But Lizzie didn't want to play another game, so I told her that after we play a different game we would play any game that she would want to play. But NO she still wanted to do what she wanted to do. Finally we really got mad at Lizzie. So we told her she couldn't play.

Well, she went downstairs and told on us!! My aunt and oncle gave Katie and me a lecture about we have to do what Lizzie wants to do because she's the youngest. Lizzie started crying and wouldn't stop until we would play the game she wanted.

Hopefully, the rest of my cousins won't be such a brat. I have about, well, about 15 cousins.

Elda Montoya

I have cousins who are much older than me but they respect me. Most of our cousins are boys. They hate playing around with my younger sister because she's such a pest. She plays so rough for an eight year old girl. They don't like playing with her because she likes to bite their ears. She loves bothering my oldest cousin who is 22 but he doesn't like playing with her because he thinks he might hurt her accidentally.

All my cousins get along with me except my cousin José who is 13 and I'm 12. He lives in the Bronx but he visits me every single weekend. Lots of times we get into fights and I love to beat him up.

I do have a favorite cousin. Her name is Yasmine and she's 21. I get along with her well. She and I like to go shopping together alot. She lends me all her things. She doesn't mind that I use something of hers that she really likes. And when ever she doesn't like something she comes straight to me and asks me if I want it. Everything she gives me is new so that's why I like her so much.

Jackson Mui

My cousins are very nice but sometimes they are a little bit mean to me. I favor one of my cousins because he is fun to play with and likes the things that I like. For example he likes Kung Fu and watching tapes about Kung Fu and I also like Kung Fu so we always have something to say to each other. He plays games with me like cards. I don't know how old he is but I know he is older than me. He used to be shorter than me when he came from Hong Kong, but no more.

Now he lives near my building and I can visit him any time I like to but I don't go to his house that much because I don't have that much time, but I do go when I have the time and when I am bored at home.

The other cousin is a girl. She is nice to but she doesn't listen to her mother or father that much. But I get along well with both of them.

I have more cousins but the names are very hard to spell out. I am 12 and a half and I am kind of happy and I plan to live a long life and have the same cousins that I have now.

Michele Pietra

I have a cousin who is very special to me. Her name is Delicia. She is 14 years old. She is special to me because she is like a sister to me. Me and her use to be with each other every day. We used to dress alike. When we used to walk in the street people use to ask us are you sisters. We both would say no we are cousins. They would say you both look alike. Everywhere she use to go I would go with her or wherever I use to go she would go. We use to tell each other secrets and we never told anybody.

We always use to stick up for each other so we can always be even. We also use to borrow each others clothes. But now she lives far away and I only see her on holidays. Sometimes I feel lonely without her. Also when I have a secret the only way I can tell her is on the phone. But I'm glad I still get a chance to see her. She lives in Lake George. She use to live in New York. But as long as I still see her sometimes I'm glad about that.

I am 13 years old and will be 14.

Josh Nowitzky

My cousin Brian is a total nuisance. I don't know what it is. We are like arch enemies or something. He is 13 years old, about half a year older than I am. Whenever I see him I think "Kill Pee-Wee Herman!!"

Brian and I used to be real close until we were about 6. That's when the war started. We always, up to this day, get in fights whenever we see each other. He never wins. My grandparents think of him as a perfect little angel. They always only know his side of the story. Brian always feels as if he has the upper hand. He thinks he has power over me. He probably knows by now that I'm the one who everyone gets mad at when something happens, except Mom and Dad.

Well, I'm probably never going to see him again so I'm not worried. At least I don't plan to. Oh, I also have a baby cousin, who happens to be Brian's brother. I hope he doesn't get influenced by that maniac.

Delmar Wilson

I have so many cousins that I don't know what to do with them but I'm only gonna tell you about a few.

Philip, 25-Philip and I get along good. He buys me anything I want. He's my second cousin and he always takes up for me. We never argue, but our relationship changed when I moved away and we weren't as close. I visit him some weekends.

Aaron, 19-He's my favorite cousin because mabe he'll treat me to some thing. He lets me wear his shirts. He drives me all over the place. We kid around with each other. We stay up all night and watch videos and laugh and play. We share our stuff. He gives me money and everything. I love him. That's why he's the best cousin.

He lives in N.C., and I visit him every holiday all year round from December's X-mas vacation then Easter vacation then in the summer.

Dyshawn, 8-He's a pest, brat, and very spoiled. He gets on my nerves. He doesn't listen. He always wants me to play with him when I don't want to play. He lives downstairs and sees me every day.

Tanya, 19-Me and her are real close. She takes me shopping and she watches out for me. We share clothes and we do each other's hair. She lives next door and I see her almost every day.

Tynisha-We are best friends. She lives on the other side of Brooklyn about a half hour away and I see her almost every week!

Desirée Serrano

I have millions of cousins but my favorite cousin is 15 years old. I hardly have any girl cousins. He's a boy and sometimes I wonder why he's my favorite one. He's nice and when we were in the same school and boys would bother me he would beat them up. I see him a lot because he lives nearby.

His parents always buy him things and he works so he buys himself things, too. I get hand me downs like bikes and skateboards.

He's a bully to me when other boys are around. One time he threw me on the floor and was going to step on me so I kicked him in the face. We fight over jobs and we tell each other our intamite secrets.

Corene Salierno

I have cousins named Marisol, Evelyn, Marina, Jessica, and Brenda.

Jessica is two years old and she is so cute. Her mom dresses her up just like me. She lives near by and I go visit her.

Marina is Jessica's mom. She is twenty-three years old. She is pretty much my best cousin. Every time she has clothes that doesn't fit her she would give them to me. She is so kind. When she goes shopping she takes me, and if she buys her daughter something, she buys me something too.

Marisol is sixteen. She is nice. We share everything. She gives me things. She takes me shopping with her, too. Her mother is really kindly to me. Marisol comes to my house to sleep and if I visit her and she has something I don't have she gives it to me. If she doesn't have something I have, I give it to her.

Evelyn recently became my cousin. She got married with my cousin. She is nice. Her aunt works doing hair and she gives me things for my hair. I like her alot. She is twenty-two.

The cousin I really hate is named Brenda. She is a brat. She thinks she smart but she is stupid. She is twelve. I hate her.

Anthony Hill

My cousin Raymond is a pain in the neck because whenever I ask him for something he says "No get away from me, leave me alone!" So I say alright just remember when you come to my house and you ask me for food I'm going to let you starve.

So then he says okay I'm sorry I didn't mean to yell at you. Take what you want, feel free to do whatever you want.

But when I go to his house on vacation he's nasty to me. He beats me up every day. Whenever I get or have money he makes me spend it on him. And what really gets me mad is when he hits me. He doesn't get me in trouble but I do get in trouble for making all the noise.

What I really like about going to his house in the Bronx is his mother. She treats me like I was a gift to the world. I get fed all the time and go shopping. But I still hate my cousin who is 15!

David Rodriguez

My cousin's name is Angela and I think she is the closest cousin I have because she is the oldest. She is sixteen and is a couple of inches shorter than me. When I was small I used to think she was a giant just because she was taller than me. I think she is the best cousin I have because on my birthday she always gets me something and on her birthday I do the same for her. Also, when I was small she used to take me to the park and stuff.

Every time she has a problem she sometimes asks me for my opinion, but if I am not there she asks my Mom. Some people think we are like brother and sister because she is kind of a little chubby like me and carry the same last name namely Rodriguez.

I think the relationship changed a little because we don't see each other that much except on holidays.

Well, before I close up this story my name is David Rodriguez and I'm 121/2 years old.

Christina Chun

I have 5 cousins. 3 cousins live in Korea and 2 cousin live in Los Angeles, California.

I went for a trip the last day in Korea. The trip was fun and nice. When I came back home, somebody took every thing of mine. My dress, my books, my piano, my phone and my favorite doll, too. So I cried. "Somebody took my everything." Soon I didn't talk to anybody. I was like a crazy person.

Next day I went to my cousins' house. My cousins names were Min Young, Min Sun, and young Kwang. They were 11, 9, and 2. I was 13. I heared the piano but they didn't have a piano, so I ran around the house. My cousins had my piano, my dress, my phone, my everything. I was very sad about that. How they have all my things? Why?

I asked my mother. She said, "We are going to another country, so we don't need it. If we need it, I could buy new one for you, all right?" I said "all right" but I didn't want to give them my favorite doll and my favorite books. So, I got those back again, and my cousins said to me, "Than you for everything you gave me."

I felt good.

Howard Kan

I have seven cousins and I am only going to talk about two. They live next door to me. I can go there any time and any day. Those two are always so stingy and selfish. Their names are Irene and Kenneth. They always bother me and my two little brothers. Irene's age is seven and Kenneth is five. They always stare at our food and always talk about it. I know what they want. They just want to eat our food. But when I ask them for food they never give me anything.

So one day when they asked me for food I said no, I'm not giving it to you. So they asked my mother and she told me to give them some. So I did and I said, if you ask my mother again and my mother said give the food to you I will not follow what she said because you are so selfish.

They both go to school…They haven't changed their attitudes yet. I want them to change so they won't be so stingy and selfish.

Mildred Mata

I have a cousin who's twelve like me but a few months older than me. Her name is Candy. I also have two other girl cousins who are like sisters I never had. I have lots and lots of other cousins but these three are my favorites.

The two sisters are Rosy (11) the oldest and the other is Wilnie (short for Wilneida). I only see them on holidays and on summer vacations because they live in upstate NY. When I see them we always stick together. We don't leave each other. We talk about everything. We play games.

Candy on the other hand is different. We talk about other things (at least we used to). She's changed a lot. She lives in Brooklyn and we don't stay in touch much. But when we leave each other she says "I'll miss you" over and over. We wrestled together and she's like a sister, too. Also, Candy and I have the same laugh and so does my aunt. We are like triplets. We laugh the same and we almost look the same. Except for me and my aunt, we're like twins.

The two sisters and Candy don't know each other at all. Candy is like the big boss. She's cool and into style. But the other two are like children. They're not like me and Candy. One time Rosy and Wilnie and me visited a friend of theirs and we went into a forest with her and we almost got lost. Rosie was so scared, and even though she's eleven and I'm twelve she thinks she's so mature for her age, but she's more like a chicken.

Me and my two cousins never had a fight ever since I knew them. Only they fight each other all the time. Candy is like a rich, spoiled girl. She has everything. But we've been together forever. So I really love my three favorite cousins.

BIBLIOGRAPHY

SINCE THE SOURCES of all quotations or references are explained in the chapters as they appear and are also listed in more detail below, it seemed redundant to list them by chapter.

The authors quoted most frequently throughout the book are Bert N. Adams, David Schneider, Robin Fox and Elizabeth Stone. In their cases, the source book isn't named every time but is always the same one (see below).

Adams, Bert N. *Kinship in an Urban Setting.* Chicago: Markham Publishing Co. 1968.

Alcott, Louisa May. *Eight Cousins.* New York: Little, Brown. 1974.

Alcott, Louisa May. *Rose in Bloom.* New York: Puffin Books (Penguin). 1989.

Anderson, Nancy Fix. "Cousin Marriage in Victorian England." *Journal of Family History,* Volume 11, Number 3. Greenwich, Connecticut: JAI Press. July, 1986.

Bennetts, Leslie. "Talent-to Amuse." *Vanity Fair,* August, 1989.

Bermant, Chaim. *The Cousinhood.* New York: Macmillan. 1972.

Bermant, Chaim. *Troubled Eden.* London: Valentine and Mitchell. 1969.

Bork,David. *Family Business, Risky Business.* New York: Amacom. 1986.

Bourgois, Phillipe. "A Night on Crack Street." *New York Times Magazine,* Nov. 12, 1989.

Bowen, Murray. *Family Therapy in Clinical Practice.* Northvale, New Jersey: Jason Aronson, Inc. 1983. (New printing, 1989).

Brozan, Nadine. "For Maria Shriver, a New Series of Engagements." *New York Times,* October 21, 1985.

Calisher, Hortense. *Kissing Cousins.* New York: Weidenfeld and Nicolson. 1988.

Capote, Truman. *A Christmas Memory.* New York: Random House. 1966.

Caro, Robert. *The Power Broker: Robert Moses and the Fall of New York.* New York: Knopf. 1974.

Clarke, Gerald. *Capote: A Biography.* New York. Simon & Schuster. 1988.

Collier, Peter, and Horowitz, David. *The Kennedys.* New York: Summit Books. 1984.

Colwin, Laurie. *Happy All the Time.* New York: Knopf. 1978.

Conway, Jill Ker. "What I Owe to Uncle Bob" (review of *Family Portraits,* edited by Carol Anthony). *New York Times Book Review,* Nov. 19, 1989.

"Cousin Marriage." *Encyclopaedia Britannica,* Vol. 6. Chicago: William Benton. 1967.

"Cousin" chart. *The World Book Encyclopedia,* Vol. 4. Chicago: Field Enterprises Educational Association. 1974.

"Cousin" word origin. *The Concise Oxford Dictionary of Current English.* 7th Edition. Ed., J. B. Sykes. England: Oxford at the Clarendon Press. 1982.

Cummings, Elaine, and Schneider, David, "Sibling Solidarity: A Property of American Kinship." *American Anthropologist,* Vol. 63. June, 1961.

Davidson, John P. "All About Steve." *Vanity Fair,* July, 1988.

Dempster, Nigel. *Heiress.* New York: Grove Weidenfeld. 1989.

Diamond, Jared. "I Want a Girl Just Like the Girl…" *Discover,* November, 1986.

Dickens, Charles. *David Copperfield.* Boston: Houghton Muffin.

Dullea, Georgia. "Lehman Wingding in Lehman Wing." *New York Times,* June 16, 1989.

Farber, Bernard. "Bilateral Kinship: Centripetal and Centrifugal Types of Organization." *Journal of Marriage and the Family,* November, 1975.

Fishel, Elizabeth. *Sisters.* New York: Morrow. 1979.

Fisher, Dorothy Canfield. *Understood Betsy.* New York: Henry Holt & Co. 1917.

Flynn, Don. "Call It His Happiest Day." New York *Daily News,* September 8, 1987.

Fox, Robin. *Kinship and Marriage.* England: Penguin Books (a Pelican original). 1967.

Gill, Brendan. "Edgar Kauffman, Jr.-Secrets of Wright and Falling Water." *Architectural Digest,* March, 1990.

Golden, Tim. "Peril in Peru." *Vanity Fair,* December, 1989.

Gordon, Mary. *The Other Side.* New York: Viking. 1989.

Harrison, G. "The Importance of Being Oprah." *New York Times Magazine,* June 11, 1989.

Irving, John. *A Prayer for Owen Meany.* New York: Morrow. 1989.

Kahn, Michael, and Bank, Stephen P. *The Sibling Bond.* New York: Basic Books. 1983.

Kenner, Hugh. "Old Possum's Postbag" (review of *The Letters of T.S. Eliot). New York Times Book Review,* October 16, 1988.

Kerr, Michael E., and Bowen, Murray. *Family Evaluation.* New York: Norton. 1988.

Kerr, Peter. "600 'Cousins' Meet to Celebrate Roots." *New York Times,* June 28, 1982.

Larson, Kay. "Pure in Spirit." *New York* magazine, December 2, 1985.

Lehmann, Rosamond. *Dusty Answer.* New York: Henry Holt & Company. 1927.

Marquez, Gabriel Garcia. *100 Years of Solitude.* New York: Harper & Row. 1970.

Martin, Douglas. "Adrift 50 Years, Holocaust Victim Finds Family." *New York Times,* June 14, 1989.

Maslin, Janet. "Iranian Director's Mournful Trilogy" (review of *The Peddler). New York Times,* March 26, 1989.

Mitgang, Herbert. "Hunch on Mary Shelley Pays Off." *New York Times,* December 2, 1987.

Moates, Marianne. *A Bridge of Childhood: Truman Capote's Southern Years.* New York. Henry Holt & Company. 1989.

Moates, Marianne. "Giving Life to a Life Story." *Writer's Digest,* April, 1990.

Moore, Jr., Barrington. *Political Power and Social Theory.* Cambridge, Mass. Harvard University Press. 1958.

Muchnic, Helen. "Two Lives Caught in History" (review of *The Correspondence of Boris Pasternak and Olga Freidenberg 1910-1954). New York Times Book Review,* June 27, 1982.

McPherson, James M. "The War of Southern Aggression." *The New York Review,* January 19, 1989.

Newman, Susan. *Parenting an Only Child.* New York: Doubleday. 1990.

Ottenheimer, Martin. *Forbidden Relatives, The American Myth of Cousin Marriage.* University of Illinois Press. l996.

Perrin, Ursula. *The Looking-Glass Lover.* Boston: Little, Brown. 1989.

Rainie, Harrison, and Quinn, John. *Growing Up Kennedy.* New York: Putnam. 1983.

Rockwell, John. "Previn Abruptly Quits Post at the Los Angeles." *New York Times,* April 26, l989.

Ruttencutter, Helen Dees. "Profile of André Previn." *The New Yorker,* January 10, 1983.

Schneider, David M. *American Kinship: A Cultural Account.* 2nd Edition. Chicago: University of Chicago Press. 1980.

Shoumatoff, Alex. *The Mountain of Names.* New York: Simon & Schuster. 1985.

Stone, Elizabeth. *Black Sheep and Kissing Cousins.* New York: Times Books. 1988.

Symons, Allene. "Looking Back." *Publisher's Weekly,* December 11, 1987.

Tester, William. "Cousins." *Esquire,* September, 1989.

Thompson, James S. and Margaret W. *Genetics in Medicine.* 4th ed. Toronto: W.B. Saunders Company. 1986.

Tolstoy, Leo. *War and Peace.* New York. Viking Penguin. 1982.

Toman, Walter. *Family Constellation.* New York: Springer. 1961.

INDEX

V

Vargas Llosa, Mario, 104

Vaughan, Scipio, 49

Vaughn, Oscar, 49

Vaughn family line, 49

Vicar of Bullhampton, The (Trollope), 111-12

Victoria (Queen of England), 103, 112

Victorian society (England), cousin marriages in, 110-16

Vinalhaven (Maine), cousin marriages in, 101

W

Walker, Berta, 1

War and Peace (Tolstoy), 103

Warwick, Dionne, 17

Wassermann, Chaim, 185

Wasserstein, Wendy, 21

Wechsler, Andrea, 74-75

Wedgwood, Emma, 112

Wedgwood, Julia, 115

Wedgwood family, 103

Weinbaum, Clare, xvi, 12, 15, 16, 17, 19, 35, 57, 66, 67, 75, 140-41, 142, 146, 155, 160

Weiner, Katie, 75, 77, 141

Wiesen, Alan, 182

Wilson, Delmar, 204-5

Winfrey, Oprah, 91

Wizard of Oz, The (Baum), 28

Women, cousin contact, 173-74

Working class families, 173-74

World Book encyclopedia, xx

Y

Youngman, Henny, 19

Z

Zimmerman, Veva, 3-4, 5, 142, 178

FAMILY INDEX

Printed in the United States
91619LV00005B/27/A